The King and the Consul
A BRITISH TRAGEDY IN OLD SIAM

The King and the Consul

A BRITISH TRAGEDY IN OLD SIAM

Simon Landy

RIVER BOOKS

First published and distributed in 2021 by
River Books Press Co., Ltd.
396/1 Maharaj Road, Phraborommaharajawang,
Bangkok 10200 Thailand
Tel: (66) 2 224-6686, 2 225-0139, 2 622-1900
Fax: (66) 2 225-3861
Email: order@riverbooksbk.com
www.riverbooksbk.com

Editor: Narisa Chakrabongse
Production supervision: Suparat Sudcharoen
Design: Ruetairat Nanta

ISBN 978 616 451 059 3

Printed and bound in Thailand by Parbpim Co., Ltd.

Contents

Illustrations

Cast of characters

SIAMESE ROYALTY

The monarchs who have reigned over Siam/Thailand since 1782 constitute the **Chakri** dynasty. The Chakri kings are customarily referred to in English using the title **Rama**, the first being Rama I and the current Chakri king being Rama X. Rama I moved the capital from Thonburi to its present location, Bangkok or, in Thai, Krungthep in 1782. The name given to the era of Chakri rule is the **Rattanakosin** period, which refers to the area of land around the Grand Palace of Bangkok. Rattanakosin literally means gem of Indra. Chakri royalty who play a role in our story include:

- **King Nangklao** or **Rama III** or **Phra Nangklao Chao Yu Hua** (1781-1851), who succeeded to the throne in 1824 as the eldest son of Rama II, even though his half-brother, Mongkut, was said to have a superior claim as the son of the queen.
- **King Mongkut** or **Rama IV** or **Phra Chom Klao Chao Yu Hua** (1804-1868), who was crowned after a peaceful transition in 1851, having spent the previous twenty-seven years as a monk where he devoted himself to rationalising Buddhist practices. He was viewed as an enlightened sovereign who opened the kingdom to western ideas and trade, though not without having to make significant compromises.

Opposite page: King Mongkut, photographed by John Thomson in 1865.

- **King Pinklao** or the **second king** or **Phra Pinklao Chao Yu Hua** (1808-1866) was Mongkut's younger brother and acceded to his throne a few days after Mongkut. The position of second king, or *uparat* (sometimes translated as viceroy), was held in equal honour to the first king, but in reality Pinklao had far less power than Mongkut and often distanced himself from current affairs. The *uparat* position was discontinued by Chulalongkorn in 1876.
- **King Chulalongkorn** or **Rama V** or **Phra Chula Chom Klao Chao Yu Hua** (1853-1910), succeeded his father, Rama IV, in 1868 and undertook substantial modernisation of the political, economic and social landscape of the country. He remains a deeply venerated figure today.
- **Prince Wongsa** (1808-71), who was a half-brother of and key advisor to King Mongkut with the title **Krom Luang Wongsa Thirat Sanit**. He was incapacitated by a stroke in 1861 and played no important political role thereafter.

The book also refers to two pre-Rattanakosin Siamese kingdoms: the **Ayutthaya** period, which lasted from 1351 until the destruction of the city of Ayutthaya by the Burmese in 1767, and the much briefer **Thonburi** period, from **King Taksin**'s establishment of a new kingdom at Thonburi (opposite Bangkok) in 1767 until the move to Bangkok in 1782.

SIAMESE NOBILITY

The main Siamese nobles who feature in this story all belonged to the same family. At the time surnames were not in use by Siamese families. After King Vajiravudh (Rama VI) required all Siamese citizens to have surnames in 1913, this family adopted the name **Bunnag**, which was the forename of an ancestor. In the nineteenth century, the Bunnag clan was by far the most powerful and influential family outside the royal family. Their senior members were responsible for making kings and held positions at the top of the civil service. The key Bunnags in our story are:

- The **Kalahom**, the most senior position in the Siamese government. Contemporaries often translated this title as prime minister, even though this was technically incorrect. Minister for military affairs would be more accurate. Today the word is used for the ministry of defence. The Kalahom who features in our story (1808-1882) was the eldest son of the Somdet Ong Yai, the previous Kalahom. Under Rama III, he held various positions; first Nai Chai Khan, then Luang Nai Sit, then Chamuen Waiworanat and finally Phraya Si Suriyawong to take charge of the embassy of Sir James Brooke in 1850. Under Rama IV he was given the title Chaophraya Si Suriyawong in 1851 although he was generally known as the Kalahom, which was his main functional role. When Rama V came to the throne he was appointed regent during the king's minority (1868-1873) and was subsequently promoted to the highest non-royal position like his father and uncle before him, becoming Somdet Chaophraya Borom Maha Si Suriyawong in 1873. His given name was Chuang and he was known as Khun Chai Chuang (today, Chuang Bunnag).[1]

- The **Phraklang**, which, along with Mahatthai, was one of the two most powerful government posts after the Kalahom. As the main agency dealing with foreign trade, the person in charge was considered equivalent to foreign minister. The Phraklang of our story (1813-1870) was known as Chaophraya Rawiwong during the early years of Rama IV and was granted the title Chaophraya Thiphakorawong in 1865. His given name was Kham (Kham Bunnag).
- The **Somdet Ong Noi**, or the **younger Somdet** (1791-1858), whose full title was Somdet Chaophraya Barom Maha Phichaiyat. Under Rama III, the Somdet Ong Noi had been granted the title Phraya Si Phiphat and served as the deputy Phraklang. His given name was Tad and he was known as Khun Chai Tad (today more commonly, Tad Bunnag).
- The **Somdet Ong Yai**, or the **elder Somdet** (1788-1855), whose full title was Somdet Chaophraya Barom Maha Prayurawong. Under Rama III, the Somdet Ong Yai had held the two most senior administrative roles in government; namely, Kalahom and Phraklang. His given name was Dit and he was known as Chao Khun Chai Dit. Today he is often referred to as Dit Bunnag.

BRITISH CIVIL SERVANTS

Charles Bell (1832-1859) was based in Bangkok from 1855 to learn the Siamese language. He became consular assistant in June 1856 and acting consul between the death of Hillier and the arrival of Gingell. He then resigned and went into private business in Bangkok, He died of a fever contracted while gold prospecting in 1859. His young wife died one week later leaving a six-month-old baby, Amy, who was sent back to England and would eventually achieve fame as the first female stockbroker in London.

Sir John Bowring (1792-1872) was appointed Britain's plenipotentiary in China, Cochin China, Japan, Korea and Siam, chief superintendent of trade in China and governor of Hong Kong in 1854, when he was also knighted. He had previously served as a member of parliament (1835-1837 and 1841-1849) and as consul at Canton from 1849-1853. He was one of the leading advocates of free trade in the nineteenth century, a prolific writer on political economics and a renowned linguist.

Lord Clarendon (1800-1870), George Villiers, 4th Earl of Clarendon, was secretary of state for foreign affairs from 1853-1858, then again from 1865-1866 and 1868-1870. He had previously held the posts of minister to Spain, chancellor of the Duchy of Lancaster, president of the board of trade and lord lieutenant of Ireland.

William Raymond Gingell (1816-1863) was consul to Siam from March to December 1857. He was a surgeon with the East India Company in India and arrived in China in 1842, where he became a consular interpreter and was later consul at Amoy and Hankow. He published several translations of Chinese texts and books on Chinese customs.

Charles Batten Hillier (1820-1856) was consul to Siam from June to October 1856. He arrived in Hong Kong in 1841 as a merchant seaman. He joined the magistrate's court where he rose to become chief magistrate from 1847-1856 before being appointed to Bangkok. He was survived by his wife, Eliza, who was pregnant with their fifth child.

Harry Parkes (1828-1885) was appointed consul at Amoy in 1854 and acting consul at Canton in 1856. He had previously worked as a translator and consular assistant in Amoy, Canton, Foochow and Shanghai. He was knighted in 1862. He would later be appointed consul-general to Japan (1865-1883), consul-general to China (1883-1885) and minister to Korea (1884-1885)

Sir Robert Schomburgk (1804-1865) served as consul to Siam from 1857-1864. He was born in Germany and was mainly engaged as a geographer and explorer until 1848 when he was appointed British consul to the Dominican Republic. He was knighted in 1845.

OTHER CHARACTERS

Dan Beach Bradley (1804-1873) was an American missionary who was stationed in Bangkok from 1835 until his death. Originally attached to the American Board of Commissioners for Foreign Missions, he switched to the American Missionary Association from 1848. He became friendly with King Mongkut and brought in Siam's first printing press. He was a qualified doctor and performed the first surgery in Siam. He also introduced vaccinations to the kingdom.

John Hassett Chandler (1813-1891) arrived in Bangkok in 1843 to work as a lay missionary, printer and book-binder at the Baptist mission. He left the mission to go into business in Bangkok in 1856. He succeeded Mattoon as acting United States consul from 1859-1862 and returned to the United States in 1880.

Charles de Montigny (1805-1868) was appointed French envoy to Siam in 1856. He had previously served as French consul to Shanghai from 1848-1853. After Bangkok, he led a diplomatic mission to Vietnam. He would later serve as a diplomat in Shanghai and Tientsin.

Eliza Hillier (1829-1886) was brought up in Batavia and then Shanghai, the daughter of the well-known missionary Walter Medhurst. She married Charles in 1846 and had five surviving children. After her husband's death in Bangkok in 1856, she moved to England in 1857. She remarried there in 1864 and had two more children.

Robert Hunter (1792-1848) was a Scottish merchant who became the principal foreign trader living in Bangkok from 1824-1844. He married a Portuguese descendant in Bangkok. After being forced to leave Siam, he returned to Scotland, leaving his wife and a son (also called Robert) in Bangkok. The younger Robert remained in Bangkok until his death in 1865.

Stephen Mattoon (1816-1889) was an American missionary stationed in Bangkok from 1847-1866, when he returned to New York. Fluent in the Siamese language, he was appointed the first United States consul to Siam in 1856, a post he held until 1859.

Antonio Frederico Moor (1807-1877) was the third Portuguese consul to Siam from 1855-1868 and retired in Bangkok. He was born in Macao and had previously worked as a doctor there for the Dutch East India Company. He also served briefly as acting French consul in 1856.

Jean-Baptiste Pallegoix (1805-1862) was apostolic vicar of Eastern Siam for the Catholic church from 1841, having been sent from France to Siam in 1828. He developed a close relationship with Mongkut during the latter's years as a Buddhist monk.

Christopher Puddicombe (1807-1895) was a master mariner based in Bombay from the early 1840s and moved with his wife and eight children to Bangkok to start a shipbuilding business in 1855. He returned to Bombay around 1861.

John Richards became a master commander in the British royal navy in 1853 when he was given command of the surveying ship HMS *Saracen*. In the mid 1850s, he surveyed some 1,000 miles of Asian coastline, including the Gulf of Siam and the Chaophraya river, enabling the hydrographic office to publish the first detailed chart of the Gulf in 1860.

Nai Seng (?-1856) was employed as the writer (scribe) in the British consulate at Bangkok in 1856. He was previously a scholar-monk at Wat Bowonniwet under Mongkut, who was then abbot of the *wat*.

VICTORIA

Introduction

British ambassador's residence, Bangkok, February 2018

Boris Johnson was working the room. He had given a short welcoming speech containing one or two obligatory faux pas and was now well into the final, glad-handing stage of the reception. The aircon was struggling to cope, but Britain's foreign secretary (as he was then) was rumpled yet unperturbed, as if he had attained an equilibrium of dishevelment. No sweaty underarm patches were visible despite his having arrived in the country only a few hours earlier.

The reception marked the first official visit to Thailand by a British cabinet minister since Bangkok's 2014 military coup. When Boris drifted over to my small group, I realised I should have something of substance to say. By then, the foreign secretary must have answered questions on Brexit at least a dozen times. His position on that was well known and I had little sympathy with it. Confrontation would be pointless.

I thought it possible no one had asked about the property we were in. I glanced at the ambassador and then down at Boris (he was surprisingly short) and, for want of something better to say, ventured: "Many Thais and Brits are concerned about the sale of the British embassy." The ambassador was looking at me warily. I ploughed on: "We all understand the need to maximise value, but will it be possible to preserve the house and the other historic assets?" But Johnson was primed: "We'll get a shiny

Opposite page: Statue of Queen Victoria in the grounds of the former British embassy at Ploenchit, photographed by Mark Bertram in 2005.

new property. Recalibrating the relationship for the twenty-first century! Onwards and upwards!" And that was it. He was already explaining to someone else the vast opportunities that Brexit would bring.

I can't say I was disappointed by his answer as I had no expectations. But a couple more conjugated verbs, or at least another pronoun, would have been nice. In fact, it was already too late: it was a done deal. The sale had been agreed. A shiny new office building for the chancery had been selected. The ambassador had yet to find a suitable new residence, but there was time for him to do so.

About one-third of the embassy site on the corner of Ploenchit and Wireless roads had already been sold some ten years earlier, and the British foreign and commonwealth office was under enormous pressure to monetise the remainder. Its value was one of the highest on their books, and releasing that value, it was argued, would enable the FCO to upgrade and build many more establishments around the world. Opposition was not intense: no petitions were organized, no marches held. Nevertheless, there was plenty of grumbling and even some outrage. And it wasn't coming solely from whingeing Brits in Bangkok. Many Anglophiles among the Thai elite – especially those who had been educated in the UK – took the sale as a personal affront, a demonstration of Britain's lack of commitment to Thailand and, for some, an act of hypocrisy as the destruction of such historic buildings would probably not have been allowed in the UK.

The economic logic was clear, but critics felt that the British government was short-changing the country by defining value in purely financial terms – based on potential investment yields or replacement costs. These methods ignored the embassy's outstanding quality, location and history which had contributed to the UK punching above its weight in Thailand, a source of its much-vaunted soft power. A sale might have been structured to preserve the "historic assets", which included the ninety-year-old ambassador's residence where the reception for the foreign secretary was being held; the statue of Queen Victoria that in less security-obsessed times, when the public had been allowed into the grounds, was a symbol of fecundity and a place of pilgrimage for Thai women seeking divine help in conceiving; and the war memorial that was a focus for the community every November on Armistice Day. But the government's bookkeepers weren't interested: the goal was to extract the highest price, and any constraints on future development could reduce bids. This argument was debatable, but the government had no appetite for the debate, so the sale went ahead as envisaged.

There was some compromise. The murmurs of discontent had reached the buyer who decided to knock down and then partially rebuild the ambassador's residence, while the statue would be relocated on site and the war memorial would go elsewhere. So some of the historic assets would be preserved on the property, but making them part of a commercial development reduced them to objects of nostalgia, features in a retail experience and backdrops for selfies. The UK had largely forfeited the soft power and heritage associated with them.

There had been suggestions that it may not have been within the gift of the British government to sell the land on a commercial basis. If, for instance, the land had been presented to the British by the Siamese government specifically for the purpose of establishing a diplomatic presence, would a commercial sale constitute a breach of this original intention, either legally or ethically? However, a cursory inspection of the documents would reveal that the British had in fact purchased the land from a Thai family and the title was therefore unencumbered by such concerns.

Prior to acquiring the current site in the 1920s, the British had established a consulate on a riverfront plot in Bangrak district, but that land reverted to the Siamese government and became the General Post Office. It now housed the high-rise head office of the Communications Authority of Thailand. The British had acquired the Ploenchit site when the location was suburban, on the outer edge of the city, but it was now prime land in Bangkok's central business district.

It was no surprise to find that the Ploenchit land was a commercial acquisition. What I didn't expect to find was that the original riverside plot in Bangrak had indeed been given to the British government by King Rama IV in 1856. Being so long ago and superseded by the second transaction in the 1920s, the 1850s gift did not pose a serious threat to the legitimacy of the 2017 sale. Yet it was also clear that history had largely overlooked the extraordinary events leading up to the king's 1856 land gift and the continued relevance of some of those circumstances in modern-day Thailand. This book tells that story.

London and Bangkok, May 1851

On the first of May 1851, Queen Victoria and Prince Albert presided over a glamourous ceremony to launch the Great Exhibition of the Works of Industry of All Nations at Hyde Park in London.

Exactly two weeks later, on 15 May, some 6,000 miles to the east in Bangkok, a more traditional royal ritual was getting underway: the coronation of Phra Chom Klao Chao Yu Hua, the fourth reign of the Chakri dynasty, known in the west as King Mongkut or King Rama IV.

The Great Exhibition showcased the latest industrial technology from Britain and thirty-nine of its colonies as well as some fifty other nations. The exhibition ran for six months and attracted six million visitors. Although it was an international event, it was above all a celebration of British innovation and imperial achievement. In contrast, the coronation of King Rama IV was steeped in the traditions and rituals that had governed royal Siamese successions for hundreds of years.

At first glance, the two 1851 events illustrated the cultural, philosophical and technological gulf separating the two countries: Britain, a forward-looking global powerhouse at the forefront of industry, focused primarily on trade as a generator of wealth; Siam, a backward-looking feudal state clinging to its ancient rituals and traditions, resisting the winds of global change.

But King Mongkut was to use his coronation to signal a change in direction. While following the time-honoured traditions of his predecessors, the king introduced European-influenced tweaks, such as a new emphasis on the crowning ritual itself, as if to demonstrate his openness to western thinking. His son, King Chulalongkorn, Rama V, was to use his own coronation in 1873 to go much further by announcing the abolition of the custom of prostration in front of the monarch. In the years between the coronations of those two great Siamese kings of the nineteenth century, the changes hinted at in Mongkut's ceremony had led to a fundamental realignment of the Siamese state and a sea change in its economy.

Siam did not participate in the 1851 Great Exhibition. However, a year before the end of the fourth reign, the kingdom took part in its first international exhibition: the 1867 Paris Universal Exhibition. King Mongkut involved himself directly in managing Siam's participation. He was keen to portray his kingdom as both a "modern, technologically developing nation, and the ancient kingdom with archaic and exotic culture".[1] The two depictions correlated to dual objectives, to "instill national pride" at home in Siam's culture, which he viewed as essential to survival, and to "inhibit foreign intervention by appearing as a civilizational equal to Western nations" abroad.[2]

There was likewise no direct participation by the British government in King Mongkut's coronation, but within five years Britain was sending its first consul to reside in Bangkok and the number of British ships entering Bangkok port each year had grown from a negligible amount at the end of the third reign to more than a hundred in the last year of the fourth reign.[3]

King Mongkut and his son, King Chulalongkorn, are generally revered in modern Thailand for their success in preventing Siam falling into the hands of the rapacious empires of either Britain or France. Siam became effectively a buffer state between British Burma and Malaya and French Indochina. Recent historical studies have tended to challenge this orthodoxy by viewing the country as having acquired a semi-colonial status through its subjugation to a series of "unequal treaties" imposed by the western powers, or even suggesting that Siam was itself a competing power that unsuccessfully vied with the British and the French for neighbouring territories.[4]

In Asia, the first of the unequal treaties was imposed by the British on China in 1842, after the war generally known as the First Opium War. The model was then used by the British to negotiate with Siam in 1855 and then further developed in the treaties of the Second Opium War with China in 1858 and 1860 and, also in 1858, a treaty with Japan. The various treaties share much common ground: the opening up of port cities to western trade at low tariffs; minimal restrictions on foreign trade; extraterritorial rights for foreign citizens; and the right for foreigners to reside in certain cities.

One important difference was that whereas foreigners in China and Japan were mostly confined to designated foreign settlements in specific port cities, in Siam the restrictions on where foreigners could live were much looser. This points to a more fundamental difference. China and Japan regarded the foreign presence as an unwanted infringement of their sovereignty; Siam, on the other hand, was much more welcoming, although equally conscious of some of the unwanted aspects of the foreign presence. Siam's compromising attitude certainly helped feed the heroic view that Mongkut and Chulalongkorn were able successfully to navigate the country through the threat of colonisation, while the greater resistance and hostility displayed by China especially is reflected in the more common modern view there of the period being one of national humiliation.

The changes to Siam's international profile initiated under King Mongkut were therefore among the most significant in its modern history. Key catalysts were the ending of Siam's tributary relationship with China in 1853 and the signing of the *Treaty of Friendship and Commerce between Great Britain and Siam* in April 1855, generally known as the Bowring treaty. The treaty was ratified and came into effect a year later.

But some of the changes ushered in by the Bowring treaty took time to take root. One incident shortly after ratification revealed the scope for different interpretations of the treaty's provisions. The incident – which we refer to as the Seng affair – involved the arrest and punishment of two Siamese subjects who the British deemed entitled to consular protection. A more serious confrontation was averted by the king's decisive, conciliatory action, but the consequence for two of the protagonists was to prove fatal.

Aside from the human cost, the episode highlighted a gulf in interpretation of the treaty's provisions that would need to be bridged for the treaty to work. In the end, the confusion over the scope of consular jurisdiction was dealt with quickly (although friction over extraterritorial rights would re-emerge later), but a less urgent matter that the incident highlighted, involving confusion over the rights of foreigners to own property, was to prove surprisingly enduring.

This book offers a detailed narrative of the incident and investigates its background and repercussions. It examines the cultural and diplomatic environment and presents a portrait of the social milieu and some of the key protagonists. Chapter 1 sets the scene by taking a fresh look at the Bowring treaty itself, principally through the unpublished account of Bowring's mission secretary, Harry Parkes, and archived correspondence. Together these shed more light on the cut-and-thrust of the negotiations than Bowring's own account and put more flesh on the debate going on in the Siamese court between the liberal and conservative factions.[5]

The second chapter concentrates on the issue of property rights that was largely sidestepped by Bowring in his treaty negotiations but remained an important issue for the Siamese. This issue is placed in the context of the development of property rights in Siam and focuses on reactions to attempts by westerners to claim property rights in the early Rattanakosin era, culminating in the property provisions in the supplementary agreement to the Bowring treaty.

Chapter 3 introduces the first British consul, describing his background and arrival in Bangkok, and presents a view of the city that greeted him. The fourth and fifth chapters look at his efforts to establish a permanent consulate, culminating in a chronology of the climactic events that appeared to interrupt these efforts and threatened to derail Anglo-Siamese friendship. Chapter 6 examines the aftermath of the incident through unexplored documents that shed new light on the king's successful management of the consequences, concluding with the eventual development of the British consulate.

The final chapter considers legacies of the Seng affair, investigating its treatment by contemporaries and historians, its role in the development of foreign property rights and the future movements of the British diplomatic presence in the kingdom.

On one level, the story carries a familiar message illustrating the unpredictability of history. The motivations and actions of leaders more often than not lack the clarity and single-mindedness of a well-thought out policy or strategy, while the heady concerns mulled over by politicians and historians are often undermined, deflected or superseded by unforeseen events. The capriciousness of history is matched by the fickleness of historiography. The diplomatic incident that forms the centrepiece of this story has been largely forgotten, as has the debate that underlay it. Despite the personal tragedies it brought about, its geopolitical consequences appear slight when compared to the great events of history. In retelling the tale, the book shines a light on a relatively obscure incident from the past and the still significant issues it brings up.

The story also suggests that there remains an important and unexplored aspect in the history of the Bowring treaty and its consequences. Much has been written on the treaty's principles of free trade and extraterritorial rights, but little on a third aspect: the development of property rights for foreigners. This is striking when one considers that while trade liberalisation has increased and deepened over the years and extraterritorial rights were eventually negotiated away in the twentieth century, foreign property rights have remained largely stuck in the nineteenth century. Indeed, in some ways, they are more restricted today than they were under the Bowring treaty of 1855.

Sir John Bowring

Chapter 1

Bowring's "total revolution"

TOASTING CHANGE

British factory, Bangkok, 19 April 1855

Sir John Bowring was hosting an afternoon dinner party to celebrate the successful conclusion of his mission to Siam. The atmosphere was relaxed and amicable, marked by "reciprocal assurances of friendship" and a number of toasts "warmly drank and responded to on both sides".

But not all the guests were feeling comfortable or celebratory. One of the Siamese commissioners, the Somdet Ong Noi, was struggling with western etiquette. Bowring observed him holding the prongs of the fork in his hand, "not knowing which end was to be employed".[1] But table manners were the least of the Somdet's concerns. His discomfort came from the knowledge that the toasts were celebrating the end of an era – his era. The Anglo-Siam (or Bowring) treaty was intended to signal the death of monopolistic business practices, the very foundation of his massive wealth. What's more, the health of his ailing elder brother, the Somdet Ong Yai, had deteriorated rapidly. In fact, the signing of the Bowring treaty was one of the last official duties in the elder Somdet's life. He passed away a few days later.

The underlying tension might have largely escaped the three British negotiators at the dinner who could be forgiven for revelling in their own success. But it was inescapable for the other Siamese commissioners. As the party broke up, Bowring's two secretaries – Harry Parkes and Bowring's son, also called John – were asked by Prince Wongsa, the only royal at the table, to accompany him to his palace nearby. The prince, a short, rotund and normally jovial character, wanted to convey a serious message to the envoys before they left Bangkok. Yes, the negotiations had gone well and the liberal expectations of the king and his principal advisors had been met, but a conservative reaction could not be ruled out.

The prince was one of King Mongkut's most trusted advisors. He and the Kalahom (effectively, Siam's prime minister) had been most involved in the negotiations, meeting Parkes and the younger Bowring every evening to go through the details, clause by clause. Now the prince wanted the British team to appreciate that the signing of the treaty did not necessarily mean that the conservatives had accepted defeat. He worried that the king "allows himself to be influenced by others", therefore his support could not be counted on. He promised that he and the Kalahom "would make every effort in their power to counteract the representations" of the anti-treaty faction (the "strong Court party opposed to foreigners, and consequently to the New Treaty") and "give the Treaty full effect", but any "untoward consequence . . . would certainly be visited upon their heads". As Parkes reported:

> It might happen that they would be unable on some occasion to withstand the cabal of their opponents and the sudden displeasure of the King, and thus they might lose their present position, which to them would be little short of destruction, for loss of office with the Siamese involves also that of income and all emoluments.

In view of the high stakes involved and the relatively straightforward character of the prince, he was not overstating the danger he and the Kalahom faced if the tide were to turn against them. However, his reason for raising the subject, he told the British secretaries, was not to seek protection for himself, but rather to make sure that the British understood the forces at work so that "the British Government would not hastily have recourse to forcible measures, but would treat their Government with indulgent consideration" while also providing protection to the Siamese if other foreign nations were to make "additional unreasonable demands with which they would be unable to comply".[2]

He was appealing simultaneously for both British restraint if Siam should suddenly turn inwards and for British protection against other western powers who may have political ambitions in Siam.

RESISTING CHANGE

Prince Wongsa's post-prandial fears that evening might appear in retrospect somewhat exaggerated. The treaty just signed gave clear proof that Siam was committed to free and fair trading practices in partnership with the great powers of the west as the route to economic growth and prosperity for its people. During the remainder of the reigns of King Mongkut and his son, King Chulalongkorn, this view would in general hold sway over the opposing voices advocating a more cautious, sometimes protectionist, world view.

Yet it was true that the conservative voices had not been completely silenced. They also believed in the virtues of trade, but for them trade was not equally open to all; it was a trade that relied on the granting of monopolies for individual commodities, and the entrenchment of those monopolies among the leading noblemen of the country. This system had persisted since the accession of King Nangklao, Rama III, in 1824, who previously had been himself a significant trader.

In the early years of the third reign, tentative steps were taken towards fostering trade with the west, most notably with the signing of the Burney treaty with Britain in 1826 and the Roberts treaty with America in 1833. But since the 1840s, liberalisation had stalled and anti-western sentiment had grown.

Siam's reluctance to enter into closer trading ties with the west bore little comparison with the isolationism of Japan that confronted US Commander Matthew Perry when he first visited that country in 1853. Indeed, Siam's economy during the third reign became more export-oriented, though not to the satisfaction of western traders who were effectively excluded from participating in the tax-farming system. Under this system individual merchants bid for the right to monopolise trade in specific commodities. The bidders were invariably prominent members of the Chinese community in Siam who were already cossetted by preferential trading rights that were not granted to merchants from other countries. In the tax-farming system, the seller was not so much an amorphous, impersonal department of state as the head of the department with the right to grant the monopoly who could and did share in the benefits derived from the bidding process. The number of businesses controlled by tax farmers grew to some thirty-eight products, including most major goods, in the third reign.[3]

Western traders, particularly the British based in Singapore, were increasingly frustrated by their exclusion from the potential riches of Siam's economy. Complaints to the foreign office were submitted by the Singapore Chamber of Commerce as well as some business associations in Great Britain in the late 1840s, culminating in a torrent of "memorials" in early 1850 from chambers of commerce, trade associations and groups of business leaders in "nearly thirty of the principal manufacturing towns" in northern England and Scotland, but also in London and Belfast.[4]

The main complaints were of specific abuses and treaty breaches allegedly committed by the Siamese as well as the shortcomings of the 1826 Burney treaty itself. Some of these perceived abuses stemmed from the treatment of the Scottish trader, Robert Hunter, who had been resident in Bangkok for almost two decades but had fallen out with the Siamese authorities and been forced to leave the country in 1844. Hunter's specific complaints were of questionable merit but were by no means the only ones; others had complained of such treaty violations as unlawful detention and unfair accusations of piracy and smuggling.

The resulting mission by Sir James Brooke in 1850, however, failed to win any concessions from the Siamese, just as had a similarly unsuccessful mission of the American envoy Joseph Balestier earlier the same year.[5] Brooke's frustration led him to conclude that only a hard line would work against the Siamese:

> I can only arrive at the conclusion that there is no other course open to Her Majesty's Government, excepting to demand the freedom of the British subjects unwarrantably detained, a just reparation for injuries inflicted, a fair remuneration for pecuniary losses entailed by violations of the Treaty, and either a more equitable Treaty in accordance with the observances of civilized nations, or a total withdrawal of British subjects and their property from Siam. . . . Should these just demands firmly urged be refused, a force should be present immediately to enforce them by a rapid destruction of the defences of the river, which would place us in possession of the Capital, and by restoring us to our proper position of command, retrieve the past and ensure peace for the future, with all its advantages of a growing and most important commerce.[6]

The other alternative was to wait for King Nangklao to pass away in the hope of a more compliant new king, who it was hoped would be Mongkut.

However, the British government had no interest in direct involvement in Siam's politics: neither gun-boats nor king-making were on the agenda. As it turned out, regime change would happen very soon anyway. King Nangklao died only a few months after Brooke had left Siam, although it took another four years after King Mongkut's accession for the next British mission to materialise.

INVITING CHANGE

King Mongkut was cut from a different cloth than King Nangklao, his half-brother. Although foreign observers often viewed Mongkut the legitimate successor to King Rama II (being the son of a queen, unlike Nangklao), he was both too young and too inexperienced in 1824 to be a serious candidate, and King Nangklao's succession was uncontested. Out of conviction or to avoid confrontation – or both, Prince Mongkut had spent the entire twenty-seven years of the third reign as a monk. He had no official involvement in the kingdom's international affairs until he was ordered to "witness all papers of communications in English and Siamese" during the 1850 Brooke mission.[7] He had, however, developed a keen interest and appreciation of both foreign languages and foreign technology, a tolerance of western religion and an understanding that the west was far ahead of Siam in terms of material progress and scientific achievement.

His accession to the throne owed much to the liberal elite in Siam with whom he was closely associated. This group understood that Siam was too weak to contemplate war with the powerful western nations. British defeats of China in 1842 and Burma in 1852 confirmed that the west in general and Great Britain in particular had replaced the traditional power brokers of Southeast Asia. By 1855, the British had control of Lower Burma, the Straits Settlements and Malaya, the Dutch had deepened their control of the Indonesian archipelago, the Spanish remained dominant in the Philippines and the French were beginning to make inroads into Indochina.

King Nangklao was certainly aware of these forces and also realised the need to reach an accommodation with the new powers. But what distinguished King Mongkut was his accurate assessment of the motivations of Siam's new western antagonists, in particular the British. As he told Wongsa in 1852, the British interest in Burmese Ava was not motivated by expansionist ambition, but rather "to get money or territory close to the sea for trade only".[8]

This understanding prompted Mongkut to regard British overtures to trade at face value, rather than as precursors to colonisation. At the same time, his own lack of direct experience in the cut-and-thrust of commercial trade gave him a more objective, less self-interested view of trade in general. He was probably as suspicious of British motives as some of his advisors but had less to fear from them economically.

As soon as he had ascended the throne, King Mongkut started to put in place a more liberal agenda by permitting rice and paddy to be exported, reducing the measurement duty imposed as a flat rate on visiting ships from 1,700 ticals to 1,000 ticals, a reduction of more than 40 per cent, and legalising the opium trade through a new monopoly. He also initiated an invitation to the British to make a return visit to Siam with the aim of concluding a treaty along the lines suggested by Brooke. Brooke received a letter from the new Kalahom in 1851 assuring him that the new king "fully understands the relations of foreign nations" and "any intercourse or consultation may hereafter be conducted in an easier method than before."[9] A new attitude now prevailed in Siam. During the Brooke mission Mongkut had written in his habitually eccentric English two confidential letters to British intermediaries. The letters contained criticism of King Nangklao's intransigent position and held out the suggestion that the next reign would be more liberal:

> I trust you will not much surprised for disappointment of English Embassy at present because Siam is now of most absolute Monarchy in the world, in which monarchy one's oppinion is no use. The others are equal of animals & vegitables in the kingdom, but I beg to assure you that His Honour Khun Phra nai Wai Wornett [Chamnuen Waiworanat; later, the Kalahom] is a good man knowing of political geography of the world. The purpose of English embassy would be succeeded on future very fairly for his preparation if he was styled or elevated in Suprime state of Siamese ministers that have ability to give advise to the succeeding or subsequent royalty in Siam but on the present none can do anything.[10]

Without King Mongkut's benign influence and open attitude, the fate of Siam at the hands of the British and other western powers could have been very different.

Good fortune also played a role. It was indeed fortunate that the British team that came to negotiate in 1855 was headed by Sir John Bowring, a disciple of Jeremy Bentham and considered "the foremost preacher and practitioner" of free trade.[11] Although his subsequent history, especially his role in the Second Opium War, would damage his reputation as an upholder of liberal values, Bowring's aversion to imperial overreach contrasted with the thinking of a man like Sir James Brooke, the White Rajah of Sarawak, the quintessential romantic action hero of Victorian Britain, who had led the earlier failed mission and had hoped to be re-appointed as envoy to Siam. Not that Bowring was averse to expressions of imperial arrogance, such as threatening aggressive action to break a stalemate or arguing for points of protocol (a twenty-one gun salute to announce his arrival; wearing swords in the inner palace) in the face of Siamese objections.[12] Yet, unlike some British officials who had preceded him as envoys to the Chakri court, his sense of British superiority was based on the material progress his country had achieved, rather than a concept of racial superiority. And this view would not have been so far from the thoughts of King Mongkut himself, who was wont to criticise the backwardness of his own people and even informed Bowring that Siam was "a half-civilized half-barbarous" nation.[13] In February 1854, Bowring was appointed Superintendent of British Trade in China, Governor of Hong Kong and Plenipotentiary accredited not only to China, but also to Cochin China, Japan and Siam. Later in the year, Clarendon acceded to Bowring's request to include Korea in his portfolio, even though "it could scarcely be anticipated that it would lead to any very important results."[14] However, Bowring's instructions were to maintain his primary focus on China. Only if the opportunity arose should he try to secure commercial agreements with the other countries under his care. It was "unquestionable" that Japan had the greatest potential outside China,[15] and this prioritising became even more apparent in June of that year after the United States had secured the opening of two ports there.[16] Siam was at best third on Bowring's to-do list.

Given its low priority, it took a combination of serendipity and political expediency to smooth the way for Bowring's visit to Bangkok. The timing was not right for a mission to Japan. Bowring was unable to get sufficient naval support for a visit due to the Admiralty's pre-occupation with the Crimean War. He was also irritated by a new British convention with Japan that was designed to open up a couple of Japanese ports. Bowring viewed the convention, negotiated by Naval Commander-in-Chief Sir James Stirling, as seriously flawed and likely to undermine his own commercial agenda. If he were to visit now, he argued, it could "lead to inextricable embarrassments, and might either compromise the Queen's dignity, or necessitate an appeal to hostile demonstrations, which I most earnestly desire to avoid".[17] Instead, he thought a Japan visit should be more fruitful in 1856, by which time the US treaty with Japan would have come into effect and duties should be more regulated.[18] On the other hand, Siam was ready and very willing to talk now.

At the same time, the collapse of the Canton trade and China's preoccupation with the Taiping Rebellion gave Bowring additional incentives to seek greener pastures for British trade elsewhere. Bowring also wanted to distance himself from the crisis in China, which he considered more likely to require military than diplomatic intervention.[19] Had the situation in China or Japan been more promising, Bowring may not have visited Siam at all or, worse, might have sent a deputy, which the Siamese had explicitly discouraged.[20]

Siam, on the other hand, offered Bowring the potential for a quick success, which he needed. Bowring owed his first China posting as consul at Canton (Guangzhou) in 1849 to the kindness of Prime Minister Lord Palmerston and Foreign Secretary Lord Clarendon, after his disastrous investment in a failed iron company in South Wales had left him dependent on loans from his sons and friends.[21] By early 1855 his finances were in better shape and his official role greatly elevated, yet he had made frustratingly little progress in developing relations with the Chinese authorities. King Mongkut's encouraging actions and correspondence suggested a much warmer welcome awaited him in Siam. At the same time, the upheaval in China was also having a negative impact on Siam's finances, which made the Siamese authorities more receptive to British overtures. As the Phraklang informed Bowring, "many of our merchants who have been in the habit of loading junks with products of the jungles and forests have been necessitated to cease trading, consequently the revenue of the country derived from duties on produce has decreased" and trade suspended "until tranquility is restored in China".[22]

So it was that Bowring left Hong Kong on 12 March 1855 and arrived off the bar in the Gulf of Siam on the 24th. He arrived with two men-of-war, the HMS *Rattler* and HMS *Grecian*, and two secretaries: Harry Parkes, consul at Amoy (Xiamen), and his eldest son, John C. Bowring, a merchant employed by Jardine Matheson. Bowring sailed into Bangkok on 3 April and left on the 22nd. But negotiations proper didn't start until 6 April and were more or less concluded ten days later.

The Kalahom (Si Suriyawong), photographed by John Thomson in 1865.

ADVOCATING CHANGE

Apart from fortunate timing, the rapid success of the mission was due in no small part to the character and ability of Bowring and Parkes, as well as Bowring's prestigious position as the first British negotiator to Siam with papers from Queen Victoria. But the main reason for the mission's success lay with the Siamese, and in particular King Mongkut and the Kalahom. While the king's desire for the mission to succeed was probably the single largest factor, the importance of the support of the Kalahom cannot be underestimated.

When Bowring first arrived in Bangkok, he was not sure what to make of the Kalahom. He had reason to expect the full support of the king from letters that had passed between them, and he knew that the Kalahom had been instructed by the king to co-operate with Bowring. But whether the Kalahom would prove to be a supporter of or an impediment to a deal could not be known in advance.

Thus, Bowring was pleasantly surprised when the Kalahom espoused a firm liberal line at their first discussion on the treaty on 5 April. The nobleman unexpectedly launched into a stinging attack on the prevailing taxation system in the country and on the vested interests that maintained it, meaning primarily his own uncle – the Somdet Ong Noi. The burden of the excessive taxes, he argued, oppressed "the poor and producing portion of the population". Taxes on virtually all commodities were not only high but could be levied multiple times. The Kalahom gave the example of sugar, which was taxed "in the course of cultivation, after the canes are reaped, on its way to market, and upon its exportation". What made matters worse was the tax-farming system, under which the government transferred its interest in the tax to the highest bidder, who would collect the tax and add a substantial profit margin in the process:

> "Under this system the country," observed the Prakalahom, "grows poorer daily, and is losing its commerce through having so little produce to export; what therefore is chiefly needed is, that the people should be relieved of their burdens, their industry encouraged, and a market provided for their produce."

The Kalahom explained to Bowring that his mission was the best, and possibly only, chance to bring about fundamental change:

> "But who has the power to effect this great change? Dare any of the ministers propose it, and brave the clamour that would immediately be awakened by those in high places, and by the numerous nobles, monopolists, &c. who are all interested in the preservation of the present pernicious system?"

The Kalahom asserted that if Bowring had the interests of the Siamese people at heart, "your influence should be exerted with the king to bring about that radical and necessary change which cannot otherwise be accomplished."[23]

Bowring was encouraged but not totally convinced by this outpouring of liberal sentiment, noting:

> Either he is a consummate hypocrite, or a true patriot: in any case, he is a most sagacious man, towering far above every other person whom we have met – of graceful, gentlemanly manners, and appropriate language.[24]

And again three days later:

> If the Kalahom be sincere, matters will end promisingly; if not, he is the most supereminent of hypocrites. He denounces the existing state of things with vehemence; says that bribery and mis-rule are often triumphant – that monopolies are the bane of the country, and the cause of the loss of trade and misery of the people. He told me I should be blessed if I put an end

to them, and encouraged me to persevere in a most vigorous persistence in my efforts for its overthrow.[25]

Bowring's wavering judgement of the Kalahom was reflected in the response of other westerners who had to deal with him. He was generally acknowledged as the most capable, intelligent and cunning of the ruling elite: in the words of the missionary Samuel House, "a man of great ability and shrewdness – the very embodiment of Siamese address and intrigue". But the same qualities could elicit a more cynical interpretation, especially among those who had failed to win concessions from him, such as the American businessman, David O. King, who judged him a "wily, deep, rapacious fox".[26]

In the end, it would appear that Bowring's hopes stood on stronger ground than his fears. The Kalahom went to great lengths to prompt Bowring on the best way to handle his older, more conservative relatives, and showed himself willing to go into battle against them when negotiating the treaty details. By the end of the process, Bowring was inclined to give the Kalahom the benefit of the doubt:

> The personal character of the prime minister is to me an object of much admiration. He is the most distinguished man of the greatest family in the empire; he was the main instrument which placed the present King upon the throne against the claims of the late King's son, and was made prime minister. . . . If he prove true to his profession, he is one of the noblest and most enlightened patriots the Oriental world has ever seen.[27]

Not everyone was convinced that the Kalahom's support for change was driven by altruism. By reducing the power of the conservative faction, the proposed changes were designed to create a fairer trading environment for all; yet privileges remained, and the Kalahom – as the most powerful minister and an owner of several cargo ships – was now both well placed and pleased to be the principal beneficiary.

Harry Parkes viewed the Kalahom even more harshly, seeing him as being motivated by a desire for greater political power. He considered the Kalahom "the most ambitious" member of the Bunnag family who "seeks for unbounded sway over the Senior King". In Parkes' opinion, the Somdet Ong Yai, the Kalahom's father, did not share his son's aims and was able to hold him in check, but soon after the elder Somdet passed away, the extent of the Kalahom's ambition was revealed:

The first act of the Prakalahom since his father's death is to commence the erection of a new palace which will exceed that of the King in size and magnificence. There all the brothers are to take up their residence and bold must the king be who dare attack them.[28]

THE COMMISSIONERS

Prince Wongsa (This photograph and those on the following page by courtesy of Tatiya Bunnag and the Bunnag Lineage Club)

The king had sensibly delegated the task of negotiating treaty details to a team of commissioners but remained the final arbiter and moral compass for the treaty. Originally the commission comprised the Kalahom and three other members of his family who had served the kings of Siam in leading ministerial roles for generations: the Kalahom's father, the elder Somdet (Somdet Ong Yai); his uncle, the younger Somdet (Somdet Ong Noi); and his brother, the Phraklang.

Prince Wongsa, the only member of the royal family on the commission, was a later addition. As one of the king's most trusted relatives, his appointment conferred a higher status on the commission even though the nominal head remained the elder Somdet, its most senior member. The prince's presence may have been designed to help resolve potential conflicts between the older and younger noblemen. Such could be expected as the two generations found themselves on opposite sides of the argument.

The Phraklang shared the Kalahom's belief in the need to reform the taxation and trading systems. Although he was less involved in the detailed negotiations than his elder brother, his criticism of the prevailing political system in Siam was at least as sharp. He elaborated his position in a passionate outburst to two young English visitors – Charles Bell and Robert Hunter junior (the latter no doubt responsible for translating

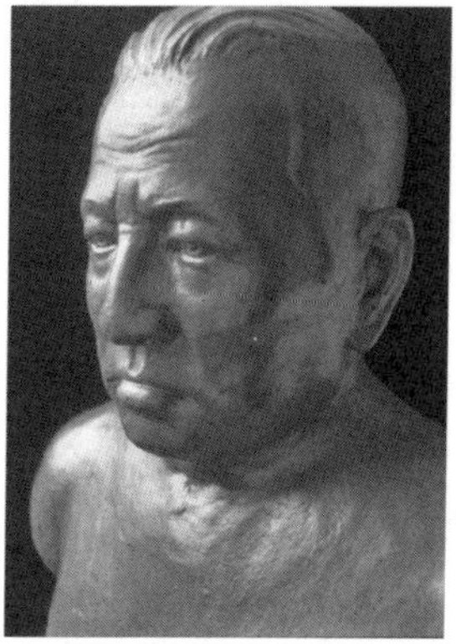

Somdet Ong Yai

Somdet Ong Noi

The Phraklang (Rawiwong)

and embellishing the Phraklang's words) – who were convinced of his sincerity:

> This country never can attain to any greatness, until the whole system of government is changed. We have hitherto given all the power to the Nobles, and what are we? Let us give a little to the people and try whether we shall not improve. Let us not have our ministers appointed for life, let them be elected for a term of years, and let their election depend on the voice of the people.[29]

The two Somdets, on the other hand, had a vested interest in preserving as much of the existing system as possible. The Kalahom told Bowring that a recent quarrel between himself and the Somdet Ong Noi "was scarcely yet healed", the quarrel having been "on account of one of his mercenary measures" which the Kalahom had "openly condemned".[30] Prince Wongsa was well-known for his amiable nature and could be a conciliator, if needed. However, he was no fence-sitter: in representing the king he also aligned himself with the liberal cause, and it is possible that his presence on the commission was also intended to shift the balance in favour of the liberal agenda.

Outside the main meetings between the British and Siamese teams, detailed negotiations were mostly conducted in a smaller group comprising Parkes, the younger Bowring, the prince and the Kalahom. While the smaller British team had clear guidelines from Bowring on what would and would not be acceptable negotiating terms, the prince and the Kalahom had to take discussion points back to the two Somdets and try to convince them to agree. Once agreement was achieved, the king would have the final say, but that proved to be the lesser obstacle.

In separate meetings with Bowring, each of the Somdets argued that Siam was a small country with limited produce. For the younger Somdet, the implication was that a new commercial treaty was unnecessary and would be of no benefit; what the country really needed was protection against the machinations of the major powers. This argument was keenly felt and held some truth: the Somdets were probably as anxious at the prospect of colonisation as their more liberal relatives. Nevertheless, their stated position was also disingenuous. The more specific reason for the Somdet Ong Noi to oppose the new treaty was understood by Bowring and by the Kalahom to be self-interest: dismantling the tax-farming system constituted a direct attack on the source of his riches.

The older Somdet appeared to hold a less adamant point of view. Under Rama III, the Somdet Ong Yai had combined the two most influential posts of Kalahom and Phraklang. Rama IV had promoted him to the rank of Somdet Chaophraya, dividing his previous posts between two of the elder Somdet's sons. Out of deference, however, the new Kalahom did not formally take that title until his father's death, preferring to style himself deputy Kalahom. When the Bowring mission delegates arrived, they considered the older Somdet "the highest and most influential noble in the Kingdom", even though they believed he no longer held any specific office. Moreover, with five ships of his own trading with China, Singapore and Java, he was considered "one of the principal patrons of and profiters by the existing monopolies".[31]

Nevertheless, the elder Somdet had been the leader of the liberal faction that had put Mongkut on the throne in 1851, and even during the Brooke mission of 1850 he had argued in favour of granting concessions to the British before being eventually overruled by King Nangklao and his other advisors.[32] His comments to Bowring perhaps indicated a more sophisticated awareness of economic realities than his brother:

> He said that Siam did not produce enough to fill the ships that come hither, and remarked that the produce might be greatly increased, and that it was by the interchange of articles that nations became rich, and strong, and respected.[33]

However, he was now an old man of sixty-eight and in poor health, giving his foreign visitors "the impression that his age had impaired the earlier powers of his mind".[34] At the key meeting of the British and Siamese negotiating teams on 9 April, the elder Somdet's deteriorating health was visible to all:

> The first Somdetch is nearly imbecile, and obviously understood very imperfectly what passed: his naked leg had a sore, and plaster upon it, which gave him some trouble.[35]

The Somdet Ong Yai did not recover from his illness and died on 26 April, only three days after the departure of the Bowring mission. Given his condition, the burden of resisting some of the changes envisaged in the new treaty fell on the Somdet Ong Noi.

The Somdet Ong Noi was four years younger than his ailing brother and in better health. Under Rama III, he may have been frustrated by his elder brother's decision not to relinquish to him the post of Phraklang when the elder Somdet added the Kalahom position to his portfolio. The younger Somdet nevertheless had managed to build a substantial fortune, effectively working as deputy Phraklang with the position of Phraya Si Phiphat, in charge of the royal warehouse department and most of the commercial activities of the Phraklang's department.

By default he was now the leader of the conservative faction, but he would have been well aware that the war was already lost: the king's strong desire for the Bowring mission to succeed meant that all he could hope for was to win minor skirmishes by negotiating for the retention of specific trading privileges.

NEGOTIATING CHANGE

There is no detailed record available of the discussions that took place among the Siamese commissioners, but Wongsa told Bowring that there had been "great contentions" among the five. He characterised the Kalahom, the Phraklang and himself as "friendly to foreigners" lined up against "others, who belonged to the ancient state of things".[36] The Kalahom clarified to Bowring the important role of the younger Somdet in the conservative group. He had warned Bowring that "from the Somdet Ong Noi much difficulty was to be expected, as all the Revenues derivable from the present Farms or Monopolies came under his superintendence,"[37] and, indeed, this

Sir John Bowring

seemed to be the case. At the 9 April meeting, the younger Somdet and the Kalahom were the main protagonists on opposing sides of the debate on revisions to the taxation system. While the details of their discussion might not have been translated in full for the British team, "it was easy to see that the former objected strongly to the destruction of a system that proved so profitable to himself."[38]

On this occasion, Bowring weighed into the argument by stating that the Siamese were already in breach of various provisions of the 1826 Burney treaty, yet Britain would be able to overlook these breaches as "the new treaty would put commercial relations on a new footing." But anyone opposing the new treaty would "incur the weight of serious responsibility" connected with past breaches.[39]

Bowring interpreted the silence that followed his intervention as acquiescence by the Somdets, but in reality the younger Somdet was not prepared to concede fully. His opposition resurfaced after the meeting when the commissioners met without the British present. The impasse that resulted constituted the most serious moment in the negotiations. The crisis was brought home to Bowring when the Kalahom informed him that the promised follow-up meeting, during which the Siamese commissioners were to present their responses to the British proposals, had to be postponed because the Kalahom "found it impossible to persuade the Commissioners and the influential nobles to accede to the conditions of the Treaty set forth by the Plenipotentiary".[40]

Although the liberals were in the majority and had the king's backing, consensus was required. The Somdets might be aging and their power waning, but the king owed them his crown and their dominance of the kingdom's commerce was as yet unchallenged. The younger Somdet may have hoped to hold out until the British mission gave up and went away, as had happened with Brooke in 1850.

Besides, even though the older Somdet was by now barely able to participate in the discussions due to his failing health, the Somdet Ong

Noi was not fighting his corner alone. Behind him, and presumably in attendance at the commissioners' meetings (as they were in the discussions the commissioners held with the British) were a large number of interested parties. At the 9 April meeting, the younger Somdet was continually consulting the pre-eminent Chinese tax farmers on the trading issues raised by Bowring. When the full extent of Bowring's proposals became clear – that he was seeking to abolish the existing monopolies – the leading tax farmer present, the "great monopolist", who held the farming concessions for some ninety articles, including opium, was said by Bowring to have "looked like ten thunderstorms on hearing what, if effectually carried out, destroys 'Othello's occupation'".[41] Bowring's sarcastic allusion to Othello's fear that his life was in danger of losing its meaning in the eponymous Shakespeare play implied a similar predicament for the tax farmer, albeit from a less noble cause. The tax farmer was identified as "Chay Sootsun a Chinese – better known by his Siamese title of Phrak Muni Chatanit" by Parkes[42] and as Koh Chun (1815-62) with the Siamese title Phraya Phisansupaphol working in the Krom Tha Sai (a government trade department) under the Phraklang by Sng and Pimpraphai,[43] although the authors considered it likely that the claim of ninety tax farms was an exaggeration.[44] Senior Siamese nobles were also in attendance at some meetings, including Phraya Chula. After the death of the Somdet Ong Yai, the younger Somdet and Phraya Chula were reputed to be "the two richest men in the kingdom".[45]

But the support of the Chinese business community could not empower the younger Somdet to defeat the liberals. The Kalahom understood that Bowring would be able to unlock a stalemate by taking a hard line against the conservatives. In essence, Bowring's threats were not markedly different from those that Brooke had suggested at the end of his unsuccessful mission in 1850. But now, with the tacit support of the king, such threats were more likely to work.

When Bowring learnt of the postponement, he decided to make his displeasure known in no uncertain terms. He complained that the delay was unacceptable and accused the commissioners of "faithless conduct" in having broken their promise to give definitive responses to his draft. He backed up his verbal attack with a threat of action that was designed to cause maximum loss of face to the Siamese while hinting at more serious military manoeuvres in the future: he would not only refuse to attend (as he had earlier promised the king to do) the royal procession to nearby Wat Arun Ratchawararam the next day, but – equally galling – he would refuse to move his man-of-war, HMS *Rattler*, down river from its anchorage opposite the British factory, meaning that it would remain visible to all the Siamese during the procession.

The prospect loomed of a major embarrassment for the king. To avoid this, the three main Siamese negotiators – the younger Somdet, Wongsa and the Kalahom – met that night and agreed to release to the British team a partial response to their draft. The Kalahom told Parkes and John C. Bowring that:

> the forcible language used by Sir John Bowring in the commencement of the evening had in reality given him much satisfaction, although he was obliged from obvious reasons to conceal this from the other Commissioners, and he appealed to the attention paid by the Commissioners that evening to the business of the Treaty as evidence of its good effects.[46]

The Kalahom, in commending Bowring's actions, was also giving himself a pat on the back for his successful strategy. From the beginning, he had primed Bowring to expect resistance from the younger Somdet in particular and had advised him not to yield, as "it was only by the Plenipotentiary adopting towards him [the younger Somdet] a strong and decisive tone, that they could hope to overcome the obstacles he would place in the way of unrestricted trade."[47]

Bowring believed it was his own negotiating genius backed by the support of the king and the Kalahom that had overcome resistance to reform in Siam. But from the Kalahom's perspective, Bowring was a useful instrument that he was able to manipulate to triumph over the conservative faction and overcome an impasse that he believed was preventing national development.

Once the impasse had been broken, negotiations moved rapidly to a conclusion. The younger Somdet could see that further opposition to the principle of free trade was fruitless. Instead, his best tactic was to accede to the overall direction while trying to preserve whatever crumbs of privilege he could in the details.

The final reading of the draft treaty on 15 April was held at the house of the Somdet Ong Yai, although the host was too ill to attend the meeting. The younger Somdet proposed that the export duty on dried fish should be removed and replaced with a transit duty. Bowring refused to accept this, "there being room to believe that the object the Somdet Ong Noi had in view was the imposition of a heavy Inland Duty on this article in the place of the moderate Export Duty of the Tariff, and it was reported that a Tender for the farming of this Inland Duty, which had been sent in to the Somdet Ong Noi only yesterday and held out to him terms very profitable to himself, was the inducement which prompted him to propose the change." The younger Somdet was unable to win this point, and the discussion moved onto three commodities on which duties had yet to be agreed: salt, sapanwood and rosewood. "The Phraklang who had the principal interest in the latter duty, consented without much opposition to its being reduced to two salungs [from three salungs per picul], but the Commissioners generally, and the Somdet Ong Noi in particular, warmly contested any abatement being made in respect to Sapan Wood and Salt,"[48] Eventually, a reduced duty on sapanwood was agreed, but the younger Somdet refused to yield on salt. As a result, salt was left out of the treaty, and as retaliation Bowring withdrew his consent for alcoholic drinks to trade under the same restrictions as opium. This compromise was to have serious repercussions in later years when the Siamese objected strongly to growing French imports of alcoholic drinks.

TREATY OUTCOMES

Even if he was unable to win all his desired concessions, the overall outcome of the negotiations could hardly have been more favourable for Bowring. He had no doubt of the significance of his achievement in Siam, claiming in his published account of the mission that:

> my success involved a total revolution in all the financial machinery of the Government, – that it must bring about a total change in the whole system of taxation, – that it took a large proportion of the existing sources of revenue, – that it uprooted a great number of privileges and monopolies which had not only been long established, but which were held by the most influential nobles and the highest functionaries in the State.[49]

His effusive unpublished report to Lord Clarendon heaps even more praise on his achievement:

> My success has far exceeded my most sanguine expectations, – and has been accomplished with a promptitude almost without example in the history of oriental nations, when neither the powers of war or conquest have been auxiliaries to the negotiators.[50]

The Bowring treaty was certainly of historic importance, marking the most significant realignment of Siam's international profile since the eighteenth century and setting the template for a large number of similar treaties that Siam was to sign with western countries over the coming years, but Bowring's assessment that it constituted "a total revolution" was a tad embellished. Terwiel, while agreeing that "the long-term effects [of the Bowring Treaty] were indeed revolutionary", made a strong contrarian argument:

> The Bowring Treaty simply made the Thai market more accessible to European traders; it did not immediately revolutionise the Thai system of revenue collection, it did not lift tax burdens, did not destroy the system of tax farms and "monopolies". The demise of the traditional taxation system would come much later.[51]

Even though it may not have been as revolutionary as Bowring had claimed, the treaty nevertheless was successful in eliminating the advantages that the king, his officials and Chinese merchants had over British merchants, which, it has been argued, was the main objective of the British.[52] Perhaps the Siamese could have won more concessions had the Kalahom supported some of the conservative demands. But for its liberal proponents in Siam, the treaty was successful in expanding international trade and, as a consequence and as intended, Siam's production base. Its failure to dismantle the tax-farming system was not a concern for them. Indeed, the three principal proponents each profited handsomely from the reallocation of tax farms in the wake of the treaty and the passing of the two Somdets: the Kalahom and the Phraklang were allocated control of the lucrative opium and spirit tax farms as well as import and export duties, while the prince controlled many of the tax farms under the royal warehouse department.[53]

Bowring had consistently emphasised that his remit was to negotiate a commercial treaty only. He informed the king in advance that his mission "has no object but the establishment and extension of useful commercial relations".[54] He therefore resisted pressure from the Siamese negotiators to introduce political issues, such as border issues with British dominions in southern Burma and the northern Malay States.

Unsurprisingly, therefore, the main changes were trading concessions. Most significantly, the Siamese agreed to replace the unpopular measurement duty with an import duty of three per cent and an agreed list of tariffs on exports, to levy only one duty on goods being traded and to abolish monopolies (except for firearms and opium). In addition, trade facilitation measures were introduced that would give British merchants free access to all Siamese ports and inland markets and the right of settlement in Bangkok, while guaranteeing British ships the same privileges as those accorded to the Siamese and Chinese. During the ratification process the following year, Harry Parkes was able to add another important measure to facilitate trade by obtaining agreement for the establishment and regulating of a customs house.

The trading provisions in the Bowring treaty were non-reciprocal, and therefore unequal. The imposition of unilateral restrictions on Siam's terms of trade without an expiration date was to become fiscally very damaging. However, it was another non-reciprocal provision of the treaty that led to the criticism of it as "unequal": the provision that empowered a British consul stationed in Bangkok to have jurisdiction over British subjects in Siam. The 1842 Treaty of Nanking that brought the First Opium War to an end was Britain's first such treaty in Asia, granting the British extraterritorial rights over five treaty ports in China. The Siam treaty followed this model – and Bowring encountered more resistance negotiating these rights than the trading privileges:

> The most difficult part of my negotiation was the emancipating British subjects from subjection to Siamese laws, and the establishment of a consul charged with magisterial functions, whose duty it would be to compel obedience on the part of all British residents in Siam to British law. This all-important object was accomplished.[55]

Siamese resistance was not to the concept of extraterritorial rights. Dealing with foreigners through their own representatives was well established in the country.[56] Ethnic communities had been self-governed in this way since the Ayutthaya period. Instead, Siamese opposition focused on having a British consul reside in Bangkok. Unlike in the established Siamese system, the foreign representative would be subject to an overseas power rather than being a servant of the Siamese state.

The Siamese claimed to be worried about this right being abused by other countries, rather than the British, and wanted to make sure that only countries with genuine commercial ambitions in the country should be allowed to station a consul in Bangkok. They were concerned to avoid opening a backdoor to piecemeal colonisation. As Parkes wrote on the first formal meeting with the commissioners:

> They were not afraid on political considerations to receive a Consul from Great Britain, for they were well aware that we had no wish to extend in the East those dominions under our rule which are already almost too large for our control. This however could not be said of other nations. They would not agree to receive Consuls from them unless they had commercial interests in Siam to call for their presence, and this course they could only adhere to in the event of its having been adopted in their negotiations with the British. They therefore begged the Plenipotentiary to duly consider the peculiar circumstances in which their country – a very small one when compared with those from the West – is placed,[57]

It was finally agreed that the British consul would be appointed only once ten ships had arrived in Bangkok, the Siamese hoping this requirement would limit such rights to the major trading powers, which Siam considered to comprise Britain, the United States and France. For the Siamese, the compromise was satisfactory. Not only did they have no fundamental objection to the concept of extraterritoriality, they even acknowledged its necessity. As Don Lord explained, the king in particular wanted to avoid friction that might arise from the application of local laws and practices to British subjects. In China, such incidents had brought periodic western interference into internal affairs. The king hoped that by granting the British consul jurisdiction over his subjects, the risk of such interference would be lessened.[58]

In addition to the trading and consular rights granted to the British by the Bowring treaty, a third area which has generally attracted less attention concerned property rights for foreigners. Under the Bowring treaty British subjects in Siam could buy or rent land and reside in Bangkok within certain boundaries. The Kalahom told Bowring prior to the full meeting with the commissioners that he was "willing to consent to the terms proposed as regarded residence and the right to buy and to sell, and to settle within twenty-four hours' distance from Bangkok".[59] As the Kalahom explained to the commission at the 9 April meeting:

> British subjects could not be allowed an unrestricted right of residence within the Siamese dominions, as the Siamese Government would be unable to extend to them protection if they wandered to distant places.

The restriction was accepted by both sides, but the commissioners were keen to pin down "many particulars as to the manner in which British subjects should acquire titles to their lands, the terms of tenure &c. &c". Bowring was able to deflect these points, arguing successfully that they should be agreed later in the detailed regulations rather than form part of the treaty.[60] However, when Harry Parkes returned a year later to ratify the treaty, the king was so concerned that the issue had not been adequately covered that the final agreement was delayed for two weeks to give time for measurements to be taken and boundaries to be better defined.

The importance of this article to the Siamese negotiators is demonstrated by the fact that it contained some of the most restrictive language in the treaty. The British were content with a general settlement right, but the Siamese went to great lengths to ensure that these rights would be as limited as possible.

The most informative records of this period are from British sources. As a consequence, the issues that mattered most to the British – particularly trade, taxes and consular jurisdiction – have dominated discussion of the Bowring treaty and its impact on Siam. In his recent study of property rights, Larsson recognised the importance of the Bowring treaty in limiting the Siamese state's control of land:

> How did the Bowring treaty affect the Siamese state's interests in regard to provision of formal property rights in land? It did so by limiting the ability of the state to tax land, the right of the state to decide who could own land where, and the jurisdiction of the Siamese government over British subjects in Siam (through extraterritoriality).[61]

However, Larsson's discussion focused on the issues of land taxes and extraterritoriality. What tends to get overlooked is that the granting to foreigners of the right to own property in Siam was in some ways the most revolutionary aspect of the Bowring treaty from the Siamese, though not from the British, point of view.

Harry Parkes

Chapter 2

Parkes and property rights and wrongs

PARKES RETURNS TO BANGKOK

Chaophraya river, Bangkok, Sunday, 16 March 1856

As Harry Parkes was sailing up the Chaophraya river on HMS *Auckland* to the centre of Bangkok, handbills were being posted in all public places in the city bearing a stark and threatening message:

> Pra Intura Tibodi Sira Tong Muang, Master of the Right Hand Office, orders Bam rung, the Officer of the Court, to proclaim to all. – That they must not sell land, gardens, or fields, being the land of the King, to Foreigners. Whoever sells will be punished severely.
>
> Those who are acquainted with the Proclamation are to inform those who are ignorant.[1]

If these handbills were officially sanctioned, they would constitute a direct violation of Article IV of the Bowring treaty, which stipulated that British subjects could rent and buy property within a specified distance of the city. Had the Siamese authorities had a change of heart? And had Harry Parkes' round trip to London been a waste of time – at least from a business point of view?

The previous year, after the Bowring treaty had been signed in Bangkok, Bowring sent Parkes directly to London from Bangkok, carrying the new treaty with him, with the aim of getting it ratified. Bowring returned to Hong Kong but was considering making a second voyage to Bangkok himself to be present for the implementation date. In the end, delays in London meant that Parkes had to navigate the concerns of both the British and Siamese governments alone, no small task for the twenty-eight-year old.

Parkes was to prove equal to the task. He was just as familiar with the details of the agreement as Bowring and enjoyed Bowring's trust. Although young, he was no novice. He had already worked for fifteen years in various Chinese treaty ports, mainly as a Chinese interpreter and translator, but had also stood in for Bowring as acting consul in Canton. According to a recent study, he was "handsome, able, ambitious and shrewd, . . . a typical example of the self-confident go-getter of modest background who seized the opportunities offered by the empire",[2] - or in the more flattering parlance of the age, he was "inspired by an unwavering belief in the imperial destinies of his country".[3] These were all qualities that would serve him well in both London and Bangkok.

In London, the queen's advocate had raised a raft of substantial objections to the terms negotiated by Bowring. Eventually, Parkes had succeeded in defending the original document against these objections and obtaining the secretary of state's endorsement. He had also been delayed (but not for long) by the process of meeting, falling in love with and, on New Year's Day 1856, marrying Fanny Plumer, the entire process taking no longer than six weeks.

The return voyage had been marred by a calamitous mishap in Singapore. Parkes had brought with him some forty-five presents for the first and second kings, the Siamese ministers and the emperor of Cochin China. A sudden squall had interrupted transhipment of this cargo from the mail steamer that had brought him from England to the *Auckland* in Singapore harbour. The poor judgement of an official from the shipping company had led to the disastrous, and entirely preventable, sinking of the boat used to tranship the presents and the loss (presumed drowned) of three of its crew. Of the presents, "some were found, some damaged, others not found". Parkes complained that the extent of the damage would have been lessened "had not several of the cases … been broken open and portions of them lost or abstracted".[4] Parkes decided to reallocate most of the salvaged presents intended for the emperor to Siamese recipients, but still had to deliver a depleted list, some in partially damaged condition.[5]

Thus, on his return to Bangkok he was bringing with him the ratified treaty, his new wife and a number of sodden gifts. He would have had every expectation of signing off the ratified treaty with the Siamese commissioners before 6 April, the date the treaty was due to come into effect. In the worst case, he wanted to make sure he could be in Singapore in time for the mail boat scheduled to leave Singapore for London on 17 May. He was also concerned that the *Auckland* would run out of provisions, although this situation would be alleviated to some extent by the British surveying ship, HMS *Saracen*, which was also anchored at the bar and supplied Parkes' vessel with bread and beef. Nevertheless, Captain Drought of the *Auckland* had told him that the shortage of provisions, especially water, meant the ship would need to leave for Singapore by 16 May.[6] Apart from these time constraints, he was also anxious to leave for Canton (Guangzhou) where he was to take up the post of acting consul for an interim period before returning to his own post as consul of Amoy (Xiamen), from which he had been absent more than a year as a result of his participation in the mission to Siam.

However, the handbills that greeted him were a sharp reminder of the unexpected difficulties that could so easily disrupt his plans. High-level opposition in Siam to some of the fundamental principles of the treaty had not disappeared. The small foreign community suspected that some noblemen had reluctantly acquiesced to the treaty and had since been running a surreptitious campaign to sabotage it.

Parkes realised that swift action was required. He had to find out if the handbills represented anything more than a last-ditch effort to stymie the treaty by the conservatives. As one of the prominent members of the foreign community, the Reverend Dan Beach Bradley, reported:

> Mr. Parkes hearing of it [the handbill] sent and had it copied and wrote to Phra Klang inquiring into it. A Conference concerning it was held in the evening at Prince Kroma Luang Wongsa, at which the Phra Klang, the Prime Minister, Phaya Yomarat, Mr. Parkes, Mr. Mattoon and myself were present. These Rulers deny that the King had anything to do with it.[7]

The senior Siamese assembled at Wongsa's palace and the king were all recognised as supporters of the new treaty and the assurances Parkes received at this meeting led him to believe that the issue had been put to bed. He had no reason to fear it would need to be revisited.

However, it became clear to Parkes quite quickly that the political landscape had altered since he had left Bangkok the year before. The most important change appeared to be in the Kalahom's relationship with King Mongkut:

> An estrangement had occurred between the first King and the Kalahom of which I could only obtain part explanation in the occasional remarks let fall by the latter. He had resigned he informed me the lead he had taken and maintained in the negotiations of the Treaty, and which had contributed so greatly to its success, for the reason that his counsel was no longer sought or listened to by the King, whilst those who advocated a less friendly course were received at Court with marked favour.

The "part explanation" deduced by Parkes was that the king had become aware that Siam had made much larger concessions to British demands than had Japan in Sir James Stirling's October 1855 convention on the opening up of some Japanese ports. More frustratingly, Bowring had failed to negotiate any treaty with Cochin China. This was no small issue for the king, who had urged Bowring "again and again" to open trade with Cochin China. Bowring had downplayed or avoided the issue during his visit. Parkes understood the king's concern to be that the Bowring treaty would be "the subject of a taunt towards" Siam. But for the king, it also represented a potential loss of face to a tributary state. The lack of a British treaty with Cochin China could also have fed suspicions that the British favoured Vietnam and might even have had a plan to allow Vietnam to take over Siam.

In addition to these issues of national prestige, the king was worried about the deleterious effect of the new treaties on his own revenues at a time when his "expenditure particularly on the female inmates of his palace was daily becoming more profuse". Parkes surmised that the King blamed the Kalahom for these failings.[8] The king might also have been attempting to check the Kalahom's power as his growing wealth, derived from his control of major sources of revenue, contrasted sharply with the king's precarious finances.[9]

Outside of Parkes' report, corroboration for an estrangement between the king and the Kalahom is hard to find. Nevertheless, there was clearly a change in the dynamics surrounding the treaty. Parkes observed that – with the Kalahom taking a step back – the other commissioners who had previously supported reform could not be relied upon. Prince Wongsa "leant more than before to the opinions or wishes of the Somdet Ong Noi, whilst the Phraklang, as greatly the junior both of the Prince and the Somdet in years and station, could seldom be induced to pronounce an independent opinion of his own, if it involved any opposition to those of his superiors" (the Phraklang thereby displaying a quite different persona to the liberal firebrand he had exhibited to Charles Bell and the younger Robert Hunter the previous year). Furthermore, the commissioners as a group – including the Yommarat (in charge of *krom mueang*, or ministry of the capital), who had replaced the late Somdet Ong Yai – "would agree no proposition, however trivial, until it had been submitted to and fully considered by His Majesty".[10] Rather than rely again on the goodwill of the Kalahom as before, Parkes realised that he would now need to establish a rapport directly with the king.

Parkes assiduously pursued the direct approach whenever possible over the next month, although his more regular interactions were almost daily meetings with the commissioners. The last obstacle he faced in the process was a potentially long delay in obtaining an approved Siamese translation of the new terms. His direct appeal to the king was successful, with the king agreeing to approve the English version, but at the cost of upsetting even the more liberal commissioners, judging from "a slight coolness observable on the part of the Prince, and the absence of the Phraklang, who reported himself ill, from all proceedings for a week afterwards".[11]

Perhaps because of his direct lobbying of the king, Parkes achieved more than might have been expected, especially given the early negative indications from the handbills and the Kalahom. Lord Clarendon had released Parkes from the obligation of considering the recommendations of the queen's advocate as deal-breakers, but he knew they were nevertheless desirable.[12] He therefore did his best to secure their inclusion in the ratified treaty – and in this he was largely successful: he secured greater clarity on which provisions of the Burney treaty were to be considered still in effect; exclusive consular jurisdiction for British subjects; and the rights to dispose and inherit property. He had also gained additional benefits tabled by neither the advocate nor Bowring, including the establishment of a customs house as well as timeframes for issuing passes and port clearances and for declaring any future prohibition on rice exports.[13] With understandable pride, Parkes reported back to the foreign office, "I think you will see that I have succeeded in settling all questionable points, as well as others that I did not think would have fallen to me."[14]

The negotiations had taken him beyond the 6 April deadline, but that was less important than winning his negotiating points. He now believed that agreement had been reached on all issues and he was anxious to leave and reach Singapore before the mailboat left for England. All that was needed was the king's stamp of approval.

Then, on 18 April, the issue of property rights was to rear its head again. The commissioners informed Parkes "by command of the King, . . . it would be impossible to issue the Proclamation respecting the Sale of Lands until they could define with accuracy the boundaries within which these sales are by Treaty permitted."

For the king and the Siamese commissioners, the geographic restrictions in Article IV of the treaty were extremely important. They had raised these concerns with Bowring in April 1855, but he had successfully deflected them, saying that these were details that could be resolved in the governing regulations of the treaty. It should not therefore have come as a surprise to Parkes that the time to sort out this issue had now arrived. The king was not looking to renegotiate property rights; he required clarity on the boundaries that would be imposed. Parkes concluded:

> It was evident therefore that until the said line should be defined, foreign merchants coming to Siam would be unable to obtain the accommodation they would at once require, namely land for their dwellings and warehouses, for as no suitable buildings are to be found ready constructed at Bangkok, these will in each case have to be erected by the merchants themselves.[15]

Unlike other negotiating points, neither a late-night session at Wongsa's palace nor a direct appeal to the king would resolve this issue. What was required was clear definitions of the two distance markers: concentric circles showing the boundaries of four-mile and twenty-four-hour travel from the city that were stipulated in Article IV. And that would require an agreement on definitions – and a physical survey.

To comprehend why this issue was of such fundamental importance to Siam, it is necessary to delve into the evolution of land law in the country and how Siamese attitudes to land tenure for foreigners had played out in a number of incidents in the recent history of Bangkok.

PRE-BOWRING PROPERTY RIGHTS

To Parkes, the king's concern about the implementation of the Article IV provisions was another example of the petty and trivial distractions from the main agenda put up by the Siamese negotiators, a testament to the "versatile [in its now archaic meaning of changeable or capricious] and dilatory"[16] nature of the Siamese people. But for the Siamese, and especially the king, the changes contemplated by Article IV were revolutionary. The article embodied the first official acknowledgement that the entirety of the land that constituted Siam was not the inalienable property of the monarch.

In reality, the king's ownership of all Siamese land was something of a myth. Tradition had given the kings of Siam a number of honorific titles, one of which was *chao phaendin* (literally, "lord of the land"). The claim that the king was the owner of all the land in the country was often repeated, but did not reflect reality, and perhaps never had:

> The Ayutthaya laws stated that all land belonged to the king and its sale was forbidden, but other clauses show that land was sold and mortgaged.[17]

Indeed, even early nineteenth century observers were aware of the limitations on the king's authority over the land. In a publication of 1847, James Low noted that occupiers held "a firm prescriptive if not an indefeasible proprietory right" in the land. For an occupier,

> although he is *not* in it vested absolutely with a right in perpetuity; still the land forms thereafter a part of his *real* property, is alienable by deed of sale, or by gift, and descends to his heirs at law.[18]

The concept of land ownership supported by documentary evidence was only beginning to emerge in the mid-nineteenth century. Large swathes of the country's land remained undocumented. Some occupiers were able to obtain documents that conferred on them usufruct (but not ownership) rights. Such documents were issued primarily to assist the authorities in collecting taxes on the land, rather than to demonstrate the rights of the holder. Thus, documents were issued only for land that was subject to tax (fields and orchards); no such documents were available for land on which houses were built because such land was not subject to tax.[19] Nevertheless, where the authorities were issuing documents, especially the *chanode tra daeng*, such documents could potentially be used as proof that the holder possessed certain property rights.

These rights were in general conferred on the person who had cleared and cultivated the land but were "less precise" than the elaborate rights that controlled ownership of manpower.[20] Despite this, a recent study has found that "traditional land rights were generally perceived as secure by landowners themselves. Evidence for this includes the ability of landowners, regardless of nationality, social class, or gender, to challenge land claims in court."[21]

While the level of security conferred by traditional land rights, with or without contemporary deeds, may be subject to debate, even the possession of deeds did not confer a "right in perpetuity". The usufruct right (literally, the right to use the "fruits" of, or make profit from, the land) was based on the occupier's continued cultivation of the land, which was liable to be forfeited if the land remained uncultivated for a defined period, usually three years. The state could, and sometimes did, take back control.

The king could also claim control over unclaimed land. King Mongkut's 1861 decree stipulated that ten square miles (16,200 *rai*) of unoccupied land on the banks of the new Mahasawat canal linking Bangkok and Nakhon Chaisi would be divided into fifty lots and allocated to his children.[22] Moreover, a royal command explaining a new decree on land rights in the same year indicated that the king still claimed his historic right to all the land in the kingdom, albeit with important new modifications. These were that land could be retained and inherited by the people under certain circumstances and that a "fair market price" should be paid by the king for any land seized for purposes other than "national defence and protection of the people".[23]

Within the overall context of underdeveloped property rights, a system had evolved which at first glance appeared to approach land ownership rights from another angle. This was the *sakdina* system. *Sakdina* has been literally translated as, for example, "power over fields". Under this system, each person was assigned a numerical value, with the number representing the amount of land (measured in *rai* – a land area equivalent to approximately 0.4 acres or 1,600 square metres) that he was theoretically entitled to possess. The king, being at the apex of the system, had effectively an unlimited *sakdina* value because his dignity "was beyond all computation".[24] The king's younger brother or son holding the rank of *uparat* had a value of 100,000 *rai* and on down to beggars and slaves with a *sakdina* value of 5 *rai*.[25] A rank of 400 *rai* or higher was reserved for the nobility (*khun nang*) appointed by the king. People at this level were entitled to receive an annual gift of money from the king (*biawat*), to attend royal audiences, to hold their offices for life and to be represented in courts of law by a third party. They and their families were also exempt from being marked and from the corvée. On their death, the king would claim a share of their personal wealth, but this requirement strengthened their legal position in regard to inheritance.

Foreigners were not necessarily excluded from the *sakdina* system. According to Jit Poumisak, the Siamese elite used the Chinese merchants as their compradors, allowing them to dominate trade monopolies and admitting them into the *sakdina* system by allocating to them a *sakdina* value of 400 *rai*, "so they would have the privilege of legal representation in their disputes with *phrai* who did not have the wit to pay the tax and to represent themselves".[26] The rank of 400 *sakdina* was considered the level "at which the real official class appointed by the king may be said to have begun", while between 25 and 400 *sakdina* applied to "petty functionaries" appointed by ministers and other high officials.[27]

The *sakdina* system dated back to the early Ayutthaya period (1351-1767) and could be viewed as a classification system for regulating the population and cementing society. However, it is unlikely that a *sakdina* value was related to an actual allocation of land as there is no evidence of actual land grants being made through the system. Instead, the ranking indicated status related to position. Nor was possession of land necessarily viewed as a key indicator of position in society, or even wealth. In fact, control of manpower conferred greater authority than control of land.[28]

Even though the king did not have absolute power over land, nor was the *sakdina* system used by him as a vehicle for land distribution, the king was nevertheless in a position to make magnanimous grants of land to individuals and even to whole communities for services rendered to the state.

Two outstanding examples from southern Siam at opposite ends of the nineteenth century illustrate how such benefits could be gained by wealthy Chinese settlers: Rama I's grant of "a large, landed estate comprising the area known today as Had Yai" to Boon Hui, a Chinese general who had defeated the forces of the Sultan of Patani; and Rama V's grant of 3,000 *rai* to Kaw Sujiang for successfully quashing a Chinese labourers' rebellion in Ranong.[29]

Moreover, since the time when Ayutthaya was the centre of the Siamese kingdom, kings had often given land to foreign communities in recognition of services rendered. Ayutthaya was an unusually cosmopolitan city before its destruction in the war with Burma in 1767. La Loubère estimated that there were some twenty-one nationalities living in their own enclaves, outside the city walls. The largest foreign community was the Chinese, but there were also significant numbers of Japanese, Malays, Peguans, Portuguese and Moors, a group which has been variously defined as "those Mahometans of Arabian Extraction, which our Ancestors have called Saracens, and whose race is spread almost through the whole Hemisphere"[30] or as "Turks, Persians, Golcondans, and those of Bengal".[31] To an extent, these communities were self-governing, although the degree of extraterritorial independence was not clearly defined and interventions by the Siamese state frequent.

The birth of Bangkok in 1782 was built around an event that encapsulated the king's powers both to seize occupied land and to make new land grants. King Rama I had decided to move the capital from Thonburi on the west bank of the Chaophraya river to Bangkok, directly opposite Thonburi on the east bank, in part because the river barrier would offer greater protection against the Burmese to the west, but also because the hastily selected development of Thonburi had serious deficiencies: "constricted confines, inadequate fortifications, and crumbling shoreline, as well as its inauspicious symmetry".[32]

The Bangkok site would address all of these shortcomings; however, the existing settlers would need to be relocated. King Taksin had provided this land primarily to Chinese settlers of Teochew ethnicity who had been encouraged to migrate from Siam's eastern seaboard and from China. Following the decision to repurpose the area as the citadel for the royal palaces, King Rama I assigned one of King Taksin's Chinese generals, Phraya Phiphit (Tan Liang), known as Phraya Rachasretthi-Chin from 1772, to oversee the operation of removing the Chinese community. He was successful in "effecting a smooth and peaceful relocation of the Teochew community to make way for the Grand Palace of the Chakri dynasty".[33] The community was moved outside the city wall to the area of Samphaeng, which is still today known as Bangkok's Chinatown.

Grants of land to ethnic minorities in Bangkok were not confined to the Chinese; many other ethnic minorities were also assigned settlement sites in and around the city. Van Roy's study identified around forty such communities in Bangkok in the first half of the nineteenth century, comprising Mon refugees, Lao war captives, Cham militias, Persian courtiers, Arab voyagers, Indian traders, Malay captives, Indonesian wanderers, Khmer exiles, Vietnamese refugees and captives, communities for each of the five main Chinese speech groups (Teochew, Hokkien, Hakka, Hainanese and Cantonese), indigenised Portuguese, not to mention a smattering of western missionaries and merchants.[34]

The Catholic communities, for instance, had benefited from land grants in Bangkok from various kings, starting from even before the fall of Ayutthaya. In the reign of King Narai, a Portuguese faction that had been expelled from the Portuguese settlement at Ayutthaya "for reasons unknown" was given "a new settlement site along the Chaophraya river at Samsen" in Bangkok on which they built the Church of the Immaculate Conception in 1673.[35] When King Taksin established Thonburi as his new capital after the fall of Ayutthaya in 1767, land was granted to the Portuguese near the king's palace and the Santa Cruz Church was built there in 1772.[36] A dissident faction of Portuguese Catholics who wanted to escape the control of the French priests of Santa Cruz moved to Ton Samrong in Bangkok in 1772. In 1786, this community was given land by King Rama I on which to build the Holy Rosary Church, also known as the Calvary Church.[37] Then, in 1834, King Rama III granted land and funds for construction of a community and church (St Francis Xavier) near Immaculate Conception Church in Bangkok for the Annamite Catholics who had arrived from Cochin China as prisoners of war. King Pinklao, the second king, was to donate more land to replace the wooden St Francis Xavier Church with a brick structure in 1851.[38]

The property rights regime for Siamese subjects that prevailed up to the Bowring treaty was essentially unchanged since the days of Ayutthaya: the king was nominally the *chao phaendin* with unlimited rights to the land, but in reality his control over the land was limited.[39] When he exercised rights over land (by, for instance, making a land grant), he was demonstrating his absolutist power rather than exercising a right derived from a concept of property ownership. However, the issuance of titles had led to the possibility of land sales and inheritance. Further moves to a rights-based transactional land system were to occur in King Mongkut's reign with the 1861 proclamation requiring the king to pay compensation to land occupiers whose land he wished to expropriate[40] and then with the promulgation of regulations on land pledging (*chamnam*) in 1865 and on conditional sales (*khai fak*) in 1866.[41]

In matters related to land, there was no evident distinction made by the state between its treatment of Siamese and non-Siamese subjects. Both were entitled to limited occupation rights and both ran the risk of losing their land without recourse, should the central authorities require the land back.

However, in the forty years leading up to the Bowring treaty, a small number of westerners were to settle in Bangkok who, unlike many ethnic minorities that already populated the city, had neither an existing community to settle into nor any intention or desire to become integrated into society as Siamese subjects. Instead, they faced a state that had no clear legal or institutional mechanism for granting them security of tenure, leading to recurrent crises in their efforts to claim the right of residence.

THE PORTUGUESE DIPLOMAT

Given the historic relationship between Siam and Portugal, it was fitting that the Portuguese should be the first western nation to establish diplomatic relations with the Siamese since the fall of Ayutthaya in 1767. The Portuguese sent an envoy to Siam from Macao in 1818 asking permission to trade and construct ships, a request that was "readily granted by King Rama II" because of the assistance the Portuguese gave to Siam in obtaining arms and ammunition.[42]

The Portuguese envoy returned in 1820 hoping to conclude a commercial treaty, but, rather than a treaty, King Rama II gave the Portuguese a land plot on the east bank of the river "with 72 Siamese fathoms along the River; 50 in depth, with two shipyards and with the privilege that all Portuguese could come to trade as His Majesty favours the Portuguese Nation more than all others".[43] The Letter of Concession specifically granted the land to "the Consul General", who was given a Siamese title (*Luang Aphai Phanit*) and recognised as "the first representative of His Majesty the King of Portugal". The purpose of the land concession was primarily for the Portuguese to construct a factory for trade between the two nations. The land is still today occupied by the embassy of Portugal.

The 1820 land grant was different in nature from the grants made to ethnic minorities, including the indigenised Portuguese. It was given to Portugal as a foreign power with the purpose of furthering Siam's new outward-facing ambitions: to house the first foreign consulate in Bangkok and to serve as a trading hub for Portuguese factors. The 1820 grant had some similarity to the land grants made in the Ayutthaya period to traders from Holland and England in that it was viewed as conferring an economic benefit on Siam, but it also carried greater permanence because it was also a non-economic, diplomatic transaction. As such, revocation of the land grant would be problematic, even if the anticipated economic benefits did not materialise.

Indeed, Siamese hopes for those trading and financial benefits were to be disappointed. From the beginning the omens were not good. The Portuguese government had originally intended to build an impressive brick consulate, but the ship carrying the finest bricks and masons from Goa "was tempest-tost in the China Seas, and finally stranded on some hidden shoal, from which the crew with difficulty escaped with their lives – the vessel went down – the bricks sunk with her, and so did the hopes of the poor Portuguese consul".[44]

Lacking the funds for a repeat voyage and with Portuguese trade moribund, the building remained unimproved, though not unpleasant. Writing in 1840, one visitor remarked that it was "very indifferently constructed with bamboos, poles, lath and plaster, but it was an extensive house, cleanly white-washed, neatly furnished, and situated in one of the pleasantest positions in Siam".[45]

The Portuguese consulate, illustration by Frederick Arthur Neale in 1840.

Nevertheless, the anticipated benefits of the new factory-cum-consulate had not materialised. Disillusionment set in almost immediately. Part of Siam's reluctance to conclude a treaty with Britain when John Crawfurd visited in 1821 was ascribed to the failure of the Portuguese to capitalise on the trading privileges awarded to them:

> In justification of the demand now made [that Britain send at least four ships per year to Siam before concluding a new trade deal], the Prah-klang observed that two years ago the Siamese had made a commercial treaty with the Portuguese, and reduced the import duties from eight per cent to six per cent. No Portuguese ships, however, had come to Siam since; and it was, therefore, a matter of some scandal to the Siamese Government that it had made a treaty, as it were, about nothing.[46]

These issues were still very much alive during Bowring's negotiations and were in part the reason for the Siamese authorities' reluctance to allow another foreign consulate to be established. In the end, it was agreed that the British could only send a consul to Siam once ten British ships had landed in Bangkok.

The diminishing importance of the Portuguese in international trade was, naturally enough, mirrored by a corresponding loss in the status and prestige of its consul. In 1821 Crawfurd was shocked to discover that the first Portuguese consul, Carlos Manoel da Silveira, had been arrested and "threatened with the bastinado" by the Siamese authorities, commenting that if a British consul were to be subjected to such treatment it would "bring on a war in less than six months". Crawfurd naturally assumed Britain would emerge victorious from such a war, thus leading to "an extension of authority and dominion incompatible with our professed policy".[47] This opinion was shared by the next British envoy to arrive in Siam, Henry Burney in 1826. Da Silveira was "un-noticed and unpaid" and had to make his living through trade.[48]

While da Silveira's successor during the time of Bowring's visit did not suffer the same humiliation, he was nevertheless largely ignored by the authorities. He was stationed in Siam more than a year before being granted an audience with King Mongkut in 1856,[49] although Bowring ascribed this to procedural issues ("something wanting in the form of his appointment") and the punctiliousness of the Siamese ("the Siamese being somewhat rigid in the observance of forms") rather than a deliberate snub. Even so, Bowring acknowledged that the consul had little of value to offer either his own country or Siam:

> The Portuguese have continued to nominate a consul at Bangkok. As they have no trade, the appointment may be deemed rather the expression of a natural national pride, the result of ancient privileges and position, than having any present purpose of utility.[50]

BURNEY AND THE SCOTTISH MERCHANT

Siam's disappointing experience with the Portuguese consulate had made it wary of granting effective freehold interests in land to other westerners. Its subsequent experience with a British merchant would confirm that leasehold arrangements offered a better way to protect valuable land from the shifting agendas of foreign counterparts.

The first treaty between Siam and Great Britain signed in 1826, generally known as the Burney treaty, gave Siamese officials "liberty to deny [English merchants] permission to stay" and authority to set terms for their residence in the country.[51] Although this power was implicit prior to the treaty, the stipulations in Article VII of the Burney treaty were its first explicit recognition. As Burney noted, its incorporation in the treaty was of great importance to the Siamese:

> The Siamese negotiators took great care in drafting the 7th Article of the treaty, to reserve to themselves the right and power of refusing the privilege of residence in Siam to British subjects.

Burney concluded that the Siamese were "utterly averse to the residence of any English amongst them". While an Englishman who was living in Bangkok when Burney visited thought this aversion was based on a fear of British spies reporting on the goings-on in Siam, Burney imputed a more underhand motive to the Siamese:

> if European merchants are allowed to remain in Siam they will acquire too great an insight into Siamese Mal-practices, and save other foreign merchants that may visit Bangkok, from extortion and imposition.[52]

Nevertheless, both Crawfurd and Burney were very aware of the exciting commercial potential of Siam, which had become more evident since the succession of King Rama II by his son, King Nangklao, Rama III, in 1824. The new reign appeared to usher in an era of greater openness to the outside world.

The first western trader to take advantage of the provisions of the new treaty and the new spirit of openness was an entrepreneurial Scot by the name of Robert Hunter. Hunter had first arrived in Bangkok in 1824 and decided to settle down. In 1825 he married into one of the leading families in the Portuguese community. His wife, Angelina Sap (or Than Phuying Sap) was reported to be a great grand-daughter of Constantine Phaulkon, the Greek Prime Minister of King Narai, and his Japanese wife through mainly Portuguese descendants.[53] When the Burney treaty introduced improved trading conditions in 1826, Hunter was well positioned to take advantage.

Hunter was to be based in Siam for two decades and achieved great wealth through trade, owning four vessels engaged in exporting commodities and importing luxury goods for the Siamese elite, and through his discovery

The British factory, illustration by Frederick Arthur Neale in 1840.

of the Siamese twins Chang and Eng, who he sent to America where they found fame and fortune. In the absence of any other British-born merchants in Siam, he became the *de facto* British representative, lending his support to visiting missions, including Burney's, and even taking an active role in negotiating the restoration of the sultan of Kedah on behalf of the Indian government in 1842 which paid him 5,000 rupees for his services.[54]

Naturally, Hunter wanted security of tenure for his residence and warehouse in Bangkok and applied to Rama III's Phraklang (who was to become Somdet Ong Yai under Rama IV when his sons became Kalahom and Phraklang) for land on which to build. The Phraklang reported the request to King Nangklao, who ordered him to arrange a place for Hunter. The king's welcoming attitude to Hunter is generally ascribed to Hunter's gift of some 1,000 muskets from India when he first arrived. The gift was greatly appreciated by King Nangklao as he was experiencing difficulties with his tributary Lao state in Viengchan (Vientiene) at the time. Largely in recognition of this welcome gift, the king awarded Hunter a Siamese title, *Luang Avudh Viset*.

However, the king was keen to avoid a repeat of what he perceived to be a mistake made by his father, Rama II, who had granted ownership rights to the Portuguese in 1820. He therefore ordered that Hunter should rent rather than own his property. The location and construction was secured with the assistance of the Phraklang:

> The Phra Klang had a piece of land in front of Wat Prayurawongse, and this he presented to the King, and in return Phra Nang Klao allowed the revenue obtained from the sale of bamboo wood to be temporarily devoted to the erection of the building for Hunter.[55]

Hunter's residence was located near Santa Cruz Church in the Kudi Chin community that housed descendants of Portuguese Catholics, including his new wife's family. It was also conveniently close to the residence of the Phraklang, who was tasked with dealing with – and keeping an eye on – foreign residents. According to Adey Moore, it "was the first building to be erected in accordance with European ideas, in the Third Reign, and was called *Tuk Farang*", (foreigner's, or westerner's, brick building) although it was more commonly known among the Siamese as *hang huntraa* (Hunter's shop or store) after its eponymous occupant[56] and among the foreign community as the British factory. Some called it the English factory, possibly reflecting the conflation of the Thai word *angrit*, which even today can denote either England or Britain, a custom that would no doubt have irritated Robert Hunter as it has many of his fellow Scots since. The building soon became a well-known landmark and a place to visit for western travellers. One visitor in 1833 noted that it was one of only two brick residences in the city (the other being the king's palace), comprising "a large white-washed brick building two stories in height, and forming three sides of a square, the fourth being closed by a high brick wall",[57] while another visitor in 1840 confirmed that it was "a very fine large prominent house" which often flew the British flag "and here every stranger found a home, for a very prince of hospitality was Mr. Hunter, as was his young partner, Mr. Hayes". Even the American envoy Edmund Roberts stayed at Hunter's residence during his 1833 mission to negotiate the first treaty between the United States and Siam.

Hunter's unique position in Siamese society was liable to exaggeration. Neale, his 1840 visitor, credited him with persuading "the Siamese Government to permit the Europeans residing at Bangkok to build houses on *terra firma*" and that "the Portuguese consul, the French bishop and missionaries, the Americans and Mr. Hunter, had all gladly availed themselves of this permission" which previously "was entirely confined to members of the royal family, and for the building of watts, or places of worship".[58] The claim is factually incorrect insofar as the Portuguese consulate predated Hunter, and otherwise highly questionable.

Nevertheless, Hunter was in the unusual position of being able to entertain important foreign guests and also provide ad hoc services to the Siamese authorities. At one time, for instance, he allowed the lower part of his building to be used to house Malay prisoners from Pattani.[59] However, his relations with the Siamese authorities were becoming increasingly strained, not least because of his own involvement in the import of opium, even though this activity was specifically prohibited by the Burney treaty.[60]

Hunter eventually fell out of favour with the Siamese government because of his belligerent handling of a business dispute. The relationship began to sour after 1840 when the king became more directly involved in trading and "caused all dealers in sugar to sell the same to him only". Friction increased when Hunter's business was affected by a series of measures: an "exorbitant" increase in duties, a restriction on the export of teak and the seizing of a sugar shipment.[61] But relations between Hunter and the Siamese authorities were to break down completely when the king refused to take possession and pay for the steamer *Express* which Hunter had shipped in at the king's request. The ensuing argument led to Hunter's expulsion from Siam and his filing of a formal complaint and request for protection by the government of British India.

Colonel William John Butterworth, governor of Prince of Wales Island (Penang), Singapore and Malacca, traced the background of the failed sale to the end of the First Opium War. The king feared that the British troops would target Bangkok on their return from China, "and every preparation was made to effect a show of resistance", including repairing the river fortifications, stretching chain cables across the river and ordering guns and the *Express* from England. However:

> The peaceable return of the British troops to India on the conclusion of the peace with China entirely changed the King's views and the whole of his attention was then and is still devoted to the accumulation of wealth. He therefore gladly availed himself of any excuse for the nonfulfillment of his engagement with Mr. Hunter for the supply of the ordinance and the steamer "Express" which had been commissioned from that firm.[62]

The king's hostility to and expulsion of Hunter arose from Hunter's response to this situation. Hunter threatened to sell the *Express* to the Cochin Chinese, a Siamese enemy, and actually carried out the threat earning 53,000 dollars in the process. Butterworth commented that "the exasperated feeling of a despotic monarch, consequent to his being told that negotiations would be entered into with his enemies, are not to be wondered at." Moreover, as he told Hunter, the Scot had only made things worse before leaving Bangkok by losing his temper and giving "the Siamese Authorities a specimen of your mind pretty freely".[63]

Hunter finally left Bangkok for the last time on 29 December 1844, leaving behind his young assistant Christopher Harvey to collect his debts, which he claimed amounted to 40,000 Spanish dollars in addition to unrealised losses from having many goods returned to him by parties he had sold them to. Among his many claims against Siam was one regarding the British factory:

> In my first settling at Bangkok I leased a piece of ground from the King for the purpose of building a house upon it, and it was agreed that I was to pay a rent of 600 ticals per annum for the ground. The buildings were erected at my own charge upon an agreement with the King that when I should give up possession he would pay me for them. Instead however of his doing so he insisted when I was about to quit Siam last month, that I should pay not only the rent for the ground but also an equal sum for the buildings. With this tyrannical and unjust demand I was obliged to comply.[64]

A later summary of this complaint from Hunter's firm, Hunter & Hayes, explained further that the original dwelling, being in a poor state of repair, was pulled down with the king's sanction and with the agreement of the Phraklang that the Siamese government would reimburse Hunter for the cost of building the new premises "by deducting the amount of the actual cost of the house from the annual rent of 600 ticals per annum until the same was paid for". Instead of honouring this arrangement, when Hunter was forced to leave the country he was made to pay not only the 600 ticals per annum rent without deduction, but an additional 600 ticals per annum which was considered ground rent for the buildings "from the day the first foundation was laid". The claim was thus backdated to 1840 and interest was then calculated on the unpaid rent. The total additional amount came to 3,575 ticals, of which 3,000 was the rent for five years and the remainder interest. Adding insult to injury, the house was then seized "without reimbursing one single fraction from the money laid out".[65]

In the end, the British authorities rejected Hunter's appeal for action against Siam on the grounds that the problems arose from a business dispute and there was no evidence of any treaty violations. Moreover, the unpleasant outcome was at least in part due to his own behaviour. The legal opinion that the authorities sought backed up their decision.

There is no evidence that the British authorities ever considered Hunter's specific complaint on the financing of the British factory. However, any such complaint would no doubt have been rejected by the British authorities as surely as they rejected all Hunter's other claims. In expelling Hunter from the country, the king was merely acting within the terms of Article VII of the Burney treaty, which gave him "liberty to deny . . . permission to stay" in the country for any reason. Whether or not Hunter had been cheated out of a refund of the construction cost was, once again, a business dispute, and it would appear that Hunter had no compelling documentary evidence to support his claim of being subject to a "tyrannical and unjust demand".

From the point of view of the Siamese authorities, the Hunter incident had been very instructive. Clearly, it had illustrated the potential risks of too close an association with independent merchants. A little less obviously, the incident had shown how useful restrictions in property rights could be in mitigating some of those risks, thereby vindicating the Siamese concerns that led to their insistence on the residential restrictions imposed by Article VII.

Even though Hunter failed to elicit the support of the Indian government for his claims in the mid-1840s, they were to feature heavily in the litany of complaints from British businesses that formed the backdrop to the unsuccessful Brooke mission of 1850.

ROBERTS AND THE FIRST PROTESTANT MISSIONARIES

Before the breakdown in relations with Hunter had proved the effectiveness of Article VII, the Siamese were already softening their position. During US ambassador Edmund Roberts' sojourn at *hang huntraa* in 1833, he was able to negotiate a far less onerous residential restriction than had Burney seven years earlier. Article VII of the United States-Siam treaty he negotiated, which inevitably became known as the Roberts treaty, stated that:

> Merchants of the United States coming to trade in the Kingdom of Siam and wishing to rent houses therein, shall rent the King's Factories, and pay the customary rent of the country.[66]

The positive language and lack of the peremptory state power of the Burney treaty gave this clause the appearance of being much more open and welcoming to foreign residents. But the language disguises its important restrictions. Under Burney's Article VII, foreign merchants had been granted the right "to build godowns or houses, or to buy or hire shops or houses", subject, as we have seen, to the approval of the Siamese authorities and under the perpetual threat of arbitrarily losing those rights. Roberts' Article VII removes the arbitrary authoritarian power, but instead restricts foreign merchants to renting only, and then only of "the King's Factories" at a prescribed rental rate. There is no provision in the Roberts treaty for any other form of occupation by Americans.

Although the residential rights in the Roberts treaty only referred to foreign merchants, the first Americans to arrive in Bangkok under the Roberts treaty were not merchants at all but missionaries. Nevertheless, the struggle for security of tenure that underlay their first two decades in Siam was traceable to the provisions of the Roberts treaty. It also stood in sharp contrast to the relatively benign experience of the French Catholic priests arriving in the country at the same time who were able to piggyback off the land grants afforded their large flock of Catholics of mainly Portuguese descent. The Protestants, on the other hand, had no congregation in Siam and were to remain notoriously unsuccessful at attracting converts among the Siamese for many years.

The solution for the first Protestant missionaries – the eccentric Pomeranian missionary, Karl Gutzlaff of the Netherlands Missionary Society and Jacob Tomlin of the London Missionary Society – pre-dated the Roberts treaty and curiously relied on the good offices of a leading Catholic in the country: the Portuguese consul. Da Silveira not only gave Gutzlaff and Tomlin a house on his premises in 1828, he also shielded them from threats of expulsion, believed to have emanated from Catholic influence at the time. Tomlin did not stay long, but Gutzlaff remained at this house for three years before moving on to China. A month later, the first American missionary, David Abeel, arrived accompanied by a returning Tomlin. They were also allowed to rent the house vacated by Gutzlaff

A typical nineteenth century missionary house.

at the Portuguese consulate.[67] Abeel's mission was to survey the prospects for a mission under the American Board of Commissioners for Foreign Missions (ABCFM), but the first permanent Protestant mission to be established was not the ABCFM. Early in 1833, only four months after Abeel had finished his tour of duty in Siam, John Taylor Jones and his wife, Eliza, from the American Baptist Board arrived. Once again, they relied upon the good offices of the Portuguese consul who allowed them to relocate the river-front house occupied by their predecessors to a more permanent location behind the consulate, which was where the Baptist mission was to develop over the following years. By 1840, the contiguity of the Baptist mission and the Portuguese consulate was a recognised feature of the Bangkok riverscape:

Dan Beach Bradley

> The Portuguese consulate and the missionaries' houses are in this part so constructed as to form a tolerably large square, extending from the Baptist chapel down to the banks of the river.[68]

The Baptists were thus able to make use of the special status accorded the land granted to the Portuguese consul. When the first permanent missionaries from the ABCFM arrived in 1834, there was no such easy solution to their residential needs. The Roberts treaty did not refer to the needs of missionaries specifically, and the new arrivals often had to make do with insalubrious, ad hoc solutions that gave them very little real security of tenure. The first two ABCFM families (the Robinsons and the Johnsons) rented a small piece of land of about thirty square metres[69] next to Wat Koh at one end of the Chinese bazaar, a convenient but not a wholesome location:

> Being at the foot of the great Bazar the mission was well located for coming in contact with the people, but a miserable place for the settlement of their families, as it was a kind of sink of the offscouring of creation.[70]

The mission had rented the land from a high-ranking civil servant called Nai Klin under a one-year lease. The missionary families erected two "rough barn-like dwellings" for themselves and, when a third family joined them in 1835, a third dwelling was squeezed onto the land. This third family was the Bradleys – the Reverend Dr Dan Beach Bradley, his wife Emelie and their adopted daughter. Bradley would become the longest serving and best known of the Protestant missionaries, but in those early days of the mission he was not warmly welcomed.

Hostility to the ABCFM missionaries soon manifested in a move to evict them from the land where they lived. Nai Klin warned the missionaries that he was under pressure to cancel their lease and they would need permission from the Phraklang to stay put. Hunter tried to help by lobbying the Phraklang. However, the Phraklang passed the buck:

> The Phra Klang pretends to have no jurisdiction over this part of the city in which we live and therefore can have nothing to do touching our residence here. He says Paya-Chai-Dook, a Chinaman and ruler of the Chinese of this city and an old and bitter enemy of the Gospel, has the control of this side of the river and that he must be consulted.

The mission was at the time located within the dense community that had been granted to the Chinese by Rama I when he displaced them from the inner city at the founding of Bangkok. The Phraklang was therefore deferring to the judgment of the head of the Chinese community, the "Paya-Chai-Dook", or Phraya Choduk Rachasretthi, which was the position within the Siamese bureaucracy with responsibility for all Chinese affairs. Hunter was equally unsuccessful in canvassing support for the mission from the Phraya Choduk as he had been with the Phraklang.

The authorities had two main complaints against the missionaries living in the middle of the Chinese community. The first was, as the Phraklang told Hunter, that they were doing too many "good works":

> That it is against the laws of Siam to "tam boon" (to do good) every day; that there were certain days designated by Government when all might give as much as they please, but to

> the priests chiefly. He assigned as a reason for this objection that we should get more merit than the people generally and would equal if not out-strip the greatest and best in the nation.[71]

If the Phraklang was concerned that the missionaries would shine as paragons of philanthropy in comparison to their hosts thereby "awaken[ing] jealousy" among the Siamese elite,[72] the Phraya Choduk had another reason for objecting to their "good works" – they could be subversive:

> He dislikes our reading Christian books to the Chinese and giving the same to them, professing to fear that we shall win their affections and instil a rebellious spirit against the Government.

The solution proposed by the Phraya Choduk was for the missionaries to relocate to one of the "three places assigned to Christians" in the city; that is, to one of the Catholic enclaves.

Meanwhile, Nai Klin was becoming increasingly anxious that he would be held accountable for allowing the missionaries to rent in the wrong place. He had failed to request permission and said he feared "royal displeasure" and could lose his head if the missionaries were still there when the king visited Wat Koh, as he was due to do in early October. The missionaries started to panic but were unable to find alternative accommodation. Five days before the king's visit, the Phraklang increased the pressure, telling them that they had to leave immediately, although "no place is designated to which we may flee."[73]

The three families were unable to find a good solution at such short notice. As a result, they were scattered to different places: the Robinsons moved into "a small Portuguese house near the Baptist Mission", the Johnsons to "a floating house . . . moored in front of the Roman Catholic Church in Santa Cruz" and the Bradleys to "a small house in Santa Cruz village".

Despite being in a Catholic enclave, the Bradleys' new home was a distinct improvement. Their new wooden house was almost the same size as the entire land plot that contained three dwellings on Nai Klin's land; it boasted two rooms, a basement for storage and verandahs[74] and was not far from the British factory where their friend Robert Hunter lived.

It would take the ABCFM another three years to find a new site and move into more permanent accommodation. This time they were indebted to the Phraklang who made good on his promise to help the

ABCFM find a permanent home on land he owned. Apart from constant pressure from the missionaries themselves, the Phraklang was no doubt responding to the support of their cause given by Edmund Roberts. After negotiating the United States-Siam treaty in 1833, Roberts returned to Bangkok in April 1836 to finalise the ratification process. Using his status to exert pressure on the authorities and make up for the failure to deal with the issue of missionaries' accommodation in his treaty, he "signed a memorial to Chao Phya P'hra Klang from the missionaries, praying that sufficient ground might be allotted to them, whereon to erect a church and suitable dwellings, with permission to appropriate a part as a place of sepulture, the same having been granted to the Portuguese Roman Catholics, Mussulmans, Chinese, and others".[75]

The new site was even closer to the British factory – on the opposite side of a canal from Bradley's house in the Santa Cruz community. A lease was drawn up under which the mission would pay rent of sixty-five ticals for the land and two large houses that were to be built at the Phraklang's expense in a style to suit the missionaries. In addition, the ABCFM would have the option to build two or three more dwellings on the excess land at its own expense. These two-storey wooden houses with verandahs were a great improvement. "Though crude, they were comfortable" and were to remain the home of the ABCFM mission for fifteen years.[76] For Bradley, moving into his new home on 8 April 1838 ended a difficult chapter. He had spent a large part of the preceding year and a half working on his accommodation issue.[77] The new premises, though far from perfect, at least allowed the mission to focus on its even more difficult task, the salvation of souls.

PROTESTANT MISSIONARIES AT THE END OF THE THIRD REIGN

The solution that emerged from Roberts' intervention held good until the end of the next decade. When the first missionaries from a third American mission, the Presbyterian Board, arrived in 1840, they would most likely have taken up residence in one of the four houses built for the ABCFM missionaries on the Phraklang's land. The second wave of Presbyterians, led by the Mattoon family and Dr House, certainly did stay there after their arrival in 1847. This cohabitation continued until 1850 when new challenges emerged for the missionaries that would affect their living arrangements.

Bradley had been on furlough in the United States and returned accompanied by two new missionary families in 1850. There would therefore be six families to house in the four dwellings on the Phraklang's land. Bradley and his new colleagues now represented the American Missionary Association as the ACBFM had decided to close its Siam operations. The Presbyterians, who had now organised themselves into the Presbyterian Church of Siam with House as ruling elder and Mattoon as pastor, tried unsuccessfully to secure the property for themselves:

> The Presbyterian Board entered negotiations with the A.B.C.F.M. for the purchase of their buildings and press, but when Dr. Bradley was accepted by the A.M.A. he succeeded in raising enough money to buy over the A.B.C.F.M. property and clearly had the first option on it.[78]

The Presbyterians would have to find their own compound. However, it soon became evident that finding someone willing to provide land would be as problematic for the Presbyterians in 1850 as it had been for the ABCFM fifteen years earlier:

> the people, fearful of getting themselves into trouble with the higher powers, were afraid to either sell or lease land for the purpose, and made all sorts of excuses.

Unlike Bradley and his first colleagues, Mattoon and his colleagues did not face forcible eviction, but their experience was equally dispiriting. Mattoon finally found "a friendly native" to sell him land, a price for the land was negotiated, the transfer arranged in the presence of the proper officials, the money paid and the Mattoons moved their floating house to the new location in preparation for the building programme, but "suddenly there was interference from higher officials, forbidding transfer of the land."[79] The rejection came shortly after the failed missions of Balestier and Brooke and was no doubt a reflection of the increased hostility engendered by those visits. The only reason given was that the new location was not appropriate because it was higher upriver than the king's palace. The affair drove Dr House to despair:

> It becomes a serious question what, as a mission, is our duty – it now being settled that no change for the better is to be hoped for. Three and a half years we have been seeking for a place where we could locate our mission, and in our way aid in bringing this heathen people to Christ. But a separate

home among them has been denied and we baffled in every attempt to secure premises on which we might build houses, gather a school and lay foundations for those that come after us. Thus far we have had no local habitation or name of our own – being merged in other societies, living by suffrance on their premises.[80]

A new option opened up after the mission of Sir James Brooke left Bangkok late in 1850. Brooke had been occupying Hunter's old British factory, and the Presbyterians were fully expecting to be allowed to rent this property once he had vacated it. Again, they were to be disappointed.

The source of this disappointment could be traced back to another property crisis for the missionaries, this time affecting the Baptists. On the night of 4 January 1851, some fourteen weeks after Brooke had left Siam, a large conflagration engulfed the Baptist mission located behind the Portuguese consulate. It was a devastating blow to the Baptists. Not only were the mission's three houses lost, the fire also destroyed the "chapel, printing-press, type-foundry, book-bindery, libraries, school and personal property. The new second edition of the Baptist New Testament printed in 1850 was completely destroyed."[81] The neighbouring residences of both the Portuguese merchant Joachim and the Armenian merchant Joseph were also burnt down.

Bradley, along with most of the foreign community, suspected arson:

> It appeared quite clear that the fire had been kindled by incendiaries . . . Strong suspicion rests upon the servants of a certain officer of the government who had taken up some of the Chinese Christians on a false charge, and had been defeated in their purpose of torturing them for money by the kindly intervention of the Baptist Brethren who placed the cause of the Chinese Christians before the Phra Klang and gained it.[82]

While the fire was catastrophic for the Baptists, it also ended the hopes of the Presbyterians to take over the British factory. The Phraklang decided that in view of the emergency created by the fire, occupation of the property would be given to one of the victims, Joachim, in preference to Mattoon and his colleagues.

At the end of the reign of King Nangklao, both the Baptists and the Presbyterians found themselves in need of permanent accommodation in Bangkok, and while the American Missionary Association had security of tenure Bradley was also keen to move into more spacious premises. The three missions had themselves suffered a decline in the 1840s, in part because of the evident hostility of the Siamese authorities but also due to the fatigue brought upon by years of an essentially unsuccessful religious mission. While a few Chinese people had converted to Christianity, by 1860 the Presbyterian mission had only one native convert, with one missionary later commenting:

> It is also just to state that there is scarcely any other field, in which modern missions have been established, where the introduction of the gospel has met with so little opposition as in Siam proper, and especially during the last reign [of King Mongkut], and so far during the present [of King Chulalongkorn]. It is equally just to say that there is scarcely any other field which has been so barren of results.[83]

As a result, some of the missionaries had abandoned Siam for the greater potential to be found in China or elsewhere. Moreover, the failures of the 1850 missions of US envoy Joseph Balestier and British envoy Sir James Brooke to extract any concessions from King Rama III had increased not only frustration but also fears of a harder line against the missionaries:

> As the intercourse between the Siamese and Sir James Brookes [*sic*] became strained, the Siamese began to cut off communications with the foreign residents. This was only a shadow of what was to come. As soon as the British fleet left, a sudden wave of arrests gathered in all who were employed as teachers at the missions . . . Next the house servants withdrew from the homes of the foreigners.[84]

These adverse forces had brought about a reduction of the Protestant cohort from a peak of twenty-six missionaries in 1841 to only sixteen at the end of the third reign. In June 1856, when the first British consul arrived, the number had reduced further to only twelve.[85]

PROTESTANT MISSIONARIES AT THE BEGINNING OF THE FOURTH REIGN

The accession of King Mongkut brought the prospect of improved relations and greater security. And indeed, that was certainly the case at the beginning of the reign. The king's more tolerant and open outlook ensured a more favourable reception for the missionaries. In addition, the king had formed close attachments with some of the brethren. Bradley and, later and more substantially, his ABCFM colleague Jesse Caswell, Jr had been Prince Mongkut's principal English language teachers in the 1840s when he was a monk at Wat Bowonniwet. Moreover, the king appreciated the medical and scientific knowledge of the missionaries, especially Bradley and House who, both being doctors, were frequently called upon to treat members of the royal and senior noble families of the kingdom.

The missionaries' hopes of a more supportive environment began to be realised as soon as King Mongkut ascended the throne in May 1851. The Presbyterians were the first to benefit: just two months after his coronation, the new king ordered land for their church to be made available on a leasehold basis. Dr House's attitude changed from despair to joy:

> A new era with us – at least the dawn of a brighter day. We have a home at last promised us, and on a really pleasant spot of ground they are going to allow us to build.[86]

The Mattoons and Dr House moved into floating houses in front of the new land to supervise construction. Two brick houses were built on the site which was located on the west bank of the river next to the old palace of King Taksin and Wat Chaeng (present-day Wat Arun). Preaching services began on the new compound in February 1853, the Mattoons moved into the first house in June, with the second house occupied by December that year. This site would remain the home of the Presbyterian mission until its move downriver in 1857.

The king was also receptive to Bradley's accommodation issues. Having performed operations on wives of both King Mongkut and Prince Wongsa early in 1852, Bradley was hoping that gratitude would be expressed by allowing his mission to take possession of the property of the Portuguese which, according to Bradley, "was to be given up". Bradley may have been referring to the Portuguese consulate land, but that property has remained with the Portuguese up to the present day, so it is more likely that he was thinking about property within the Portuguese community at Kudi Chin. Whichever plot he had in mind, Bradley's hopes went unrealised. Instead, gratitude for his medical assistance came first of all in the form of lower rent on his existing property, with the Phraklang reducing

Bradley's rent from 780 ticals to 500. Further gratitude was expressed in the form of a more substantial offer from the king conveyed to Bradley by Wongsa: "in view of his long and friendly acquaintance with me and the many services I had already performed for this people and for this kingdom" and because he approved "of the proposition made by the mission to establish a boarding school for Siamese boys and girls", the king "was well pleased to purchase" a plot of land slightly upriver from Wongsa's residence on the west bank "for our mission which he would rent to us at a cheap rate". Later in the month, Bradley reported that the rent had been agreed with Wongsa at the same rate as the Presbyterians were paying: 320 ticals a year.

The premises were measured and an agreement on the lease was signed with the Kalahom on 23 February. The lot was divided into four dwelling lots of equal size and two other lots for mission purposes. The house lots were allocated by casting lots and Bradley moved into his new house on 3 August of the same year.

The king's magnanimity to the Protestant community extended further still. On 19 April of the same year, Bradley recorded that:

> A meeting of European merchants and mariners and American missionaries was held at the house of Mr. Ashmore to take into consideration a very generous proposition of the King of Siam that we make choice of a site for a cemetery, for him to purchase and give to us and those whom we represent in future years.[87]

A second meeting was held at the home of B. Joseph a week later and by December a site had been found and Bradley and Mattoon were measuring it with officials from the Phraklang. The following July, the deal was "consummated". Bradley described the plot as follows:

> It is about four miles in the country on the East bank of the river, a very pleasant place for the purposes for which it was given and would be a good location for a Mission Station if the object should be to establish a boarding school. The King will have no objections to having the surplus ground used in this way. I suppose there are nearly two acres of it.[88]

During Bowring's mission two years later, however, the cemetery still required further work as it lacked a wall. Bowring reported that a subscription had been opened to pay for a wall around the cemetery at a cost of 4,000 ticals. Bowring subscribed for 500 ticals "on behalf of the

British Government", which was similar to the amount contributed by British residents.[89]

But even with Mongkut there were misunderstandings. The missionaries were soon to learn that their new-found security of tenure was less a treaty right than a traditional grant based on the king's benevolence, and therefore subject to arbitrary withdrawal. The most serious misunderstanding occurred in 1854 after the 12 September edition of the *Straits Times* in Singapore reprinted two letters from Bangkok that were "strongly condemnatory of the King and his government".[90] The anonymous correspondent opened his 12 July missive with a damning indictment:

> The King, whom all thought would be a good one and rule his country and order things for the benefit of his subjects, so as to be beloved by them, is now very unpopular, and all and everyone in the country, from the highest officer, to the lowest slave, are disgusted at his conduct. It is now nothing but *Tax, Tax,* and oppression in every way, and farm, to squeeze money out of the People, to furnish himself the means of appeasing a most *ferocious appetite*, he has at present for *diamonds* and *women*.[91]

For reasons that are not now known, the king suspected the source of the story to be one of the American missionaries, specifically the Reverend Samuel J. Smith of the Baptist mission. He told Bowring that he suspected the intention was to bring about a Christian government in Siam which would enable the missionaries "to promote their system among our people very easily".[92] The king threatened to banish Smith from the kingdom and was reported to have issued orders to that effect.[93] However, if he did they were not acted upon.

Dr House from the Presbyterian mission conducted his own investigation into the affair and reached the intriguing conclusion that "the letter was doubtless gotten up between Josephs (the Armenian merchant) and Capt. Eames, a friend of Captain Trail, with the knowledge of the prime minister, who was piqued at the king".[94] According to House, Captain Trail, a commander of one of the king's vessels, was motivated by his anger at being arrested and incarcerated for several days in a Siamese jail after a complaint from the British consul in Singapore about Trail's firing of an unauthorised salute in Singapore. The offending article does indeed refer to Trail's "false imprisonment". The suspicion of the Kalahom's involvement is harder to credit, although we have seen that Parkes also noted a breach in his relationship with the king about one and a half years later.

The king's anger at the missionaries was fueled a couple of months later when he discovered the property dealings of another Baptist, John Hassett Chandler. Chandler had first arrived in Bangkok in 1843 as a lay missionary employed in the printing works of the Baptist mission as machinest and printer. Following the destruction of the Baptist mission in January 1851, Chandler had been sent back to the United States to raise funds for the refurbishment. However, he soon decided to break with the mission when he ran into opposition to his plan for bringing back a steam-powered printing press. While in America, he started to develop plans to introduce steam machinery into Siam. He ordered a steam engine for the Kalahom that would be used to power Siam's first substantial steamship, the *Royal Seat*, that the Kalahom would build for the king. After returning to Bangkok on 24 June 1854 he also became a successful agent for shipowners engaged in the purchase of Siamese rice for sale in China. Newly wealthy, he acquired a plot of land on which to build his house soon after arriving back in Bangkok. But the way he had concluded the land deal met with unexpected opposition.

Chandler had rented the land from Nang Chang, a member of the Baptist church and a nurse to some of the missionary children. The king was "much displeased" with the way Chandler had obtained occupancy of the land and became even more upset that he did not know about it "until passing through the new canal at the time of the celebration of its completion" on 4 December. Nang Chang was arrested and faced two charges:

> first, that she had sold that lot to Brother Chandler which is contrary to the law of the land, and second that it had occasioned the King to be highly insulted by refusal on the part of Brother Chandler to allow the King's servants to cut off three fathoms width from the bank of the new canal on which his lot bounded.

Nang Chang and two others were put in chains and stocks, but within three days she "was liberated from prison, the charges on which she was arraigned having been found false". Nevertheless, over the next few days

Chandler was prohibited from entering his building and many of his and other missionary servants fled, while some of the missionary teachers "were seized and thrust into prison".

The missionaries were especially dismayed by the king's harsh reaction to the Chandler lease because they believed Chandler had obtained the proper approvals. Bradley noted that some three months previously the king had told Chandler and other missionaries that they should be given permission "to rent house lots where they pleased". On this basis, Chandler had rented his plot and had even received approval and assistance in acquiring the land from the Kalahom. Bradley surmised, however, that the Kalahom had never discussed the matter with the king.

The Chandler incident, following shortly after the critical letter in the *Straits Times*, added to the king's frustration with the missionaries. On 25 December Wongsa visited Bradley to tell him that the king "evinced great displeasure at all the Protestant missionaries", saying that they should be "prohibited traveling in any direction toward the sea beyond the sentinel stations", that "they may be shot without offense" if they resisted his officers, and that "he would be glad to have them go" out of the country.[95]

By the end of the year, the king's anger had dissipated to some extent and the proclamation naming Brother Smith was not issued, although the restrictions on missionary travel were enforced.[96] The missionaries were to stay out of favour for a few more months. It wasn't until Bowring arrived that the opportunity for a reprieve presented itself. Bradley asked Bowring to intermediate on behalf of the missionaries with the king, and Bowring obliged in his audience with the king on 17 April 1855. Bowring's intercession brought about an almost immediate return to cordial relations between the king and the missionaries. The very next day the proclamation restricting missionary travel was withdrawn and some of the missionaries called on Bowring and "warmly expressed their obligations" to him.[97] By the end of May, Bradley's teacher had returned, having kept away out of "fear of being seized by the government and made to pay another heavy bill of lawyer's fees for teaching the missionaries", and in September the Kalahom offered to give Chandler a plot of land to build on near his own residence, an offer which appears not to have been taken up as Chandler completed his large residence on the plot he had originally targeted.[98]

The American missionaries suspected that the turbulence they had encountered in 1854 arose from the work of forces within the Siamese government that were exploiting incidents such as the *Straits Times* letter and Chandler's land deal to undermine their standing with the king. Whether that was the case or not, the experience did demonstrate their absolute dependence on the goodwill of the king for their own security. When relations with King Mongkut were good, permission and even support to rent land and build residences and mission facilities was easily obtained. But when relations turned sour, the fragility of their situation was immediately apparent. While the missionaries (other than Chandler and Smith) did not face the immediate threat of eviction in 1854, it was clear that the lack of a legal basis for their living and working premises rendered them as much at the mercy of the authorities as they had been in the early years of the mission under Rama III.

THE BOWRING TREATY SOLUTION

In the light of the many problems that merchants and missionaries faced in securing residences in Siam, it is hardly surprising that the issue was on Bowring's agenda. Contemporary western opinion generally subscribed to the view that the Siamese aversion to conferring property rights on foreigners reflected "the repugnance which the Siamese entertain towards the permanent holding of land by foreign residents in the immediate vicinity of the capital".[99] The unfortunate experience of Robert Hunter's fall from grace was certainly one reason behind this. But more recent arrivals had, if anything, re-enforced the negative image that many Siamese leaders had of most westerners. As one of the Siamese nobles commented to Captain Mellersh of the *Rattler*, one of the two ships that had brought the Bowring mission, the two captains of these ships "have given me a very different idea of an English 'Sea Captain' from what I had before, as all the English Captains who come here drink and fight and make such disturbances".[100] But the more liberal leaders in Siam, while perhaps sharing some of these concerns, had a more complex view of the benefits and dangers of allowing foreigners to hold property in Siam.

The solution encapsulated in Article IV of the Bowring treaty was simultaneously more liberal and more restrictive than Article VII of the Roberts treaty. It was more liberal in providing ownership rights for British subjects where Roberts had only contemplated a rental right. But it was more restrictive in limiting the rights to own and rent to specific geographic regions where Roberts had in theory allowed rental rights throughout the kingdom.

The right to own property had also been a key component in the treaty that Sir James Brooke proposed to Siam in 1850. Article II of Brooke's draft treaty would have repealed Article VII of Burney, which, Brooke complained, had often been interpreted by the Siamese authorities in such a way "that a British merchant may, at a moment's notice, be turned out of house and home and his property thrown into the street". Such action, Brooke argued, "is inconsistent with the ordinary degree of permanency requisite for the conduct of trade". Brooke's proposed new clause would have given British subjects "full liberty to reside in and trade with all parts of the dominions of His Majesty the King of Siam". Brooke elaborated that "'reside in' clearly implies the necessity of a sufficient space for a residence and warehouses" and, although the draft clause did not specify ownership or rental, his meaning was that "the ground thus bestowed by His Majesty the King may be leased for a term of years at a just yearly rental; or British subjects may be permitted to purchase ground sufficient for dwelling-houses and stores, or shops, or other buildings necessary for carrying on their business." To allay what he assumed to be Siamese fears, he further clarified that "reside in" did not "imply any right to buy land for estates or plantation, or for other purposes beyond what is herein defined".[101]

The Phraklang's response to the proposed clause illustrated that Brooke was very far from appreciating Siam's real concerns. The Phraklang pointed out that other races had lived in Siam for generations and were "intimately intermingled and become the same as the other inhabitants of the land". They were allowed to cultivate gardens, fields and plantations, and if they break the law they face the same penalties as the Siamese. Rather than worry about English access to productive land, the Phraklang's reason for rejecting Brooke's proposal was based on fear that it would lead to conflict. The experience of the "overbearing and insolent" Robert Hunter who had to be expelled from the country still rankled and implicitly underlay the Phraklang's concern that:

> If the English should come in large numbers and reside in Siam and should pass about in the provinces, controversies and quarrelling would rise and proceed to blows, and an

> Englishman or a Siamese be killed, and then the matter would become serious.

Brooke's Article II was thus rejected on the grounds that if British subjects were to reside in Siam under its terms, "it would prevent the quiet of the country and cast a shade on the subsisting friendship."[102]

Five years later when Bowring arrived, King Mongkut's greater openness than his predecessor facilitated major concessions to British demands in regard to trade and extraterritorial rights. However, on British subjects residing in the country, the position of the Siamese government had hardly moved at all. The overall change in direction meant that Bowring's equivalent of Article II could be accepted, but only because it addressed the concerns raised by the Phraklang in 1850. The key for King Mongkut was to restrict the geographic scope of British property rights in return for granting the concession of ownership. His rationale used strikingly similar language and was essentially an elaboration of the Phraklang's message of five years earlier:

> As the physical appearance, language and traditions of the English are different from ours, if we let them live far from Bangkok, locals who have never come across English people may see them as strange and gather together to attack them. If the English travel far to isolated places, people may rob or even kill them. When that happens, it will be very difficult to investigate and find the truth because the English will not know anyone there. But if the English buy land near the city when they first arrive and they know nobody, the higher density of the city may lead to quarrelling and being attacked by Bangkokians.[103]

The geographic solution proposed by the Siamese involved defining three concentric circles around the city of Bangkok, in each of which different rights applied. Article IV of the Bowring treaty stated:

> British subjects coming to reside at Bangkok may rent land, and buy or build houses, but cannot purchase lands within a circuit of 200 *sen* (not more than 4 miles English) from the city walls, until they shall have lived in Siam for 10 years, or shall obtain special authority from the Siamese Government to enable them to do so. But with the exception of this limitation, British residents in Siam may at any time buy or rent houses, lands, or plantations situated anywhere within a distance of 24

hours' journey from the city of Bangkok, to be computed by the rate at which boats of the country can travel.[104]

Within the middle circle – more than four miles but less than twenty-four hours' travel-time from the city – British subjects were to enjoy the same rights as other citizens (in fact, given the codification through the treaty, it could be argued that they would have greater security in such areas than locals); closer in, foreigners could only buy land after ten years' residence and would otherwise have to rent; further out, they had no right of residence under the treaty.

The new geographic constraints were not a concern for the British negotiators. Bowring stated that "the restrictions within a short distance from the City of Bangkok are quite unimportant,"[105] while Parkes viewed them as "an instance of the absence of useful aim or purpose which characterizes many of their [Siam's] proposals". Instead, the important concession was the right to reside in the Bangkok area either on a leasehold or freehold basis. Parkes believed that the constraints "will probably have a very limited application, as the right of leasing land within this circuit is not forbidden, and may have nearly the same effect and value as the immediate right of purchase". Meanwhile, the limits established for the twenty-four-hour circuit would be more than adequate to satisfy British commercial needs as the permitted areas "comprise a very large portion of the fertile delta formed by the four rivers which flow into the bend of the Gulf".[106]

Even in the middle ring where both foreign ownership and rental was to be permitted, access to property was not completely unfettered. Article IV still required British subjects to apply through the British consul to the Siamese authorities for permission to "obtain possession" of land and houses, but the wording made clear that if the British applicant had "honest intentions", the Siamese authorities would provide help in securing "equitable" terms, give "protection", impose only "just" regulations and set the same tax rate as would be levied on a Siamese subject. The Siamese, however, retained the power to expropriate the land if it had not been cultivated or improved within three years, which was in line with the standard term applied to Siamese usufructs.[107] Nevertheless, from the British point of view the Bowring terms were a marked improvement on those of the Burney treaty.

For the Siamese, the residential rights enshrined in the treaty constituted a reasonable compromise. The headline concern – to keep aggressive foreigners out of remote regions – was addressed. In addition, the royal city and its environs were protected from an influx of foreign buyers. As one historian noted, "the designated area was where the government thought they would be able to control foreigners without endangering the security of the people."[108] It is more difficult to understand the rationale for the twenty-four-hour travel time, although it has been suggested that it was based on a Chinese model.[109] Perhaps it reflected the reality of the king's limited mandate: it has been argued that "Bangkok exercised direct rule only over an area within a radius of two days"[110] and that longer distances in premodern Siam tended to be "measured by human experience", such as travel times, while shorter distances could more easily follow the western concept of a firm boundary line.[111] Siam's real concern was that the British might use random attacks on their subjects as an excuse for embarking on more direct intervention in Siam, even perhaps its eventual subjugation. In his more reflective moments, the king reasoned that the British focus in Siam was on trade, not conquest. By 1863, when the French annexed Cambodia, he was prone to take a less benign view, suspecting a Franco-British hidden agenda ("We have no means of knowing whether or in what way they have contrived beforehand to divide our country among themselves."[112]). But in the honeymoon period of the mid-1850s he appeared more wary of the unforeseen consequences of accidental misunderstandings than suspicious of ulterior motives.

Later in the nineteenth century, the combination of foreign property rights and extraterritorial rights would cause justifiable alarm among the Siamese authorities when a large number of Asian subjects of the western powers claimed protection from the western consuls in Bangkok. As a result, the Siamese showed a willingness to further liberalise property rights for foreigners in exchange for the rescinding of their extraterritorial rights.[113]

But in the 1850s this double threat was far from clear. Indeed, although Bowring reported that the issue of consular jurisdiction was the most difficult part of his negotiation, the Siamese authorities acknowledged the need – and, to some extent, the desirability – of granting consular and extraterritorial rights to the British. Siam focused instead on restricting those rights to countries who could be major trading partners and who would not have an ulterior political motive. The *quid pro quo* for extraterritoriality in 1856 was primarily trade, not property rights.

PARKES MEASURES BOUNDARIES

The first property dispute of the new treaty era had arisen between the Siamese authorities and another American, this time not a missionary. David Oliphant King, an enterprising American merchant, had first arrived in Bangkok in November 1855. He was based in Shanghai, where he was also Prussian consul, and he had additional trading offices in Canton. According to a note in the American envoy Townsend Harris' journal, King "had freed some Siamese vessels that had been captured by the Chinese at Shanghai, and the King of Siam had in gratitude appointed him Consul and Commercial Agent of Siam at Shanghai."[114] He had quickly established himself as a significant trader. When Harris sailed into Bangkok on 21 April 1856, the ship's surgeon, William Maxwell Wood noted: "On our way in, we passed several merchant ships at anchor, all of which were being loaded by Mr. King, an enterprising American merchant of Bangkok."[115]

When Harris arrived in Bangkok to negotiate a similar treaty to Bowring's, the purser from the *San Jacinto* stayed at King's Bangkok residence. But King had identified a large plot of land on the river that he wished to buy and turn into a dockyard. He had negotiated a good price and was waiting for official permission to buy under the new American treaty (naturally labelled the Harris treaty), the property terms of which were identical to those in the Bowring treaty. King claimed the land was more than four miles from the city walls; the Siamese authorities said it lay within the restricted zone and therefore could be rented but not bought. King wrote to Harris complaining of his treatment in Siam, a correspondence which was characterised as "a tirade against the Prime Minister",[116] who King believed to be hostile to him, possibly because of this land dispute.

Parkes was well aware of the dispute during his visit. He attributed the king's sudden insistence on marking the Article IV boundaries to the dispute with the American, noting that the discussion between King and the Siamese authorities "was still pending" and that the Siamese authorities were holding up King's land purchase until it could be ascertained whether the land was within or outside the four-mile line.

To satisfy the king's request for clarity on where the boundaries fell, Parkes' options were limited. He could leave without resolving the issue and entrust it to the new British consul to resolve, but then his hard work in negotiating other points would be at risk. Besides, he did not know when the new consul would arrive. The best option, he decided, was to bite the bullet and complete the survey with the help of a British survey ship that had been engaged in surveying the Gulf of Siam since arriving on 6 January 1856:

> I knew that Her Majesty's Surveying Vessel "Saracen", was at this time outside the Bar, and that I might look to her Commander, Mr. Richards, for professional assistance – a very important advantage which the Consul himself might not have been able to command at a future period.

Parkes also felt it advisable to get "public and unmistakeable refutation" of the rumoured prohibition on land sales to foreigners, rather than relying on the "personal explanations of the Commissioners, made known only to myself and not to the people".[117]

Having decided on his strategy, Parkes borrowed a boat from the king and went to the bar to talk to Captain Richards. Richards immediately assigned two officers for the survey team to accompany a Siamese team of thirty to forty men led by two of their officers – one from the first king, the other from the second. The Siamese also provided the boats required for the exercise. As the king was to explain in his proclamation on the new regulations, the Siamese officials had been instructed to "work with British officials to measure 200 *sen* from the city and put stone columns in the ground in each of the four directions to delineate the circumference of the circle around the city, with additional stone columns on both banks where the circle crosses the river".[118] The operation got underway only one day after the commissioners had told Parkes that it was needed and was completed by the end of April, some eleven days later.

Parkes had to clarify two points to bring the exercise to a conclusion. The treaty stipulated that the restricted zone should be within "a circuit of 200 *sen* (not more than 4 miles English) from the city walls", but Parkes calculated that "four English statute miles amounted to no more than 159 Siamese *Sen*. Thus, two hundred *Sen* would have been upwards of five English miles." Parkes persuaded the commissioners to use the English measure as the base. Second, the commissioners tried to argue that the starting point of the measurement should not be the existing city walls, but a proposed wall planned to be built a further one and a half miles outside the current walls. Again, Parkes objected and won the day.

While the survey was being undertaken, Parkes and the commissioners agreed the methodology for establishing the twenty-four-hour travel boundary:

> The Commissioners proposed various rude methods of estimating the distance . . . In their opinion nothing less than actual travel, with all its contingent accidents and uncertainty, was to be adopted as to the means of testing the length of the journey, and it was not until I argued the point successfully with the King, that I persuaded them to accept five miles as a fair average rate of one hour's travel by boat, and to agree to the multiplication of this rate by twenty four to obtain the total length of the twenty four hours journey.[119]

To simplify this exercise, the two sides agreed on specific districts or geographical features that would define the extent of the twenty-four-hour boundary in all directions.

In the end, the boundaries were agreed and enshrined in the supplementary agreement that was signed on 13 May. Given the reliance on river transport in the city, the most important co-ordinate to emerge from the survey was locating the point at which the four-mile circuit intersected the Chaophraya river to the south of the city. This is defined in Article X of the Supplementary Agreement dated 18 June 1856 as follows:

> The pillars marking the spot where the circuit line crosses the river below Bangkok, are placed on the left bank 3 *Sen* [120 metres] below the village of Bangmanan, and on the right bank about one *Sen* [40 metres] below the village of Banglampulaem.[120]

With the measurements completed, Parkes was able to quickly wrap up the agreement and left Bangkok for China via Singapore on 15 May. In Singapore, he was to cross paths with Charles Batten Hillier who was on his way from Hong Kong to Bangkok to take up the post of British consul. Hillier replaced Parkes on the *Auckland* and arrived in Bangkok less than a month after Parkes' departure.

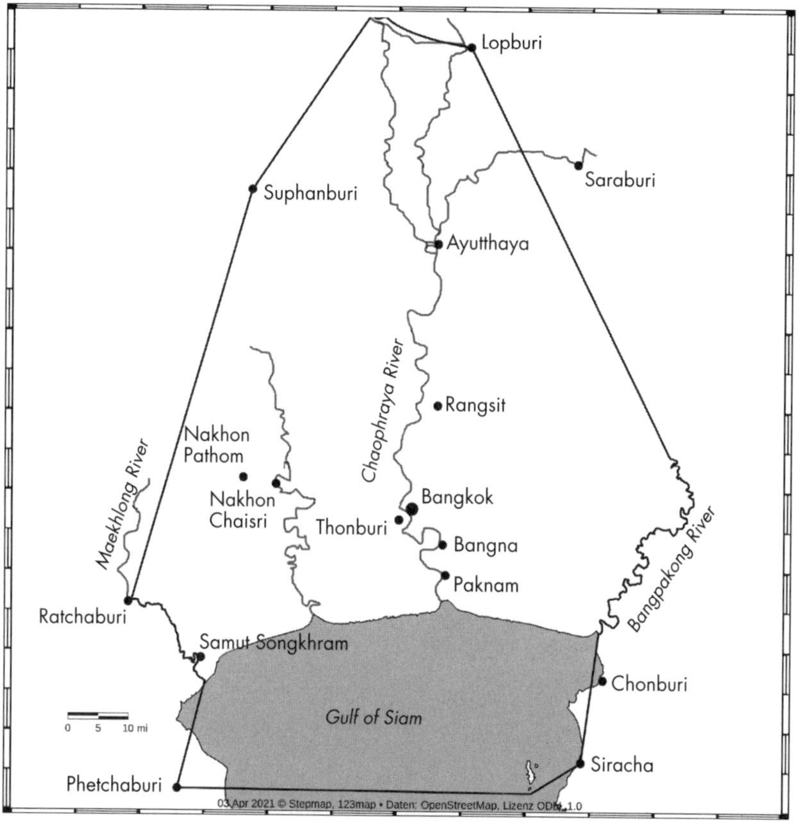

Map of central Siam, showing 24-hour boundary, 1856

The districts that formed the boundary of the twenty-four hour zone were defined as: "1. *On the North.*– The Bangputsa Canal from its mouth on the Chow Phya River, to the old city walls of Lopbary, and a straight line from Lopbary to the landing-place of Tha Phrangam, near the town of Saraburi on the River Pasak.

2. *On the East.*– A straight line drawn from the landing-place of Tha Phrangam to the junction of Klongkut Canal with the Bangpakong River; the Bangpakong River from the junction of the Klongkut Canal to its mouth; and the coast from the mouth of the Bangpakong River to the isle of Srimaharajah [i.e. Siracha], to such distance inland as can be reached within 24 hours' journey from Bangkok.

3. *On the South.*– The isle of Srimaharajah and the islands of Se-chang on the East side of the Gulf, and the city walls of Petchaburi, on the west side.

4. *On the West.*– The Western Coast of the Gulf to the mouth of the Meklong River to such a distance inland as can be reached within 24 hours' journey from Bangkok. The Meklong River from its mouth to the City walls of Kagpury [presumably, Ratchaburi]. A straight line from the City walls of Kagpury to the town of Swbharnapury [i.e. Suphanburi]; and a straight line from the town of Swbharnapury to the north of the Bangputsa Canal on the Chow Phya River."[121]

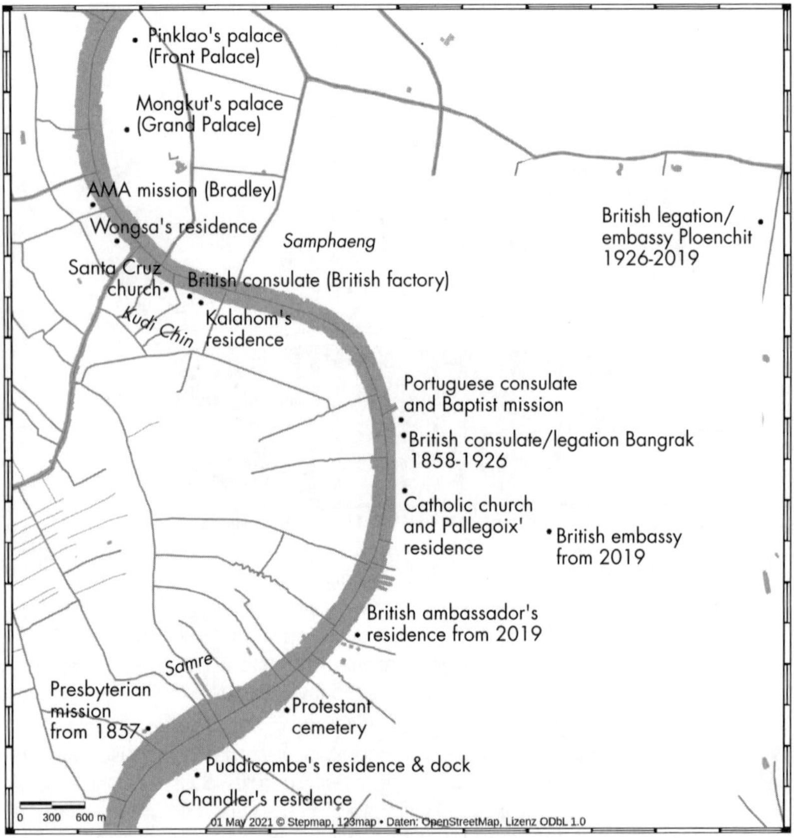

Map of Bangkok, showing prominent buildings, 1856, and future locations of British diplomatic missions.

Chapter 3

The Hilliers in Bangkok

THE HILLIERS ARRIVE IN BANGKOK

HMS Auckland, Singapore, Wednesday, 28 May 1856

After an unsettling two weeks wait in Singapore, Charles and Eliza Hillier were finally setting sail with Maudie, their three-year-old daughter, for Bangkok. Charles was under instructions to get to Bangkok as quickly as possible to take up his new position as the first British consul in Siam. He had ended his official duties in Hong Kong, packed up his household and left the colony – all "with little more than 48 hours notice"[1] – and embarked for Singapore on 10 May. Seven days later the Hilliers arrived in Singapore where they were to intercept the HMS *Auckland*, which would be arriving from Bangkok four days later carrying Harry and Fanny Parkes.

The arrival of the first British consul at a new post was not a matter to be taken lightly. An impressive show of strength was deemed essential to demonstrate British military heft and superiority. The rationale as it applied to Siam had been well summarised by the secretary of the Singapore Chamber of Commerce to Sir James Brooke in 1850, who explained that:

> an imposing display of Force calculated to impress the Siamese with a due sense of the power of Great Britain and its earnestness on this occasion will much facilitate negociations and avert a risk of failure. The Chamber believes also that such a Force would offer the best security against any hostile collisions, which on every consideration it is desirable to avoid.[2]

Hillier was therefore under instructions to arrive in Bangkok on a ship of war. The best option turned out to be the *Auckland*, a naval steamer requisitioned from the Indian navy to help suppress piracy in the South China Sea. The choice was not ideal but served the purpose. The selection had been made by the Commander-in-Chief of the Royal Navy's East Indies and China Station, Rear Admiral Sir Michael Seymour. Although the Treaty of Paris ending the Crimean War against Russia had been signed on 30 March, Seymour had not yet received "decisive intelligence" that the peace agreement had been finalised and was therefore reluctant to send one of the China squadron vessels to Bangkok.[3]

The two weeks in Singapore had been well spent. The Hilliers were able to get first-hand reports from Harry and Fanny Parkes on what was awaiting them in Siam and employ staff as they had heard that "it is absolutely impossible to get servants of any description" in Siam.[4] Parkes also briefed Charles on the operations of a consular office, which gave the new consul a very useful grounding as he had not had time to visit one of the Chinese consulates before leaving Hong Kong.

When the *Auckland* finally set sail on 28 May, the sense of excitement and anticipation was overshadowed to some extent by the difficult relationship between Charles and the ship captain, Captain H. A. Drought, which had started off badly in Singapore and did not improve. Hillier and Drought's first clash concerned Edward Forrest, one of the two student-interpreters (the other being Charles Bell) brought to Siam by Bowring in 1855 to learn the language. Forrest had arrived in Singapore from Bangkok on the *Auckland* as the private guest of Drought. Hillier, worried that nobody would be available to assist him when he arrived in Bangkok as Bell was due to be out of town, wanted Forrest to return with him on the same ship as a private passenger. Drought, however, "having apparently taken umbrage at something that occurred on board on the way down" refused, forcing Hillier to ask the Senior Naval Officer in the Straits Settlements at Singapore, Captain Sir William Hoste, for permission for Forrest to travel on the public account. Hoste gave his permission, to Drought's displeasure.

Hillier was further frustrated at Drought's insistence that he would return to Singapore as soon as the Hilliers had disembarked "and could not make it square with his duty to yield to my official request in writing that the vessel might be detained for 48 hours after my arrival at the

Consulate, to enable me to prepare the necessary Despatches".

The journey itself was without serious incident, despite some misgivings among its passengers arising from Captain Drought having orders "to clear the Malaysian coast of pirates".[5] In the event, Eliza recorded, "much to my comfort, they remained invisible". The only incident of note on the journey was a stop at the port of Terengganu on the Malaysian east coast, a tributary of Siam, where they met the sultan. The *lingua franca* for this encounter was Malay. Eliza, being the only one of the visiting party who could communicate in this language (owing to her childhood in Batavia), "rose to my position" and informed the sultan of the Bowring treaty and the appointment of a British consul to Siam, which was news and "of some interest" to him. However, he was even more fascinated by three-year-old Maude who was "much noticed and honoured by a place on the great man's knee".

The *Auckland* arrived at the sandbar at the mouth of the Chaophraya river on 5 June. Hillier's annoyance at Drought was here compounded when Drought informed him not only that he had "strict orders not to enter the river with the vessel" (either to avoid causing alarm among the Siamese or to avoid getting stuck in the city as it could be several weeks before the bar was navigable again), but also by that fact that the *Auckland* had no tenders, leaving the party totally reliant on the Siamese to provide transport to the city – thereby considerably diminishing the imposing show of British sea power that was supposed to herald the consul's arrival.

For want of a tender, the Hilliers and the *Auckland* "remained tossing and rolling [at the bar] four long days, vainly expecting some means of conveyance up to Bangkok". Apart from the physical discomfort, the wait on the *Auckland* was emotionally stressful because of the strained relationship between Charles and Captain Drought:

> We were anxious enough to be out of the steamer, for we were wretchedly uncomfortable in her, and indeed had scarcely enough to eat – the Captain was a most unpleasant person, and Charles every moment feared a row of some sort.

Eventually, two boats arrived, arranged by the Phraklang, to convey the family to Bangkok. To add insult to injury, "though the Captain knew that we had at least a twelve hours' journey before us he allowed us to leave the ship without even so much a biscuit."[6] This part of the journey was at least entertaining, with Eliza impressed by the sixty royal oarsmen:[7]

> They rowed standing, and at each stroke of the paddle the sixty gave a stamp on the deck with one foot. The steersman occasionally varied the performance by uttering, in a high key, a prolonged yell, to which the other fifty-nine responded by a short sharp bark. Only kings and nobles have the right, in Siam, to indulge in howling boatmen.

This voyage was also a revelation for Eliza. Despite having spent most of her life in Asia, she was immediately inspired by the beauty and unflagging charm of the scenery. The attractions of an unfamiliar landscape were no doubt enhanced by the thrill of experiencing the esoteric Siamese rituals that attended their arrival. However, the journey upriver took twelve hours, including two stops – for breakfast and lunch. At the first stop at Paknam, Charles was welcomed by the Phraklang's brother, Phraya Racha Nu-prapan, who had been sent especially from Bangkok by his brother for the purpose, while Eliza and Maude were provided with "a kind of meal" for breakfast ("but I was not up on pigs' insides, curry etc and therefore made but a sparing breakfast. Dear Maude ate a good meal in her innocence," noted Eliza) and were able to inspect the fortifications. Despite the grandeur and glamour of the royal boats, their vocal oarsmen and the temporary relief provided by the two stops, tedium soon set in:

> For the first quarter of an hour we were amused by our new friends; but, as we proceeded, and the hours wore on, the natural effect was produced by such continued howling and stamping on our wearied nerves and aching heads. When, however, at our request, the boatmen left it off, they also relaxed in their pulling, so that we, finding their exertions to depend upon the noise, submitted to the renewal of it; and, for ten mortal hours the greater number of them endured under a burning sun – we submitted to be yelled and barked over.

Moreover, as the Hilliers were to find, not far below the surface brilliance of the landscape, a harsher reality awaited them. When they finally arrived at their new home, the British factory, at nine o'clock that night, "nobody had expected us till next day, so we found the house empty and dark and dismal". First Assistant Bell finally arrived but on gaining admission, "we found there was one bed and one table upstairs (or rather up ladders) and into these I speedily consigned poor Maude."[8]

The "empty and dark and dismal" property that greeted them on the night of their arrival was, in the cold light of day, in "a very dilapidated and uncomfortable state, and unsuitable for a public office".[9] Eliza believed it would take "the united energies of the British Consulate for an entire month to make the house clean".[10]

The challenge was too much for the Hilliers to face in those first days, so they made the decision to find lodgings elsewhere until the house could be made more welcoming. Options were thin on the ground, there being very few brick houses built on solid ground. As Hillier was to write a month later:

> To hire a house is at present impossible, and the only alternative in prospect in case of ejection is to build a floating house, or one composed of mats, a contingency which, for the sake of the public service and the health of the Consular establishment, I trust to be enabled to escape.[11]

The two young assistants, Bell and Forrest, were not so fortunate as both had been living in floating houses moored on the river since their arrival. As Harry Parkes remarked, both assistants were in poor health during his visit, "and living as they have been in wretched little floating houses, I am scarcely surprised at it".[12]

The only western-style accommodation, apart from a few houses built by the Siamese elite, were the simple residences belonging to the missionaries, and it was in one of these that the Hilliers found refuge. The morning after their arrival, their neighbours, the Reverend Stephen Mattoon and his wife, Mary, came to offer help, which Eliza was glad to accept: "the arrangement is that we are to sleep and eat there till this place can be cleaned and made

Eliza Hillier (© Hillier Collection, by courtesy of Andrew Hillier and Historical Photographs of China, University of Bristol)

habitable."[13] This course of action may have been suggested to them by Parkes who had rented a room at the same place for his wife, Fanny, two months earlier as he also considered the British factory "by no means suited to the requirements of a lady, or in accordance with the English ideas of cleanliness or comfort".[14]

One difference now was that between the time Parkes had left Bangkok on 15 May and the arrival of the Hilliers some four weeks later, Stephen Mattoon had added to his responsibilities. As well as his duties with the Presbyterian mission in Siam, he had somewhat reluctantly accepted the post of first American consul and therefore, since 30 May, was using his residence as the *de facto* American consulate in Siam. Hillier was to start his posting in Bangkok as a tenant of the American consul, a fact that he failed to mention in any of his verbose dispatches to either Sir John Bowring in Hong Kong or Lord Clarendon in London.

THE HILLIERS IN HONG KONG

The inauspicious start to their Bangkok sojourn would not long dampen the sense of optimism at the start of the couple's new adventure. For the Hilliers, apart from the enhanced prestige of Charles' appointment, the posting offered the prospect of a return to England where their sons were at school, which was what the couple really wanted.[15] In addition, the new posting had the advantage of taking them away from Hong Kong. A change from Hong Kong's unhealthy climate was desirable but made even more welcome as the six months leading up to their departure had seen a series of family tragedies: from the death of Eliza's brother-in-law in Batavia, to their own daughter Maude contracting smallpox and coming close to death in late 1855 and culminating in the death of their new-born child in February 1856. It was also a great relief to escape relatively unscathed from the cut-and-thrust of colonial politics in Hong Kong. Eliza told her sister that Charles was "overjoyed" with the appointment and "luxuriates in the relief from tiresome duties, and the change of scene".[16]

Hillier came from a naval family and had served in the Indian Mercantile Marine from the age of fifteen, arriving in Hong Kong during the First Opium War in 1841. He stayed on, joining the newly-established magistrate's court in 1842 and rising with remarkable speed to acting magistrate just six months later. In 1847 he was appointed chief magistrate.[17] His meteoric rise in Hong Kong owed much to his close relationship with Major William Caine, the colony's first chief magistrate, who regarded him as "almost a child of my own", and Governor Sir John Davis as well as the support of recently-retired Shanghai Consul Captain Balfour, who had praised him as "a zealous officer" who had "well qualified himself for the performance of his police duties by acquiring the Chinese language" in a report to Parliament on the China trade.

He had married Eliza Medhurst in May 1846 in Hong Kong. Eliza was born in Batavia and spent almost all her young life either there or in Shanghai. Her father was Dr Walter Medhurst, the famous missionary for the London Missionary Society who had moved his family to Shanghai as soon as it had been opened as a treaty port in the wake of the First Opium War. She had first met Charles in Hong Kong while en route to China when she was just fifteen years old. They were married two years later and in their ten years in Hong Kong were to have four children. The three older boys were all sent away to school in England, while the youngest, Maude, was the only one with them when they eventually arrived in Bangkok.

In 1854, when Hong Kong Governor Bonham retired, Sir John Bowring was appointed his successor and Caine took over the new position of lieutenant general. Hillier applied to take over his mentor Caine's role as colonial secretary, but instead William Thomas Mercer (former Governor Sir John Davis' nephew) was appointed, leaving Hillier, according to one historian of Hong Kong, feeling "estranged and embittered".[18] Caine clearly favoured Mercer for the role, reporting to the secretary of state for war and the colonies that "there is no Gentleman here more fitted for the Post of Colonial Secretary". Hillier's application letter was actually dated some eight days after Caine had made his recommendation of Mercer to London, but Caine was certainly aware of Hillier's ambition for this position as he had made a similar application to serve as acting colonial secretary during Caine's absence from Hong Kong in 1851. When Caine received Hillier's application, he did forward it to London with glowing praise for Hillier's "zeal, ability and usefulness", but failed to offer any comment on his suitability for the job.[19]

Bowring was similarly complimentary about Hillier in his note on the application to the secretary of state, commenting that "Mr Hillier is indeed a very valuable public servant, and has most successfully devoted himself to the study of the laws, language & literature of China. He is one of those who desire encouragement and promotion as the recompense of zeal and industry." Nevertheless, he confirmed his support for the opinion of Caine and Bonham that Mercer had "the superior claim" to the post.

Perhaps Caine's reluctance to promote his protégé was partly due to his awareness that the Hilliers were keen to move out of Hong Kong. Only two months earlier, Hillier had written directly to Prime Minister Viscount Palmerston, with a letter of support from outgoing Governor Sir George Bonham, asking to be considered for a post in the new police force that was being developed in England. His desire to relocate was so strong that he was willing to take a significant reduction in salary – from his current level as chief magistrate and member of the Legislative Council of £1,000 a year to £600. He gave as his main reason for requesting the move back to England as "the ill health of my wife and eldest son, which has compelled me to remove my family to England, where my children at least must necessarily remain for many years, there being no means of education here":

> Their training and advancement in knowledge I consider of such paramount importance, that I should be willing to make great sacrifices both of social position and pecuniary advantage, in order to secure to myself the privilege of bringing under my own more immediate supervision their progress from childhood to youth and manhood.

There would not have been time for Hillier to receive a reply from London before he submitted his application for the post of colonial secretary two months later. Caine may therefore have considered it somewhat half-hearted. To soften the disappointment, Bowring proposed Hillier for the additional post of emigration agent to oversee implementation of the Colonial Passengers Act which increased his salary by another £200, bringing his earnings to the same level as those of the new colonial secretary.[20] It should be noted that the salary increase came at a time of considerable pressure from the British parliament on the Hong Kong administration to reduce expenses. In the wake of Bonham's departure, some senior posts were consolidated and senior salaries reduced by one-third. The salary of the colonial secretary, for instance, was reduced from £1,800 to £1,200.

But Hillier was not to be consoled. Unsuccessful in both his bid for a more senior role in Hong Kong and a lesser role in England, his miseries were to be compounded by a new adversary. At the end of March 1856 Hillier's professional competence was sharply criticised by the new Attorney-General Thomas Chisolm Antsey, who was to become a major critic of the colonial administration over the next three years. In a court hearing in front of the chief justice, Antsey accused Hillier of taking depositions on a burglary case that were "the most slovenly and careless depositions that I ever saw". Hillier's defence of his own actions was unconvincing. Finding himself in a deep hole, he unwisely said: "If the Government are not satisfied with the way in which I discharge my duties, let them get some one else to do them," to which Antsey readily agreed, suggesting that the chief magistrate would be better served by "a regularly educated lawyer".[21] Antsey would eventually get what he wanted when a qualified barrister, Henry Tudor Davies, was finally appointed Hillier's successor.

Bowring was later to claim that the quarrel with Antsey "was one of the principal causes which led to his [Hillier's] removal from the Colony".[22] This statement came in 1858 when Bowring had finally had enough of what he saw as Antsey's argumentative, reckless and malignant behaviour and suspended him from office. In defence of his now-deceased protégé, Bowring wrote:

> Mr. Hillier, the Chief Magistrate, a most painstaking and praiseworthy officer, but not a lawyer by education, had discharged the duties of his office for more than ten years without a word of censure, but within two months of Mr. Antsey's arrival here, he made a most virulent attack on the Chief Magistrate in open Court, because the depositions had been taken in a somewhat informal manner.[23]

Whether Bowring was being deliberately economical with the truth or his memory was fading when he wrote this, we cannot know. It is true that Hillier was held in high regard by many in Hong Kong for the strong line he took as chief magistrate of "severity linked with a complete impartiality".[24] In this he was following the lead of his mentor Caine who believed strong measures were needed to combat the atrocious lawlessness of the colony. The Chinese residents, so often the victims of his harsh judgements, evinced respect for Hillier's firm-but-fair approach to his duties, even holding a grand procession in his honour at his departure.

However, it is certainly not true that his years as a senior magistrate had been "without a word of censure": he was often criticised not only for his lack of legal knowledge and his consequential errors of judgement, but also for what appeared to be harsh and arbitrary sentences. Ironically, in 1846, when he was Member of Parliament for Bolton, Bowring had himself voiced criticism of Hillier for sentencing a large contingent of Chinese men to twenty strokes of the rattan and the cutting off of their queues, tabling this question in the House of Commons:

> Whether the attention of the Government had been called to the frequent application of flogging, as a punishment for petty offences, in the island of Hong-Kong, it being stated that no less than fifty-four persons were so punished on Saturday, the 25th day of April last, for not having obtained tickets of registration; and after such infliction, were deliverd [*sic*] over to the Chinese authorities to be subjected to further penalties under the criminal code of that empire?[25]

Bowring's claim that the Antsey affair was the principal cause of Hillier's removal was also spurious as the chronology shows: Bowring had proposed Hillier for the post in Siam to Clarendon on 4 December 1855 and Clarendon's approval was dated 6 March 1856, some twenty-five days before the courtroom drama with the attorney-general.[26]

Instead, Bowring had chosen Hillier for the Siam posting for several reasons: to defuse a conflict among his senior staff in Hong Kong, to demonstrate his support for one of his key lieutenants and, most important of all, to fulfil a personal promise he had made to King Mongkut that he would appoint a suitable person for the post, or at least so he hoped. Hillier had survived almost a decade as chief magistrate without any legal training. Now he was to take on a diplomatic challenge in an alien environment without any diplomatic training. Despite this, Bowring proclaimed his confidence in Hillier's ability to rise to the task although he did suggest that a vice consul with diplomatic experience also be appointed, a suggestion rejected by Lord Clarendon:

> I know of no one to whom I should be so much disposed to confide the Consulship as Mr. Hillier, the present Chief Magistrate of Hongkong. His judicial experience would be of great value, his knowledge of China and Chinese, especially useful, but I think he should be aided by a Vice Consul who has been trained to the details of Consular business as conducted in China[27]

In view of the events that led up to their relocation to Siam, it is no wonder that the Hilliers were looking forward to starting their new life in a new environment. The hurried departure from Hong Kong had not allowed them to speculate much on what life would be like in Bangkok, but it is fair to say that before arriving they would have had limited information on their new home and no inkling of the kind of impact it was to have on their lives.

BANGKOK SOCIETY, 1856

On first arriving in Bangkok, Charles and Eliza, despite their relative youth (Charles was thirty-six years old, Eliza twenty-seven), could rightly claim to be old Asia hands. Yet Bangkok was a completely novel environment for them, exotic and alien to a degree Charles had not experienced in his fifteen years in Hong Kong, nor Eliza who had spent most of her life till then in Batavia, Shanghai and Hong Kong. Possibly unknown to her, her arrival in Bangkok fulfilled a curious family legacy. Both her father and brother had failed to participate in separate historic visits to Bangkok. One of the earliest American missionaries noted that "to the Rev. W. H. Medhurst it is believed belongs the honor of first projecting a Protestant mission to Siam."[28] In 1828, Medhurst arrived in Singapore to accompany Karl Gutzlaff and Jacob Tomlin on that first mission, but they had already left for Bangkok. After an unsuccessful search of the Malay peninsula for them, Medhurst gave up and visited Borneo instead.[29] Some twenty-seven years later, Eliza's brother (also called Walter), who had recently become consul at Foochow (Fuzhou), was appointed secretary to Bowring's 1855 mission, but had to drop out due to his wife's illness and was replaced by Harry Parkes.[30]

Eliza would add more substance to the legacy soon after moving from Siam to England in 1857. Once there, she embarked on a brief writing career and had three articles published in Charles Darwin's *Household Words* magazine. The fact that all three articles were on aspects of Siam, where she had lived for only six months of her life, illustrates the profound effect the country had on her. Like many European visitors at the time and since, she found plenty to both delight and repel her in her encounter with Siam. While her husband's actions would often typify the patronising attitude of an imperial elite, Eliza's sense of British superiority was more likely to brush up against her instinctive fascination with the exoticism of Siamese culture.

View of Bangkok, photographed by John Thomson in 1865.

The Bangkok that welcomed the Hilliers in 1856 was already a large, bustling city. It had grown rapidly from a small customs post and garrison outpost for Ayutthaya into an important city since King Rama I had inaugurated it as the nation's capital seventy-four years previously in 1782. For the Hilliers, a large part of the exoticism may be attributed to its unusual multi-ethnic population mix. In 1854, the French Bishop Pallegoix estimated the total population of the city at some 400,000. Even though probably an overestimate (a more recent analysis of various estimates concluded that 50,000-100,000 was a more likely range),[31] Pallegoix's description of the population is interesting for identifying and providing estimates of the size of the main ethnic groups. As with several other estimates in the early nineteenth century, Pallegoix believed the number of Chinese (200,000) far greater than Siamese (120,000).[32] On the ethnic mix of the city, Van Roy commented:

> Old Bangkok could well be described as a city dominated by non-Thai ethnic minorities, ruled by a tiny Thai ruling class. The city's colourful reputation rested heavily on its diverse assortment of Chinese, Mon, Lao, Khmer, Malay, Cham, South and West Asian, Vietnamese, Burmese, and indiginized Portuguese communities, plus a sprinkling of Western expatriate newcomers[33]

It has been estimated that the vast majority of the Siamese in Bangkok were slaves. While Pallegoix claimed that "slaves constitute at least a third of the population", a later visitor reported being informed that "nine-tenths of the non-Chinese inhabitants of Bangkok were slaves".[34] Although probably an exaggeration, it was the case that most Siamese living outside Bangkok could not freely move to the capital and freemen attached to nobles were mainly left on their patrons' provincial estates.[35] As a result, Siamese in Bangkok were mostly slaves or retainers of the elite class and that "tiny Thai ruling class" would have been the main Siamese interlocutors for foreign residents in the capital.

The inner city was surrounded by a wall that contained the palaces of the two kings. While King Mongkut was the undisputed monarch, his younger brother, King Pinklao, was officially the second king, or the king of the front palace, and was entitled to equal honour and ceremonial rights as his older brother, but with far less effective power. A number of other royal palaces were also located in the inner city. By mid-century the continuing fecundity of the senior royals had created such pressure on available space that more new palaces were being built on land outside the inner city than within it. By 1851, when Rama IV acceded to the throne, some forty royal palaces had been built in the inner city and another twenty-nine in the adjacent city areas.[36] Among these was the palace of Prince Wongsa, which was situated on the Thonburi side of the river opposite the walled city, near the Kudi Chin community and therefore a close neighbour of the new British consul. The residences of the principal non-royals in the noble quarter surrounding the inner city were often indistinguishable from those of their royal neighbours. Both the Kalahom and the Phraklang, for example, each had substantial residences in the noble quarter, situated approximately one and a half miles downriver from Wongsa on the west bank.[37]

Siamese communities would often be dependent on specific royal or noble figures and be situated close to their palaces. There would also be communities associated with the many temples (*wat*) whose roofline and *chedi* provided the city with its most characteristic panorama. A total of fifty-four *wat* with an estimated 3,606 monks in the city of Bangkok were shown on the map Bradley included in the 1860 edition of his *Bangkok Calendar*.[38]

Among the other ethnic groups, the Chinese dominated commerce, as they had throughout the Bangkok era. Parkes observed that "almost every undertaking requiring skill, enterprise, and industry is in the hands of the [Chinese], they are the principal traders, planters, shipbuilders and farmers of the Revenues, and either through fear or favour, enjoy greater privileges than the people of the soil."[39] The more important Chinese merchants often had houses on either side of the river, stretching well into the noble quarter and even within the walled city itself.[40] Other wealthy Chinese merchants had built their houses on either side of the mile-long, bustling market known as the Grand Bazaar, which boasted one of the few brick-paved roads in the city outside the royal palace area.

The distinctive journey up the Chaophraya river that all visitors experienced and had so inspired Eliza was remarkable not only for its lush greenery and gilded temples, but for the large number of floating houses moored along both sides of the river, becoming denser and multi-rowed as the city grew nearer, with the hectic daily traffic of large and small boats plying their trade on the river. This dramatic entrance to the city led many to overstate the preponderance of floating houses. Even the king complained that one of the four fixed ideas wrongly believed by English residents of Bangkok was that "three quarters of the houses in Bangkok are built in water". The other three misconceptions, according to King Mongkut, were that "the river running through Bangkok has no other name but 'Menam'", that nine-tenths of the population are Chinese and that "the First King is a decrepit old man, so weak and thin and stupid as to be entirely incapable of conducting any official business." [41] At least Townsend Harris chipped away at the myth of a city built on water with his April 1856 estimate that there were only around 7,000 floating houses and that "more than nine tenths of the whole city is built on terra firma".[42] These floating houses usually doubled up as shops and other commercial premises and were often occupied by Chinese traders.

View of Bangkok, photographed by John Thomson in 1865.

Non-Chinese ethnic minorities generally lived in their own communities. Van Roy elaborated on how these communities were distributed in roughly concentric circles around the city, based on their "political ranking, social status, and occupational skills":

> First, a ring of leading refugee settlements (Mon, Portuguese, Cham, Persian, Vietnamese, and Hokkien) occupied preferred sites directly adjacent to the Thonburi and Bangkok citadels. Second, ranking settlements of war captives (Lao, Khmer, Malay, and Cham) were situated along the outer periphery of the Thonburi and Bangkok city precincts. Third, a string of "sojourner" settlements (Chinese, South Asian, and Western) stretched along the river well downstream from the walled city. And lastly, small settlements of hereditary slaves (Karen, Khmu, and other nondescript "tribals") were relegated to the more distant hinterlands, though small groups were assigned to menial service in individual elite households and some of the city's royal temples.[43]

In the limited time the Hilliers were in Bangkok, it is unlikely that they had much, if any, interaction with most of these communities. Exceptions may have been the occasional meeting with members of the "indigenized Portuguese" community neighbouring the British factory (who, although forming one of the five sizeable Catholic enclaves in the city with some 700 souls,[44] had "become almost assimilated to the people of the countries in which they live".[45]) and wealthy merchants from the Chinese and Muslim communities.

Although the strange local customs, ceremonies and attire accounted for much of the exoticism of Siam for the new arrivals, other cities in Asia had an abundance of similar attributes, although perhaps not with the same degree of multi-ethnicity. For the Hilliers, an important difference between Bangkok and other cities in Asia they had experienced was the extremely small western community and the lack of familiar amenities. As a result, they were required to confront the unfamiliarity of local customs to an extent far greater than in the relatively cosmopolitan city of Hong Kong.

A reasonable estimate of the size of the western community in mid-1856 can be made from contemporary sources. The visiting American envoy, Townsend Harris, noted that when he attended a Sunday service in late April that year at Bradley's house, "all the missionaries and most of the white population were present, numbering between thirty and forty."[46] Bradley's own account of his congregation at this service named many of the attendees, including "our usual number of missionaries" (i.e. about eight families), eight officers from Harris' ship, the *San Jacinto*, British envoy Harry Parkes as well as "Captain Smith, Captain Phillips, Mr. Grenon, four other strangers, Mr. C. Puddicombe and his sisters"; in total, some twenty-five people who were neither from the visiting American or British ships.[47] A few of these were likely to have been passing through, but on the other hand several western residents of Bangkok were clearly absent. Naturally, none of the French Catholic priests were there, nor it seems were the two young student-interpreters that Bowring had sent over. Other western residents absent from Bradley's service that day included the mainly British community of merchants and mariners, such as the owners of recently-established ship-building yards, John Baxter and Christopher Puddicombe and his wife (parents of probably six Puddicombe children in attendance at the service); Thomas Knox, an Irish military advisor to the Siamese army who became an interpreter at the British consulate in 1857, eventually rising to the position of consul-general in 1868; Robert Hunter the second, the son of the Scottish merchant who had built the British factory; James Hayes, Hunter senior's former partner in Hunter & Hayes who had stayed on after his partner's ignominious ejection from the country; and a handful of merchants and ship captains with occasional residence in Bangkok, such as Shanghai-based American, David O. King.

Another contemporary source is a list of Bangkok's foreign residents compiled by Hillier's successor as consul, William Raymond Gingell, in May 1857. Gingell estimated how long each resident had been in Bangkok, and from that calculation the western population would have been some forty-four adults when the Hilliers arrived in June 1856. The backbone of the community was the eight Protestant families and six Catholic priests that were associated with the various Christian missions in the city. There were five merchants, five master mariners (all British captains working on Siamese ships), a couple of shipbuilders and a handful of others. Almost half the community was British, but except for the Protestant missionaries, there was only one other married couple apart from the Hilliers (the Puddicombes). Even this small community of around forty to fifty westerners constituted an increase over the preceding decade. While the number of Protestant missionaries had declined, Hunter had reported only five British businesses in the city in 1844, of which his was the only one with British-born subjects involved, the others being run by Anglo-Indians.[48] By the late 1840s, only two western merchants remained in the city.[49]

In the years after 1856, a more substantial expatriate community was to develop. Individual merchants were beginning to arrive, although not necessarily to settle, in the wake of the new treaties. Branch offices of import-export houses were being set up, most notably that of the Borneo Company in May 1856 under Samuel Gilfillan which would grow into one of the largest businesses in the country. At this point it was operating simply as a branch office of its Singapore parent securing its first rice trading contract in September of that year. As well as the German trading houses of Pickenpack, Thies & Company and A. Markwald, other businessmen setting up operations in 1856 included the traders J. S. Parker and D. K. Mason and the shipbuilder Daniel Maclean.[50]

Growth in this community was really to manifest itself in the years immediately after 1856 when business opportunities created by the new treaties led to a moderate influx of merchants. By 1859, Bradley's first edition of the *Bangkok Calendar* indicated that the population of Europeans and Americans had more than tripled in three years, with a total of 143 male residents listed. Of the total, twenty-six of the males had no occupation ascribed to them, but of those that did eight were Protestant missionaries (seven with families), ten Catholic missionaries (none, naturally enough, with families), forty-two merchants or master mariners – sometimes both (six with families), twenty-four office clerks or employees (all single), thirteen full-time diplomats (only one with family), with the remainder comprising mainly engineers, shipbuilders and storekeepers as well as a couple of compradors, a surgeon and a bookkeeper.[51]

However, in the 1860s, the rate of growth slowed. The final edition of Bradley's *Calendar* in 1873 listed 312 western residents, just over double the 1859 total, and this included some twenty-three living outside Bangkok mainly as missionaries and sugar-factory engineers. The composition of the western population remained dominated by missionaries, merchants, mariners, diplomats and office clerks, but there were also a few new professions represented – watch-repairers, hotel and tavern proprietors, auctioneers and even a bandmaster. But the increase in the population largely came from growth in shipping, with over one-third of the total (120) described as mariners, mates or pilots, many on ships owned by Siamese royalty and nobility.[52]

Only fifteen of the 1859 total and forty-three of the 1873 total were accompanied by their families. The single men who dominated the western population were sometimes of questionable character. Hillier commented that "Europeans in Siamese employ are not always the most respectable or moral, and they will probably give more trouble than others of the Consul's countrymen."[53] One would be found guilty of indecent exposure and assault on the young daughter of another business owner, who was himself regarded by Bradley as a "scoundrel". Many died through drink, some drowning in the river, and would often leave behind at least one and sometimes several Siamese wives and mistresses. As William Bradley observed, "*delirium tremens* seems to have rivalled smallpox as the most common disease amongst Westerners."[54]

The small western community in 1856 was mainly clustered in two areas: one, on the east bank of the river about two and a half miles downriver from King Mongkut's palace, including the Portuguese consulate, the Baptist mission and the senior clergy from the French Catholic priesthood; the other, on the west bank around King Taksin's palace, about one mile downriver from King Mongkut's palace, included the British factory and the Presbyterian mission which were within the Portuguese Santa Cruz community. Bradley's AMA mission, which had been in the second cluster until 1852, was now upriver, alongside King Taksin's palace, while some of the new business owners had set up dockyards and trading operations in new locations, over four miles downriver from King Mongkut's palace.

THE DIPLOMATIC COMMUNITY

On his arrival in Bangkok, Hillier was immediately the senior foreign diplomat in the country. Given that there were only two other foreign consuls, this was not particularly remarkable, other than as an indication of the nascent state of foreign relations at the time. The two other consuls were the Reverend Stephen Mattoon representing the USA and Antonio Frederico Moor who was both the Portuguese consul and acting French consul. Unlike Hillier, both these men were at best part-time consuls engaged in time-consuming activities outside their consular roles.

Stephen Mattoon

The appointment of Mattoon was one of the last acts of US envoy Townsend Harris before leaving Bangkok on 31 May 1856. As soon as he had signed the Treaty of Amity, Commerce, and Navigation, Harris was anxious to leave Bangkok as quickly as possible. He was scornful of his hosts, labelling the Siamese a "false, base and cowardly people" and their king "pedantic beyond belief, and that too on a very small capital of knowledge".[55] He was also anxious to get to Japan where he was to serve as the first American consul.

Harris' selection of Mattoon was pragmatic. The United States was keen to enjoy similar privileges and status as Great Britain in emerging trading countries such as Siam but was not ready to commit long-term resources to the task. This view was compounded by the fact that the earlier treaty signed with Siam (the Roberts treaty of 1833) had not led to any substantial increase in trade. Finding the most suitable resident

American was the most logical course of action, and in 1856 in Bangkok that meant one of the Protestant missionaries.

Bradley was the most senior and longest serving of the American missionaries, and Harris may have considered him a candidate for the post of consul. However, in character he was a more divisive figure than Mattoon, and besides would most likely have turned down the role as being a distraction from his missionary work. Bradley noted in his diary that he had thought the appointment of one of the missionaries as American consul "would scarcely be possible".[56]

The choice of Mattoon was also guided by Harris' experience in Bangkok, where Mattoon served him as advisor and translator, and he witnessed at first hand the high esteem in which Mattoon was held by the Siamese elite. In fact, by appointing Mattoon he was taking on board the advice of the Somdet Ong Noi, the Kalahom's uncle, who told him that Mattoon "was a discreet good man; that they [the Siamese] had full confidence in him; that *he never lied*; and that he never got angry".[57] Mattoon had been resident in Siam for almost a decade and, like Bradley, was fluent in the language.

Mattoon himself was a reluctant appointee, calling his position as consul "entirely unexpected and unsought, I had almost said, undesired".[58] Nevertheless, he did accept, arguing the need for someone to take on the duties negotiated in the treaty and the difficulty of finding a "good man" to do so in view of the limited pay and the restriction on trading the post entailed. He was also to allow the Presbyterian mission to become the location for the American consulate in Bangkok.

Hillier's successor as British consul, Raymond Gingell, acknowledged Mattoon's "considerable" influence on the Siamese authorities, which he attributed to "his intimate knowledge of the Siamese language", but also believed that Mattoon's fellow citizens did not "recognize his right to exercise judicial authority" and as a result "many irregularities are committed by American ships and citizens with comparative impunity".[59]

Of the three accredited foreign consuls in Bangkok in 1856, only Moor could claim any experience in the field of diplomacy. However, since his arrival in the city on 22 February 1854, he had had few opportunities to deal with the weighty affairs of state. Portugal was a shadow of its sixteenth-century imperial grandeur and its position as a trading power had been eroded in the face of Dutch, French and British competition.

Jean-Baptiste Pallegoix

The Portuguese consul in Siam was largely ignored by the Siamese authorities, who were said to "hold his position in no very high esteem",[60] and forgotten by the Portuguese. Like his predecessors, Moor had taken to working as a merchant to make ends meet.

Unlike America and Portugal, France had a growing strategic interest in Southeast Asia, but was focused on the countries on Siam's eastern border – Cochin China and Cambodia – rather than Siam itself. The French community in Bangkok was also composed almost exclusively of missionaries, and the most obvious choice for French consul would have been the leader of that community, Bishop Jean-Baptiste Pallegoix, the vicar apostolic of eastern Siam. He had been resident in Bangkok since 1830 – even longer than Bradley – and had become a fluent speaker of the language and a close friend of Mongkut during his time as a prince in the monkhood when Mongkut and Pallegoix were living close to each other (Pallegoix at the Church of the Immaculate Conception; Mongkut at Wat Samorai until 1836 and then at Wat Bowonniwet) and exchanged language lessons – Latin and some French for Mongkut, Pali and no doubt some Siamese for Pallegoix. However, even before arriving in Bangkok, French envoy Charles de Montigny had developed a strong resentment of Pallegoix because of what he considered his uncooperative attitude, which he concluded was due to his having been in Siam too long and "had become a Siamese and let the native government treat him like their head priest".[61] He also believed that Pallegoix's influence over the king and elsewhere in Siam was overrated.

Outside the priesthood, there was no obvious candidate of French nationality for de Montigny to select. It was essential to appoint a Catholic, and the Portuguese Catholic community presented the most promising source. De Montigny decided to appoint Moor, the Portuguese consul, as acting French consul after the signing of the French treaty with Siam on 15 August 1856 as a temporary measure until a permanent

French representative could be sent in. Unlike the American appointment of Mattoon, France's selection of Moor was not popular with the Siamese authorities who viewed the appointment of "only a merchant from a small nation" as an indication of French contempt for Siam.[62]

Aside from Mattoon and Moor, the two junior assistants in the British consulate could be considered members of the minute diplomatic community. Charles Bell and Edward Forrest had both emerged from the recently-established pipeline for the China consular service being provided mainly by King's College London. A few months of training in Chinese at King's had given them at best a very rudimentary knowledge of the language: Bell was only able to write six Chinese characters and explain the meaning of twelve in his final exam.[63] They were nevertheless appointed by Clarendon as "Supernumerary Interpreters on the China Establishment" in October 1854[64] and sent to Hong Kong to learn the trade and for further assignment in consulates in China. Arriving in Hong Kong at the beginning of March 1855, Bell was to be taken to Siam almost immediately as part of the Bowring mission. The intention was to leave him there "where he may have an opportunity of studying Siamese, and where the multitudes of Chinese settlers will I hope enable him to make some progress in the language of China".[65] Of course, once in Siam there was no real opportunity to maintain his Chinese studies, but he did make some progress in Siamese. Forrest requested to be sent to Siam to join Bell, which was agreed and he arrived in Bangkok towards the end of 1855. As well as being designated student-interpreters, Bell was given the post of first assistant and Forrest of second assistant in the new consulate; Bell at the tender age of twenty-three and Forrest only nineteen.

Despite his lack of first-hand diplomatic experience, the fact that Hillier had been posted to Siam specifically for the role gave him the aura of a professional diplomat. Moreover, by establishing quickly his consular court he was looked upon as the chief upholder of justice for the small western community. Bradley recognised the importance of the appointment, writing in his *Journal*, "I am very glad that this important station has been so soon provided for. May it prove to be a good election."[66] The king also understood the importance of Hillier's role, remarking at one time that "no foreign officer of similar rank had ever before resided permanently in Siam."[67]

ELIZA SETTLES IN

As it turned out the Hilliers were to enjoy only a short period of time in Bangkok, but despite the challenges it would appear to have been a rich experience for them – at least until Charles' deteriorating health took over their lives. In those few months, the Hilliers' responses to Bangkok – as evidenced by Eliza's letters and articles in *Household Words* and Charles' dispatches to Bowring and Clarendon – give an interesting, though necessarily partial, picture of their life in the city.

Eliza viewed her time in Bangkok prior to Charles' illness with her natural enthusiasm and a positive outlook. She wrote in generally glowing terms on the beauty and exoticism of daily life. From her first day travelling by boat to Bangkok in June, she had found the landscape captivating. At Paknam, about ten miles upriver from the bar, she was struck by its "temple prettily decorated, gleaming like a pearl in its bright-green setting", and then further on "the eye is relieved by a great variety of foliage" with numerous bread fruit and cocoa-nut palm trees – "the one, with its large, curiously indented leaf offers a tempting shade from the glare of the tropical sun, while the other, with its feathery crown, towers aloft over its companion in the forest", while the "graceful bamboo, in all its beautiful varieties, also fixes the attention – seen at one time in short full clumps, then again with its drooping branches and long stem of lance-like leaves quivering in the breeze". All this, while the "peculiar beauty of the picture is much enhanced by the variety and richness of tints of an eastern sky glittering in the sunlight".

She even found the climate better than expected. Her friends in Hong Kong had warned her that the climate in Bangkok was "intensely hot and very damp, and that a poisonous miasma hangs over the shores of the river", concerns that she said "proved unfounded" as "even during the most unpleasant months" the heat was less than that of the north coast of China and Hong Kong during two summer months. Although she did not experience the hottest months of March and April, having arrived in June and leaving before year-end, the missionaries had confirmed to her that "the heat never is distressing". Likewise, the intense rains from May were not unpleasant, bringing "deliciously fresh and cool" air, new growth and "even self-willed English constitutions appear as though it were incumbent on them to thrive and rejoice in the great huge washing-day of nature." The climate, in her view, brought health benefits for foreigners

King Pinklao, photographed by John Thomson in 1866.

in the city, all of whom "look healthier and more robust than the majority of those at Hong Kong or in the northern ports of China", with illness rare, except – from her personal experience – "the much dreaded dysentery" which is "almost invariably fatal" for Europeans.[68]

Nevertheless, even for the optimistic and energetic Eliza, the business of maintaining a household in Siam was extremely challenging. Unlike Hong Kong, the foreign community was miniscule, amenities unavailable and the lifestyle, customs and governance systems completely alien.

Before leaving Hong Kong, she had told her sister that "we must take every single thing in the way of furniture with us."[69] The British factory where the Hilliers were to live was not only lacking furniture, it was also barren of appliances: "There were no pots or pans, none of the numerous conveniences the value of which is scarcely known or heeded till the want of them is understood." Improvisation was required: using a packing-case and an empty beer-bottle in place of a board and roller to make pastry or engineering two large unbaked earthen pans in place of an oven. Essential foodstuffs, such as poultry, eggs and fruit, were in abundant supply, but the market "offered so little variety of food that the task of keeping a good table was no easy one". Ingenuity was required to overcome the obstacles presented by routine tasks in an unfamiliar environment, whether it be preparing meals, getting furniture made or overseeing the Siamese servants, whom she regarded as having "a real fear of labour".

She was full of praise, however, for most of the Siamese royals, noblemen and their wives who she met either at dinner parties or on more formal occasions. She was particularly taken by the Kalahom:

> Such a nice gentlemanly little man, he really behaved as if he had been accustomed to dine in English fashion all his life, and I was fairly taken by surprise when he asked me to take wine with him in the most finished style possible. The effect of having a gentleman to dinner who wore no jacket or upper garment of any sort was in some degree peculiar . . . it would however be no loss if all who claimed to be gentlemen had as much right to the title as this Kalahoma, although he chews betel and wears no jacket.[70]

She also praised a young prince who was a frequent guest for displaying "the ease and polished manners of a gentleman", while often sitting with his legs "tucked … up into the chair, frequently cuddling his knees with his long bare arms. In this manner he would sit for a long time, talking excellent English, - instructing us, amusing us, and winning our respect."[71] Eliza did not identify the prince by name. One possibility is Prince Chookiati, who Fanny Parkes called "the best specimen of a Siamese noble" and "really gentlemanly in his manners". She observed that he was unfortunate enough to speak and write English and, as a result, was constantly employed by the king: "He told me that when he first learnt English, 'he like it, but now he hate it very much'"[72]

Eliza's opinion on the two kings of Siam, whom she also met, was also generally positive:

> Both are remarkably in advance of their age and country; highly intelligent men, who have cast aside entirely the self-satisfied spirit of a half-wild people.

Like many in the western community in Siam, Eliza displayed stronger admiration for the second king than the first. She contrasted the pomp and garishness of King Mongkut's palace with the more restrained European-style elegance of King Pinklao's and concluded that the latter "far surpasses his royal brother, not only in literary and scientific attainments, but in moral character". On meeting the second king at a luncheon at his palace, she wrote: "I was pleased by his manners, which were peculiarly courteous and gentlemanly, and at the same time unassuming."[73]

Her praise for the Siamese nobles often extended to their wives. The Kalahom's head wife she considered "a very interesting woman" who exhibited "perfect propriety and good breeding". Coming from a Hong Kong society where women played a more circumscribed role in entertaining local officials, the role of women in Bangkok in general astonished her. She was surprised to find that "it is not uncommon in Siam to find women able both to read and write" and that:

> The occupations of the females are various and far less circumscribed than in many parts of the East. In fact, the women in Siam occupy a moral position many degrees superior to that of their sisters in neighbouring countries. The wife of a Siamese has no unimportant voice in the domestic arrangements of the family. She is cash-keeper and seems to possess the right to

claim all her husband's earnings. The women, as a race, are very intelligent and observant; those belonging to the higher classes seem to have pleasing and modest manners.[74]

However, her admiration did not extend far down the social ladder, dismissing "the lower orders" as "quiet and unobtrusive in their manners".[75]

Aside from the occasional meeting with the higher echelons of Siamese society, opportunities for social interaction were limited. For Eliza, the opportunity to socialise with ladies of a similar standing and background – as she would have been accustomed to in Hong Kong – was particularly limited. The small western community was predominantly male. The only cohort of western women was the American missionaries. As the daughter of the missionaries Walter and Betty Medhurst, Eliza's upbringing had much in common with the missionaries'. Even though her father had fallen out with the American missionaries in Shanghai over the correct Chinese terminology for God and the Holy Spirit,[76] the Medhursts' non-conformism would have had more in common with the American Protestants than Charles' Anglicanism.[77]

Eliza's view on the missionary women was more positive than might have been expected given a general antipathy for Americans that she expressed during her time in Hong Kong. That antipathy may have stemmed partly from her father's doctrinal dispute, but also from Charles' bruising clash with the American consul in Hong Kong over the harsh treatment meted out to a British sailor on an American ship. Nevertheless, in Bangkok, she had kind words for the American missionary women: "They are all good kind people and constantly beg me to 'be sociable' and 'run round when I have a mind to'."[78]

Eliza's closest bond would have been with Mary Mattoon, with whom she had stayed on her first night in the city and whose house was near the British consulate. The fact that both had consuls for husbands would have necessitated relatively frequent socialising. The only other English woman known to be living in Bangkok at the time was Margaret Puddicombe, the wife of Christopher, but the Puddicombe's lived over four miles downriver, a journey of at least an hour against the tide.[79] Besides, the Puddicombes had in tow seven children.

Nor was there much opportunity to entertain international visitors, aside from the occasional merchant or ship's officer passing through. The only diplomatic mission to visit during their time in Bangkok was the French mission of Charles de Montigny, who was well known to Eliza from when she lived in Shanghai where de Montigny had been French consul. But even that was a disappointment. Eliza complained to her sister that de Montigny, "forgetting what a very small individual he was at Shanghai" declined a dinner invitation at the Hilliers because, she surmised, "it would be infra dig for an Ambassador to dine with a Consul."[80] To compensate for the snub she invited some other French people to a dinner where, as usual, the challenge was in providing the food, "all the material one has to work upon being chickens *ad libitum*. I was obliged to send far and near yesterday to secure a joint of beef and in order to get one piece must take a whole leg."

But outside of formal dinners, social interaction would have been very limited, and not particularly easy. As Pallegoix noted, "there is not a single carriage in the city; everybody goes around by boat. The river and canals are almost the only roads used."[81] The Chaophraya river, as Bradley wrote, was the "broadway of Bangkok, while the canals are the inferior streets".[82] The consequent dependence on the availability of boats and oarsmen made spontaneous visits difficult. It is hardly surprising that Eliza told her sister "visiting is not one of the pleasures of Bangkok so I indulge in it but little."[83] The lack of roads also made the favourite European activity of taking walks impossible: "to exercise the body regularly by going for a stroll was not known among the well-to-do Thais."[84] Nevertheless, the more leisured pace of life was appealing to both Charles and Eliza after the intensity of Hong Kong:

> My time passes in a quiet way, totally free from excitements of any kind, and yet I do not find it hang heavily on my hands. We both like the place really very much, and Charles seems to enjoy his quiet leisurely sort of life. He has plenty to do in his office, but not too much, and is able to get through his work generally by four o'clock – when we dine and afterwards go out for a pull in the boat, returning to tea.[85]

Kalahom's wife, photographed by John Thomson in 1865.

Although Charles enjoyed his leisure time, his new role as consul was not stress-free, and any ease he had found would soon crumble before disruptions that would affect both his official duties and his family life.

Charles Batten Hillier (© Hillier Collection, by courtesy of Andrew Hillier and Historical Photographs of China, University of Bristol)

Chapter 4

Hillier gets to work

HILLIER'S INSTRUCTIONS

The Grand Palace, Bangkok, 17 April 1855

The evening before the signing of the Bowring treaty, King Mongkut invited Bowring and his party to the Grand Palace. He had arranged to entertain them with an elaborate play involving a cast of about a hundred people featuring some of his wives and concubines. Shortly before midnight, the king interrupted the performance to invite Bowring to his private rooms. The terms of the treaty had been agreed and the execution document was being prepared for signing. The king was anxious to address some issues on the implementation of the treaty, raising three specific concerns he had on the appointment of a British consul.

First, the king wanted assurance on the character of the consul, asking Bowring to "not allow any intemperate man to come and cause quarrels". Second, he asked Bowring "who would control the consul, and to whom he could complain if he behaved amiss." Bowring confirmed that it would be he who would have this task, to which the king responded: "but when you are gone, there may be some one who is not my friend." On these two points, Bowring could only reassure the king that "a fit person would be sent".

Finally, and probably having in mind Siam's experience of Portuguese consuls turning active traders, the king wanted to make sure that the British consul would not be allowed to charge fees for services, which could lead to "abuse and extortion". Bowring was able to promise him that no fees would be levied, that the consul would not be allowed to trade and that he would be "handsomely paid, and a person so educated as to be worthy of his Majesty's confidence". Although the king expressed satisfaction with these reassurances, Bowring noted:

> I can perceive how distasteful the nomination of any consul is in Siam, and I doubt if anything but prompt persistency at an early period would have carried this point; the Second and First King being alike indisposed to welcome any foreign authority whatever in Siam.

At a dinner to celebrate the conclusion of the treaty two days later, the two principal supporters of liberalisation, Wongsa and the Kalahom, reiterating the king's main concern, "begged us [the British] to bear in mind the difficulties they had to encounter, and especially to arrange that a just and wise consul should be sent".[1]

In appointing Hillier, Bowring could be reasonably optimistic that he was fulfilling his promise to the king to send "a fit person". In Hong Kong, Hillier had earned a reputation for being "if not the brightest, certainly one of the most honest, conscientious, and straightforward" of its civil servants.[2] Although he was unflatteringly described as "not a man of colourful personality",[3] even this characteristic might satisfy the king's requirement for a man of moderation. On the other hand, Hillier had also acquired a reputation for dispensing stern discipline and had made some high-profile enemies. His personality, however uncolourful and incorruptible, was also uncompromising. Bowring would be less confident that Hillier would meet the king's request for a person who would not "come and cause quarrels".

A year after his discussion with the king on the consular appointment, Bowring was writing detailed instructions to Hillier which indicated that the king's concerns were still fresh in his mind and that he was aware that Hillier's character was not necessarily best suited to allay them. His letter to Hillier was designed to set the tone of the consularship and ensure it would preserve the British government's policy of non-confrontation with Siam. The need for caution and compromise was a recurrent theme. Hillier would have to adapt to a very different dynamic from what he was used to in Hong Kong. After all, Hong Kong was a full colony; the relationship with Siam, on the other hand, was based on a treaty arrangement not dissimilar to those that governed British involvement in the Chinese treaty ports, but unlike in the treaty ports the British relationship with Bangkok had been achieved through delicate negotiation, not conflict.

Indeed, the treaty with Siam was one of Bowring's proudest achievements: it was a personal triumph that had greatly enhanced his own reputation. Apart from his formal duties, therefore, Bowring needed Hillier to be aware that his new job involved protecting that positive reputation. Bowring told Hillier of "the deep interest I feel in your success" and "the responsibility I have taken upon myself in recommending for the Consular Office, to the Earl of Clarendon, in your person, a gentleman new to that particular service". He would therefore give Hillier "every co-operation and counsel, which may help the peaceful, progressive, and prosperous development of the advantages of the Siamese Treaty".

In tacit acknowledgment of Hillier's tendency to be intransigent, Bowring was at pains to point out the need to "treat with consideration and indulgence difficulties which may present themselves and whose removal will be best accomplished by gentleness mingled with calm determination". And although it was important to ensure obedience to the consul's legal authority and protection of British rights and privileges, at the same time, "no needless offence must be given to the people" of Siam, any new regulations should be discussed "amicably" with the Siamese authorities and friendly relations maintained with the Kalahom and the two kings. Again, even though it must be a priority for Hillier to set up a consular court, "it is desirable that friendly mediation should be looked to for the settlement of all questions at issue," even when cases involved British subjects only. Finally, Hillier would have to "take care to avoid engaging in religious controversies, or giving umbrage to the Siamese authorities by interference with the religious rites of the people".[4]

Bowring's message could not have been clearer: make friends, respect your hosts, avoid conflict and find solutions through compromise wherever possible. Such should be the guiding mantra of Hillier's consulship.

HILLIER STRUGGLES TO GAIN RESPECT

During his time in Bangkok, Hillier would find it challenging to abide by Bowring's guidelines consistently. Consular affairs were to involve a series of irritants that made his life far from stress free; a sharp contrast to the tranquil idyll portrayed by Eliza. Apart from the sorry state of his intended accommodation, Hillier had to establish consular operations from scratch with very limited resources, no real on-the-ground support and a drawn-out approval process.

Hillier's new position required him to transfer from the colonial office under Secretary of State for the Colonies Henry Labouchère to the China consular service under Secretary of State for Foreign Affairs George Villiers, 4th Earl of Clarendon. He would now be reporting to Bowring in the latter's capacity as plenipotentiary accredited to the court of Siam rather than as governor of Hong Kong but would also need to send reports directly to Clarendon in London. Interestingly, Hillier and Bowring (who had previously served as a member of Parliament) were the only two senior appointments made from outside the China consular service, all others being promoted from within.[5] Bowring warned Hillier on more than one occasion not to commit to any new expenses nor exercise his judicial authority before receiving official authorisation from Clarendon in London, which would take several months to arrive.[6]

Even more disconcerting for Hillier was his sense of being slighted by his Siamese counterparts. He complained to Clarendon that his reception in Bangkok had not "appeared in any degree cordial":

> The officers of Government seemed suspicious of my objects and doubtful of my disposition and appeared to shun rather than seek my society.

He attributed this to an "anti-English feeling" that he believed had arisen since the departure of Parkes, particularly in the mind of the Kalahom. Parkes himself believed that any such attitude had been "sown by our American friends" in the Harris mission after his own departure.[7] Both Parkes and Hillier were no doubt influenced in this by Charles Bell's report on the reception of the Harris mission, in which the student-interpreter had reported that "the greatest friendship was shown towards the Americans, whilst on the contrary a most violent antipathy exhibited itself towards the English".[8]

The fact that the Kalahom had distanced himself from the Parkes negotiation but played the leading role in the Harris negotiation could be seen as indicative of his new-found preference. However, both Harris' culpability and the Kalahom's new partiality are far from certain. Harris himself viewed the Siamese expressions of distrust of the English as a reaction to Parkes' aggressive negotiating strategy rather than claiming any role for himself:

> I learned in the evening that a grand row had taken place, about the business of Mr. Parkes who had so wearied the King by his letters, etc., that he got enraged, blew up all his court and ended by closing the palace against all the world.

Moreover, Harris was to find that his own negotiations would not necessarily benefit from any anti-English sentiments in and around the court. He was soon complaining that "the Phra Kalahom, who had always affected to entertain the most friendly feeling towards Americans, was my chief opponent." A few days later the Kalahom told Harris that he considered the English "rapacious tyrants who were seizing on the whole of Asia" while praising the Americans as they were not "seeking conquests in the East" and their missionaries had been "of vast use" to Siam. However, the Kalahom's main objective was to win a negotiating point, reminding Harris that as friends "surely you will not ask as much from us as we were forced to give to our enemies?"[9]

Whether the Kalahom's stated views on the relative merits of the English and Americans reflected his true feelings or his negotiating strategy, Hillier was soon to come to the conclusion that he was not being accorded the status and respect that should accompany Queen Victoria's principal agent in the country. In his dispatches both to Bowring and Clarendon, he pointed out that his efforts to further British interests in Siam were hampered by his own lowly position in the hierarchy, especially when dealing with senior nobles and royalty. He was acutely conscious of his status in his dealings with the king: "the disparity of rank is too great, the bond of union is too weak for such a connection to resist the first outbreak of the Royal displeasure caused by a plain statement of truth, and the discontinuance of intimate relations once established, in this manner, would have mischievous effect."

As a solution, he told Clarendon that he would be prepared to step down as consul in favour of "an officer of higher standing than myself, either divested altogether of the consular character, or at least clothed with additional powers as an inferior political agent, and possessing right of access to the King's person", while routine consular duties could be handled by a vice consul.

While some officials in London may have interpreted Hillier's suggestion as a disingenuous attempt to engineer his own promotion to consul-general, there was clearly a wide gulf in understanding between Hillier and the senior Siamese officials. His first audience with King Mongkut only lasted fifteen minutes, unlike the lengthy audiences granted to his predecessors. At one point he reported to Clarendon that "I have been told on several occasions by the Chief Officers of State that I must deport myself as a high Siamese Noble, 'one of themselves'." Even the king was on his case:

> His Majesty's caution against any possible attempt on my part to unduly magnify my office, has at times almost assumed the form of insult, while he seems to be, at other times, equally solicitious [*sic*] lest it should be thought among his subjects, that Her Majesty has sent an officer of low rank to represent British interests here.[10]

Hillier's insecurity over his position coloured much of his dealings in Siam. Even the appointment of boatmen was determined by the need to project the correct status, arguing that "it would not be at all politic for the Consul to appear on public occasions with a less number while natives of small rank are pulled by from 20 to 40 men:"

> He might be told by the authorities, as was once the case in China, that if he expected them to secure proper respect to his office he must be accompanied by those outward signs of authority to which alone the natives are taught to pay deference.

A few weeks later, this view was validated when the Phraklang "quite spontaneously, took me seriously to task for not using such a mode of conveyance as alone among them, betokens rank" and warned him that if he continued to use a small European, four-oared boat instead of a Siamese boat with many more rowers, "I must not expect to be treated with the respect that was my due by the Siamese."

Subsequent consuls complained in similar terms of the tendency to be dismissed as lowly by the Siamese elite, although not in the case of Sir Robert Schomburgk (consul from late 1857), whose knighthood and direct appointment by London (rather than through Hong Kong) gave him sufficient prestige in the eyes of senior Siamese officials. Thomas Knox was to argue successfully for an upgrade in his position to consul-general in 1868 by making similar points to those made by Hillier.

By late August Hillier's situation appeared to be improving. Having won an important concession from the Siamese on the siting of the new consulate and excited by the king's confirmation of his desire to send an embassy to England, he was much more positive towards the country. He began to extol the economic prospects of Siam, the particular interest in its development that Britain should evince given its neighbouring territories and the laudable liberality of its leadership:

> From a people in a low condition materially and morally, have arisen a monarch and one or two nobles almost self taught, admiring the science and civilization of the West, which their respectable attainments enable them to appreciate, desiring to raise their country to a similar elevation of material wealth and mental progress, but lacking the knowledge and administrative ability to this end.

He also praised the important strides made by Siam – without the threat of external force and in the face of domestic opposition – in opening up to western trade and giving up partial judicial sovereignty. Nevertheless, he stressed the need for the treaty powers to provide educational and institutional support to guide Siamese society to its bright future within the "family of nations". Otherwise, Siam ran the risk of "political annihilation" as its liberality could be subverted by an influx of foreign workers and capitalists.

Importantly, he could report in early September that his "relations with the Siamese Authorities, are, I am happy to say, in a more satisfactory condition than on my first arrival". The Phraklang and the Kalahom had made several visits to the consulate "and conversed with the greatest freedom" and the Hilliers had entertained both, as well as Prince Wongsa, at dinners. Moreover, the Kalahom "so far overcoming the habits and prejudices of Eastern life, as on two occasions to send his wife and sister to spend the morning with the wife of the Consul".

Nevertheless, Hillier was all too aware that he was being tolerated rather than respected:

> This state of things has not however, been brought about without some trouble, and it is occasionally easy to see that my distinguished visitors had to struggle with their dignity before determining to visit the Consul on equal terms, and even now are somewhat doubtful of the policy of such a proceeding.

While Hillier recognised that his lowly social and political status impeded his acceptance in Siamese high society, there was no acknowledgment of how his own behaviour had exacerbated the problem. Like Bowring, Mongkut had urged Hillier "to cultivate friendly relations with the highest Ministers of State" from their first meeting.[11] However, in a short time, Hillier's relations with the king and his ministers had become strained, which the king attributed to the consul's disagreeable personal attitudes. In 1857, comparing the newly-arrived British consul (Schomburgk) with his predecessors, Mongkut wrote scathingly that Hillier was a sulky presence from his first arrival, describing him as *na bueng ban bueng*, which suggests a frowning, grumpy presence, or, in Bradley's contemporaneous definition, a person who looks serious and unsmiling, a person who is angry, resentful and does not laugh.[12] As Mongkut commented:

> After only a couple of days he started demanding this and that. If we didn't respond quickly enough, he would make accusations and threaten to immediately bring in a ship of war, using every issue to threaten Siam every day.

Mongkut also pointedly contrasted the gracious manners of Schomburgk with the aggressive Hillier, whose behaviour he described as *ekkrek kaeka*, which could be translated as loud trouble-making.[13]

Hillier's dispiriting encounters with Siamese officials fed his own insecurities. Unprepared for the challenges of his new position, his feeling of being unequal to the task was no doubt compounded by his isolation from the network of senior colleagues that had guided him in Hong Kong. His confrontational oubursts would only further alienate the king and his officials, whose approach to foreign relations reflected a political and cultural tendency to compromise and conciliation. Rather than ingratiating himself with the Siamese elite, he fell back on the hard-nosed doggedness of imperial bombast that was more likely to repel them. In the end, he would achieve some of his objectives, but never earned the respect of his Siamese counterparts.

HILLIER ESTABLISHES HIS PRIORITIES

Neither Clarendon's notice on Hillier's appointment[14] nor Bowring's detailed instruction letter to him made any mention of the need to obtain new premises for the British consulate. While Bowring's letter covered many issues, only the need for establishing a consular court was mentioned as a priority. As court procedures were well within Hillier's area of expertise, this was accomplished quickly. Hillier heard his first case in early July 1856 and a total of ten by mid-September. The cases involved non-payment of debt, assault or desertion. Plaintiffs and defendants were mostly British or Anglo-Indian seamen, with the exceptions being four cases against British sailors brought by Anglo-Chinese, American and French plaintiffs.[15] No cases involving Siamese subjects were heard by Hillier.

Apart from the general duties of the new consul, Bowring had mentioned several areas where new regulations may be required: "the rights of settlement, travelling in the interior, the landing or shipment of articles of commerce, Custom House and harbor arrangements".[16] Such topics did register as matters to be pursued by Hillier during his brief tenure at Bangkok, but he clearly spent a great deal more time and effort on acquiring a site for the new consulate. Despite Bowring's failure to cover this topic in his letters, Hillier referred to "verbal instructions" that he received from Bowring before leaving China "to make it one of my first duties to procure a suitable piece of land on which to erect a Consulate",[17] a claim he would certainly not have made if it were not the case.

Harry Parkes had also made it clear to Hillier when they met in Singapore in May 1856 that he "attached much importance" to the objective of securing new premises for the consulate.[18] Parkes' view was in part coloured by his own negative impression of the British factory, which had been prepared for him by the Siamese government on his arrival, and his awareness of the Siamese government's desire to take back possession of the building. After Hunter's ignominious departure from Bangkok – and following a short tenancy by a Portuguese merchant called Joachim – the Siamese authorities, acutely aware of the shortage of suitable accommodation for foreign dignatories in Bangkok, had taken possession of the British factory. It was used to accommodate Sir James Brooke in 1850 and then, during the early years of King Mongkut's reign, repaired with the intention of using it for the reception of distinguished international visitors. When Sir John Bowring came in 1855 to negotiate the treaty under which Hillier had been appointed consul, he was put up there and had evidently been quite satisfied with his lodgings, considering it to be "in good order", with its "large and airy" sitting room, "newly papered" and richly ornamented bedroom and pleasant amenities: "Jars of fresh water are placed on my table, with bouquets of roses; and a Siamese servant speaking English has me in special charge."[19]

Parkes had inspected the property a few days before Bowring arrived and reported to Bowring that it was "scantily but still sufficiently furnished", concluding that it would "serve very well for the lodgement of all the officers accompanying you to Bangkok".[20] However, a year later Parkes had changed his mind. It was now inadequate, especially for his new bride:

> The arrangements, though as good perhaps as the Siamese had it in their power to make, were by no means suited to the requirements of a lady, or in accordance with the English ideas of cleanliness or comfort, and I had therefore to procure accommodation for my family in the house of an American missionary [Mattoon], making use however of the factory for the transaction of all my public business.[21]

During his sojourn in Bangkok, Parkes had been made acutely aware of Siam's need for the property. When Townsend Harris, the American envoy, arrived in April 1856 to negotiate the US-Siam treaty, the Siamese authorities tried to persuade Parkes to vacate the property for Harris. The Siamese would have seen Harris as the more senior diplomat and therefore entitled to the choice accommodation, but Parkes refused to move. Harris was willing to accept alternative accommodation with the option of moving to the British factory when Parkes left. Parkes himself advised Harris to apply to stay in the house of the recently-deceased Somdet Ong Yai ("the late Phra Klang").[22] The Siamese authorities, however, were reluctant to set a precedent of using the houses of noblemen for foreign envoys and quickly provided an alternative building for Harris' use. They had also built a similar structure for the upcoming visit of the French ambassador.

Before leaving Bangkok, Parkes had negotiated a one-year lease on the British factory for use as the British consulate. Despite this, shortly after Hillier took possession, like Parkes before him, he was put under pressure by the Siamese authorities to make way for a more senior diplomat.

This time, the occasion was the arrival of French Ambassador Charles de Montigny to conclude the Franco-Siam treaty on 14 July. Again, the Siamese were thwarted by the intransigence of the British incumbent. The French were, at first, equally resolute and had rejected the alternative that had been erected for de Montigny. Bishop Pallegoix had written to the king informing him of de Montigny's "determination not to land until His Majesty had placed at the disposal of the French Mission this Consulate (the British Factory) which was the building occupied by Sir John Bowring, or its full equivalent".[23] The French insistence on following British precedent is not without irony given that Bowring and Parkes had insisted a year earlier that the Siamese had to accord their mission the same status and procedures as those enjoyed by the French ambassadors from the court of Louis XIV in 1687.[24] In the end, the Siamese compromised and the French ambassador and his family were housed in the late Somdet Ong Yai's palace, which de Montigny deemed suitably prestigious for the king he represented.[25]

The implied precedence to be given to the French envoy in spite of Parkes' one-year agreement in favour of the British was foreshadowed at Hillier's first arrival. The Phraklang had informed him while he was still on board the *Auckland* at the bar that the king had intended "to have offered the Factory to the French Plenipotentiary in case he had arrived first", but as he didn't Hillier would be allowed to "take temporary possession".[26]

Hillier thus found himself in the unenviable position of fighting for possession of a property that not only failed to meet "the requirements of a lady", as Parkes had remarked, but also fell short of meeting the requirements for a British consulate.

While the pressures on Hillier to solve the accommodation issue were certainly strong, it does appear that he pursued this particular mission with a zeal not necessarily applied to some of his other priorities. Only six days after his arrival in the city, he was writing to Bowring:

> I have the honor to request that, if Your Excellency see fit, I may receive immediate authority to purchase a piece of Land for the erection of Consular Buildings here, and to incur the necessary outlay in fencing and drainage; so that, on the approval of the building plan, which it will be my duty to submit, no time may be lost in preparation.[27]

SITE SELECTION

Four days after requesting approval for developing the new consulate from Bowring, Hillier called on the Phraklang to expedite the process. Hillier was under the impression that the site selection would have been already completed because Parkes had received "a distinct promise" before he left Bangkok in May that a suitable piece of land would be allocated. He was therefore somewhat taken aback by the Phraklang's suggestion that Hillier should choose a suitable site and the Siamese authorities could then check its availability as certain land (that owned by nobles) would not be available for selection. Hillier saw this as a repeat of a delaying tactic used on Parkes who, two months earlier, had initially selected three or four sites which he was then told were unavailable. He reminded the Phraklang that Parkes had already gone through this process and that "on my arrival, therefore, I expected to be called upon, not to make the application but to signify my approval of the selection."[28] Moreover, Hillier pointed out, "it was impossible for me to discover at once, without great difficulty, the real ownership of the property" and he refused "to enter upon an undertaking apparently so uncertain and so profitless".

The king had also promised Parkes "that as the English were the first in the field, they should be first provided with ground suited for consular purposes". However, Hillier was aware that the Americans were close to acquiring a site for their own consulate, which would, in his view, contravene the king's promise.

The Phraklang then presented a map showing the ownership of various plots of land south of the Portuguese consulate, and Hillier selected the site immediately adjacent to the Portuguese. He then went to visit the land, approved it and was told that "the matter would be laid before the King and I should receive a speedy answer."[29]

Although the site had a narrower river frontage than he would have liked and it appeared to be smaller than the ideal size indicated to him by Bowring before he left Hong Kong, Hillier considered the site adequate because it was in line with guidelines established during the visit of Parkes. The assurances given to Parkes by the king specified that the British consulate plot should be "equal in size to that on which the Portuguese Consulate is built – about 450 feet by 252 feet by Siamese account" and the price should be "not more than one tical (2s.6d) the square fathom, this being the price at which, by a recent law of Siam, real property, that of the nobles excepted, can be returned for public purposes".

In terms of its location, Hillier selected the site next to the Portuguese consulate for several reasons. First, it was near the land designated on the map of the Phraklang for the future customs house. Second, Hillier believed the plot to be the only one in close proximity to the city that could be bought for the target price:

> Nearer the city no ground could be purchased but at a very exorbitant price – probably, if The Government objected, not at any price -, nor lower down, on the same side, is any available at a moderate rate.

Third, the only other plots identified as viable in terms of size and probable price were those located on the east bank either "immediately above and adjoining" the land being acquired by the American merchant David O. King, that was now planned to house the new American consulate as well as King's businesses, or even further down river. These plots were considered by Hillier too far from the city – "from an hour to an hour and a half, against the tide" for King's land – for the conduct of consular business and for "the collection of reliable information respecting the resources of the country and its political and social condition".[30] The location for the American consulate would, in Hillier's opinion, "probably, for a long time, be the extreme limit of the Foreign Settlement".[31]

Furthermore, both Parkes and Mongkut had endorsed the selected site,[32] and Bowring would concur, informing Clarendon that "the site he [Hillier] proposes is convenient, being in the neighborhood of the ordinary places for shipping and unloading goods, close to the river, and sufficiently adjacent to the city for all useful purposes."[33]

Had Hillier presented this site as the only choice, London could well have suspected that failure to provide comparable properties for consideration indicated a lack of transparency. In essence, there appeared to be two other choices, and Hillier's approach to disclosing those showed that he had already mastered some of the dark arts of diplomacy.

The first alternative, as we have seen, was a site adjacent to the proposed new American consulate in a part of the city called Samray (or, today, Samrae sub-district in Thonburi district),[34] which Hillier believed to be too far from the city centre. But if it was suitable for the Americans, why not the British? To pre-empt this question, Hillier had to explain the peculiar background behind the American decision. In fact, as he pointed out, the selection of the American consulate location was not in any sense a decision by the state department in Washington. Hillier explained that since the US government had no policy "permitting the acquisition of land in foreign countries at the cost of the State",[35] the consul had struck a deal with David King, a private investor, to fund the land acquisition. This would presumably be the same land that King had tried to buy under his own name by persuading the Siamese authorities that it lay outside the four-mile circuit within which foreign sales were prohibited.[36] The definitive survey undertaken by the *Saracen* must have proved the falsity of King's claim. His approach now was to hitch himself to Mattoon who would be eligible to purchase the land once he reached the milestone of ten years' residence in Siam on 22 March 1857. When the Siamese commissioners had negotiated the US treaty with Townsend Harris, they had tried to make the ten-year residency requirement prospective rather than retroactive.[37] Had they succeeded, Mattoon and other long-serving missionaries would not have been eligible for ownership rights until 1866.

Mattoon was keen to move the Presbyterian mission to more spacious premises. King intended to put the land in Mattoon's name, which would suit Mattoon well. The mission would thus get the land as a "free gift"[38] on which to build new premises which would also be used as the American consulate during Mattoon's tenure in that post. Should there be a new consul, it was likely that new premises would be required. King, who had secured the land at the remarkably cheap price of "75 dollars (£15.12s.6d.) an acre" (equivalent to around 0.25 ticals per square *wah*, or one-eighth of the standard official rate for more centrally located land), intended to use the remainder of the site for docks, warehouses and dwelling houses.

If that was not enough to undermine the case for a location near the land of Mattoon and King, Hillier provided further intelligence which suggested that the fate of the American deal was still in the balance. Although he understood that the earlier difficulties caused by "delays of the authorities and the fears of the owners lest they should be visited with penal consequences for thus disposing of their land to a foreigner" had now been overcome and the deeds were being prepared, both he and Mattoon remained skeptical:

> But, at the time of my arrival, the purchase was supposed to be equally near its consummation, and, on one occasion, Mr. Mattoon informed, me, that he feared the Siamese

> were endeavoring to avoid the sale of land altogether, as their prejudice against its alienation to foreigners was so overpowering; or, at least, that they intended, in all cases, to purchase the land on their own account at a cheap rate, and charge the fixed Government price:- and, it is possible, that, in regard to suburban lots, such intention may still exist.[39]

Perhaps the delay also resulted from the fact that Mattoon still had to be resident for one more year to qualify for ownership rights. For Hillier, however, the location was clearly inferior to the site next to the Portuguese consulate that he recommended to Bowring and Clarendon, although he diplomatically – or shrewdly – conceded that if Clarendon thought the vicinity of the American consulate more suitable, he would move ahead on that basis.

The second alternative was the British factory itself. While the existing premises were not fit for purpose, the location was suitably close to the city, and redevelopment was conceivable. Hillier elaborated on this idea in a letter to Mongkut, proposing that "the piece of ground on which is erected the British Factory, added to the waste land adjacent, might, though small, not be unsuitable for the purpose, the present buildings being removed & the cost of erecting them refunded to the Siamese Treasury."[40]

Just as Hillier had half-heartedly proposed the location of the American consulate as a less desirable option, he now unenthusiastically gave the Siamese a fall-back option. He could be quite confident that the Siamese would not take the option seriously in view of their need to get hold of the British factory for their own purposes. Nevertheless, the fact that he failed to even mention this albeit somewhat unlikely option to his own superiors suggests that he did not want to create false hopes that could lead to further delays.

PROCRASTINATION

If Hillier's letters reveal a somewhat surprising degree of tact in his management of expectations, it was unfortunate that his diplomatic skills did not always extend to his personal dealings with the Siamese bureaucracy. From his first month in Bangkok, the process of securing land for the consulate sorely tested the spirit of compromise and empathy that Bowring had urged him to display.

The Phraklang was the nominated conduit for all business between Hillier and the Siamese state. But having finalised the site selection process with the Phraklang, he was left waiting for official confirmation, which failed to come. So, "after waiting for seventeen days", he decided to write directly not only to the Phraklang but also to the king. He knew that writing to the king was both a contravention of the stipulated procedures and a provocation to the Siamese officials. He therefore needed a strong pretext to justify his course of action. His ostensible reason was to seek verification of the personal promise made by the king to Parkes in regard to the consular land, "believing that this would be more acceptable to His Majesty than to make his personal communications with Mr. Parkes the subject of official correspondence".[41] In other words, because the king's promise to Parkes was of a private nature, Hillier was claiming that he needed to discuss it in a private note to the king rather than in an official letter to the Phraklang. That this claim was specious can be gleaned from Hillier's own statement to Bowring that he had in fact already discussed the king's promise to Parkes in a meeting with the Phraklang on 20 June.[42]

Hillier clearly spent a great deal of effort in constructing his note to the king to ensure that it struck the balance he wanted between friendly diplomacy and the gloved fist. The letter reflected not only the somewhat verbose and convoluted diplomatic style of the times, but also a sophisticated ability to convey multiple messages:

Hillier opened by suggesting that a failure to supply land for the Consulate would not only create "anxiety" for the king's friend, Bowring, but could also be deemed an obstruction to the implementation of the treaty provisions. He then reminded the king of his promise to Parkes "that before any ground whatever was sold or disposed of to foreigners, the British Consul shall be provided by the Siamese Government, at Government price, with a site suited to his wants".

Hillier was not averse to pointing the finger of blame at the Phraklang directly, moving from the more conciliatory general statement that, "owing perhaps to some misapprehension on the part of Your Majesty's servants Your Majesty's kind intentions have not been carried into effect", to a more specific accusation that, although some land was about to be sold to foreigners, "the Phraklang informs me that none has yet been set aside for a British Consulate" and specifically in regard to the site next to the Portuguese consulate "I have received no official reply."

Hillier, by framing the Phraklang's lack of response as a potential (though "perhaps" unwitting) breach of the king's promise, was implicitly justifying by-passing agreed procedures. He also sought to distinguish his position in ethical terms from that of both the Siamese officials and the cohort of foreign consuls in Bangkok. On one level, Hillier was merely stating the obvious when he wrote that as a foreign diplomat he was not in a good position to find out information on land ownership in Bangkok. But his choice of terminology (disclaiming any "private interest in this matter" and reminding the king that as "a public officer" he was "prohibited from trading") implied a comparison between the ethical standards of a British government official and those prevailing in Siam.[43] From his experiences in Asia, Hillier would have been aware that officials may seek to benefit from an indirect sale by creating their own profit margin on the deal. Indeed, the practice was enshrined in much of the Siamese bureaucracy. Back in the Ayutthaya period, "nobles were not paid and were expected to remunerate themselves through the powers of their office."[44] Hillier was also aware that the Siamese state may benefit from acting as intermediary, as Mattoon suggested might have been the case with his own proposed land, in order to control pricing levels. Hillier might also have been keen to impress upon the king that he was in a very different position to the other foreign consuls in the country whose other interests could derive benefit from land transactions – particularly Moor as an active trader, but also Mattoon who was attempting to help his missionary work through the acquisition of consular land in collaboration with a merchant.

In view of the circumstances outlined in his letter, Hillier concluded that "nothing would be easier" than for the Siamese government to purchase the land and transfer it at a suitable price to the British government.

We do not know how the king reacted to this letter, but the negative views he later expressed on Hillier could have emanated from or been re-inforced by the veiled criticisms and implied condescension of this and Hillier's subsequent letters to him. Whatever the king's feelings, he did respond quickly, sending a letter to Hillier the very next day. While no copy of that letter has been found, much of the content can be gleaned from Hillier's response to it of the following day, 9 July.

The king had obviously tried to compel Hillier to communicate through the Phraklang, rather than directly. In addition to the procedural breach, the king complained of the difficulty of deciphering Hillier's handwriting. Hillier offered an apology and assured the king that he would try to write private communications more plainly while more public communications would be transcribed by one of the consular assistants. But his defence of the need to write directly to the king had now developed into a surprisingly robust extension of the points raised in his previous letter. Apart from repeating the spurious contention of protecting the confidentiality of the king's promise to Parkes, Hillier now moved away from the more measured criticism of the king's officers in the letter of 7 July to a more explicit exposition of his concerns. He now claimed that there was a need on hopefully rare occasions for him to write directly to the king because "the nobles & high officers of State are unacquainted with the English language or customs & in consequence are likely to doubt mistrust and misapprehend the intentions of the Consul." What had been expressed as a possible and unspecified "misapprehension" on the part of the king's servants in the letter of 7 July, had crystallised into probable distrust of Hillier's intentions by the nobles and high officers of state two days later.

Rather than leave the point there, Hillier took the opportunity to push for what the king could have regarded as unwarranted privileges, asking the king to inform his ministers that "although business must be transacted through the Foreign Minister yet they are without fail to forward immediately to Your Majesty any written statement in the English language, which the British Consul may think it his duty to deliver." Hillier clearly suspected that vital messages from him were not getting through to the king. The Phraklang, as the younger brother of the Kalahom, would probably have taken any serious matters to his elder brother. Hillier's distrust of the Siamese bureaucracy, however, appears to have included the Kalahom.

Hillier's letter finally took on a pedagogic tone in lauding the superiority of the democratic spirit of the British monarchy over the fear and suspicion surrounding the Siamese court, with Hillier making a far-fetched claim which the king would probably suspect as bogus but would be unable to disprove:

> In Great Britain the meanest subject claims a right to reach the royal ear with his complaint. I feel assured that it is Your Majesty's intention to accord to the British Consul a greater

> privilege than this; but he will actually enjoy a less if Your Majesty's servants in fear of unpleasant consequences to themselves refuse to present his communications for Your Majesty's perusal.

Hillier then concluded his letter with more positive comments on the continuing friendship between the countries, but the tone is relentlessly patronising, even implying a correlation between allowing Hillier direct access to the king and the nation's prosperity.[45]

On the same day, Hillier also wrote to the Phraklang appealing for a resolution to the "unexpected difficulties and delays" on the land issue. The letter repeated most of the points made to the king, including reminding the Phraklang of the selection process undertaken by Parkes and himself at the Phraklang's request. As in his letter to the king, Hillier felt the need to remind the Phraklang that as he was "not a merchant, but a public officer prohibited from engaging in trade" and as negotiations and promises had already been made before his arrival, "I have no doubt that I will not look in vain for your cordial cooperation."

Hillier was aware that the king had given an order to the Phraklang to provide assistance in resolving the land acquisition for the consulate. But at this point he appeared not to be aware of the extent of the problems the Siamese faced in trying to deliver the land in its entirety at the targeted price.

THE NOBLEMAN'S LAND

Like the American consul, Hillier suspected that the obstacles to closing land acquisition deals were largely artificial barriers being thrown in his way by Siamese officials with either political or nefarious motives. As the American missionary Chandler had experienced, foreigners' difficulties acquiring land had not disappeared during the fourth reign. The handbills that greeted Harry Parkes' arrival earlier in 1856 proved that opposition to foreign land ownership remained strong. A Singapore newspaper was expressing the common view of Siam's western community when it wrote of "the repugnance which the Siamese entertain towards the permanent holding of land by foreign residents in the immediate vicinity of the capital".[46]

However, in the case of the site selected by Hillier, there is little reason to suppose that either the king or his officials were standing in the way of the deal. Instead, as Hillier should have realised, the problem was very specific to the land plot selected and arose because he had not followed the king's advice in choosing a site.

On 13 June, three days after Hillier had arrived in Bangkok at his first audience with the king, the king had made clear to him that "the property of the nobles could not be obtained", but Hillier believed that the king was only saying this "for the satisfaction of the nobles rather than for my information".[47] Hillier assumed that despite the king's professed inability to assist in the purchase of land owned by the nobility, this obstacle could be overcome. Indeed, he repeatedly underplayed the difficulties that the Siamese faced in resolving the issue, referring to the area owned by a nobleman within the chosen site as "an inconsiderable piece of the corner occupied by a limekiln & an excavation for a native dock, both of small dimensions" in writing to the Phraklang[48] and as "only a very small portion . . . (just a corner)" of the overall site in a letter to the king.[49]

From Hillier's point of view, acquiring the nobleman's land was essential to the success of the deal. In terms of size it was not significant – by Hillier's calculation occupying only about seven per cent of the total estimated site area. But excluding it from the deal would have made the site unworkable as consular land. There were two main issues. The first was the potential disturbance to the consulate of its ongoing use as a dock yard and, in particular, for the production of lime. As Hillier pointed out to Clarendon, "without the possession of [the limekiln and dock], the rest, owing to the thick smoke of the kiln and the odour of the shells of which the lime is made, would be scarcely, if at all, habitable,"[50] a point he had already made to the king: "it would I fear be quite impossible to live there by reason of the smoke that the kiln continually emits."[51]

The second issue was the positioning of the lime kiln and dock on the river. Hillier estimated that it occupied some seventeen fathoms, or approximately 102 feet, of the site's total river frontage, which he in turn estimated at 300 feet. (A more detailed survey the following year calculated the total river frontage at 330 feet or 100 metres.) The location of these industrial activities damaged the integrity and security of the quadrilateral site, which would otherwise be bounded by a creek separating the site from the Portuguese consulate to the north. The corner occupied by the lime kiln and dock would complicate any development on the remainder of the site, compromising the functional efficiency of any buildings to be erected. Aesthetics were also a concern: as Bangkok was essentially a city without roads, the river front would constitute the principal access to the consulate, important for communication, visibility and prestige.

The king wrote again to Hillier on 17 July with a detailed explanation of the difficulty he faced in delivering the plot in its entirety:

> The quarter part of the piece of land in neighbouring place of the Portuguese Consulate is belonged to many Malayan and Burman people who are very common native inhabitants here. I will compel them all the owners of that part of land to sell their land to you in customary price of every one Tical for every one square fathom according to the modern Siamese law and Royal custom or little lessening of the part thereof, which were or are useless to the possessors before. But I am in a difficulty for a part of that land wished and pleased by you, in which the limekiln is included or enclosed, as the said part of that land belonged to His Excellency Phya Bhirabal Sombattha, who is noble minister of His Majesty the Second King, and not of mine so his land is in right to be in dependent to the Second King. I have no right to compel the owner or possessor thereof to sell to you in the foresaid price.

Since the nobleman owed allegiance to the second king, Mongkut's advice to Hillier was to write to the King Pinklao "for his consideration and assistance".[52] But the real issue was not power but money. Phraya Bhirabal Sombattha was quite happy to sell the land, but not at the government-mandated price of one tical per square *wah*. Instead, he "was asking no less than fifty catties (4,000 ticals or 500£st), or at the rate of $7\frac{35}{100}$ ticals the square fathom"; that is, over seven times the government price.[53] Hillier calculated that the total land price would come to some 10,400 ticals: 4,000 ticals for the nobleman's land of around 20,000 square feet or 544 square fathoms; 6,400 ticals for the remaining area of some 230,000 square feet or 6,400 square fathoms. At eight ticals to the pound, the total budget for the land would be not more than £1,300.

Rather than wait for further clarification on the pricing of the nobleman's land, Hillier decided to immediately make his proposal to Clarendon for the acquisition of the entire site on the same day as he received the king's inconclusive reply. He confessed to Clarendon that he had "not yet succeeded in arranging the price at which the whole of the piece of ground selected as the most suitable for a Consulate can be obtained", but he was so aware of the need "to avoid the contingency of summary ejection from my present quarters" that he was requesting permission to purchase at "the extreme limit of expenses" that would be incurred. This he had estimated at £1,300 for the land and £5,000 for construction of the buildings.[54] In making his funding request to Clarendon, he decided to assume that the full asking price for the nobleman's land would need to be paid.

When Hillier responded to the king's letter near the end of July, it was clear that he was still set on trying to get royal support to reduce the price of Phraya Bhirabal's land. Relations with the Phraklang had understandably deteriorated in view of Hillier's criticisms of him, and Hillier now blamed the Phraklang for his own slow response to the king as the Phraklang "declined to receive any communication addressed to Your Majesty and I was at a loss to discover the proper channel through which a letter might reach Your Majesty's hands". After expressing his gratitude to the king for agreeing with his suggested land plot and "for the trouble Your Majesty has taken and is taking in this matter", he went on to report that the nobleman had approached him ("as I understand, by Your Majesty's command") and confirmed that the lowest price he could accept was fifty catties or 4,000 ticals. Hillier told the king that he had already written to Clarendon on the land and that "it was for His Lordship to decide whether the H.M. Government would pay so high a price".

Rather than negotiate further directly, Hillier tried to shift the responsibility for getting a better deal onto the Siamese authorities. He said that he did not "feel myself at liberty" to take up the king's suggestion to appeal to the second king with a view to getting "the Phya Phrabum to part with his land at a lower price than he considers just" as the British government would want to pay "the full and proper market value so that both buyer and seller may be benefited".

Hillier concluded with a new proposal to the king to resolve the pricing of the nobleman's land, which was to adopt the British system in which "if the ground is required for the State then the price may be assessed by a jury of twelve indifferent men acquainted with the real value of land in that neighbourhood."[55]

It would appear that the king did not respond to this final request from

Hillier. The suggestion revealed the depth of Hillier's ignorance of how Siamese government worked: not only was the proposed tribunal alien to Siamese traditions, it was also impracticable in view of the complex relationships of the first king, the second king and the nobleman. Besides, the Siamese knew that Hillier had already requested approval to purchase the land at the asking price, so there would be little point in convening a land tribunal before a view had been obtained from Lord Clarendon. If the foreign office approved the asking price, there was nothing more to be said on the matter. For these reasons, Hillier's letter may not have warranted an immediate response.

RESOLUTION

Nevertheless, Hillier's appeal was not ignored. Instead, a response came from the Phraklang just over three weeks later. The Phraklang's letter effectively resolved the issue by placing it in a clearly defined Siamese structure, rather than adopting the British tribunal advocated by Hillier. Moreover, the Phraklang's conclusion was that Hillier would get what he really wanted: the whole area of land at the price of one tical per square *wah*.

The Phraklang explained that, rather than convening a "jury of twelve indifferent men", as Hillier had suggested, the "high officers of Government consulting together" had resolved the matter. This intervention, it was made clear, was directed by the king because, after being in the country for two months, the British consul "was not able to negotiate a bargain for a place". Furthermore, the Phraklang reported to Hillier that:

> Mr. Consul Hillier having come to reside in Bangkok and not having obtained a place of residence, and being an officer of H.B.M. Queen Victoria it is the same as though he was a Siamese officer, and the question should be decided as in the case of Siamese officers.

And, referring to the Siamese custom of granting land to appointed or promoted Siamese officers:

> It has been the custom when a Siamese officer had not a place suitable to his rank, and desired the assistance of His Majesty the King to procure such a place, for His Majesty to direct the proper officer to arrange the purchase.

The Phraklang's letter explained the rationale for the pricing conclusion. He pointed out that the price of one tical per square *wah* was applicable to land which was "not occupied by brick buildings but only such wood dwellings as temporary buildings as may be easily removed". As the nobleman's land was occupied by a limekiln and dock and "is not a place of residence" and "can easily be removed", it did not qualify for a higher price. While the remainder of the site was occupied by residences, these also would not qualify for a higher price because "there are no large or permanent dwellings, and the owners can easily remove and buy other places of residence". The letter also made clear that this conclusion was a special favour being granted to the British consul and was not be "taken as a precedent".

Based on the measurement referred to in the letter of an area of "1 *sen* 9 *wa* and 2 *sok* in length and 17 *wa* broad",[56] the total area of Phraya Bhirabal's land (assuming it was more-or-less square) would be around 500 square *wah* (21,000 square feet or 2,000 square metres) and he would therefore be receiving about 500 ticals for his land compared to his asking price of 4,000 ticals. The Phraklang informed Hillier that he was to pay directly for the land. The detailed justification for the lower price in the Phraklang's letter would have suggested to Hillier that the nobleman had been either persuaded or coerced into accepting the lower price, but it is also feasible that a separate agreement had been reached to compensate Phraya Bhirabal.

The Phraklang's letter did not mention a total price for the land, but it did remove potential ambiguity by referring to an agreed measurement undertaken by representatives of both the Siamese and British governments:

> The proper officers proceeded with Mr. Bell, measured the ground, and found it 2 *sen* and 15 *wa* wide on the river, and on the upper side extending back from the river 4 *sen*, and the lower side of 6 *sen*, and 4 *sen* 2 *wa* broad on the back side of the lot.[57]

Based on the assumptions of one *wah* being equivalent to six feet (1.8 metres) and twenty *wah* equaling one *sen*, the total area of the site would have come to approximately 230,350 square feet (21,400 square metres), or 6,400 square *wah* (or square fathoms). At one tical per square *wah* and £0.125 to the tical, the total land price would have been £800, some £500 below Hillier's maximum estimate if he had had to pay Phraya Bhirabal's asking price.[58]

Hillier's response to the Phraklang was dated 3 September, Hillier noting that he had only received the Phraklang's 21 August letter that morning. By that time, as we shall see in the next chapter, Hillier's health was beginning to suffer, which may account for his terseness in tone. Although he must have been pleased with the good news from the Phraklang, he merely repeated his position that he was not empowered to make a final decision on buying land, only to select a suitable plot, enquire about the price and submit the particulars for a decision to London. He did, however, request the Phraklang to "tender my thanks to The King for the trouble His Majesty personally has taken in arranging this affair".[59] There was not a word of thanks to the Phraklang or the other senior officers for their efforts in finding an amicable solution to Hillier's problem.

The official approval from the British government for the land acquisition and development was sent by the treasury to Clarendon on 1 October. Clarendon forwarded the news to Hillier a week later, informing him that he was allowed to spend a sum not exceeding £6,000 on the land, buildings and fittings.[60] The budget was achievable based on the discounted price for Phraya Bhirabal's land, which would not have been known in London at the time of setting the budget, but fell short of Hillier's proposal of £6,300. It could have been much worse. Parkes had estimated the cost of the land at £1,000 and the buildings and fit-out at only £3,000, while Bowring had first estimated that a budget of £5,000 should be sufficient.[61]

Of course, the approval letter would not be received in Bangkok until much later. The day after the treasury letter approving the deal was sent to Clarendon in London, the ailing Hillier was enduring a long boat ride in Bangkok to meet his fellow consuls and deal with events that had unfolded in a dramatic new direction that would change the proposed project in unexpected ways.

As a portend to those events, in mid-September a consulate employee (referred to by Hillier as "the office coolie") was arrested by the Phraklang while obtaining an official seal for a ship's pass at a public office. The reason for the arrest was never explained, except that he had "made, in his ignorance, some mistake". The punishment to be meted out involved a flogging, but this was forestalled by Hillier's demand that "the man should be allowed, without the slightest delay, to go back with me to the Consulate, where, if he had been guilty of any offence against Siamese law, I would in terms of the Treaty, and in the presence of the P'raklang, if the latter so desired, investigate the case, and then if the offence were manifest, hand the delinquent over to be punished". The man was released, the Phraklang grumbling that it would be better if consular servants wore "some distinguishing dress or they could not be known" and that he should be given a list of their names. The Phraklang's response suggests he was aware that his action could be deemed a violation of the treaty, which he would not have made had he known the man's employment status. Hillier, however, made his position clear:

> Such a clear infraction of the Treaty as the summary seizure of one of the Consul's public servants, I said, I could not for a moment permit.[62]

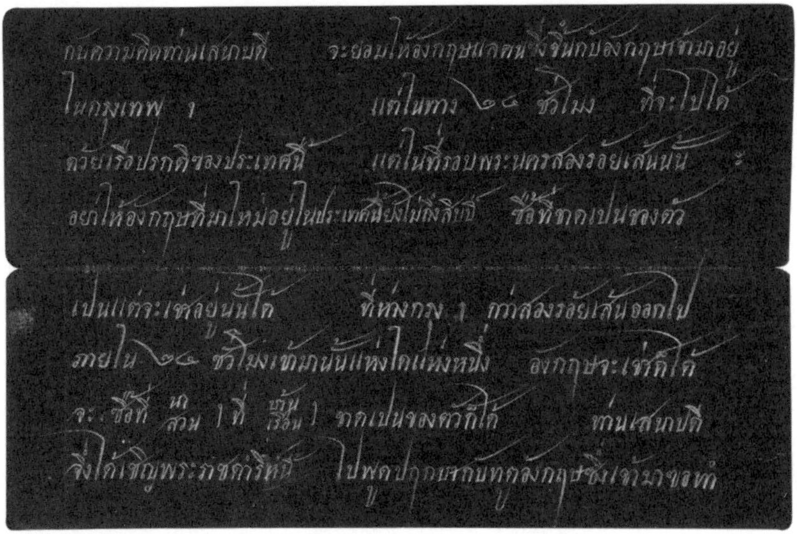

กับความคิดท่านเสนาบดี จะยอมให้องกฤษแลคนซึ่งขึ้นกับองกฤษเข้ามาอยู่
ในกรุงเทพฯ แต่ในทาง ๒๔ ชั่วโมง ที่จะไปได้
ด้วยเรือปรกติของประเทศนี้ แต่ในที่รอบพระนครสองร้อยเส้นนั้น จะ
อย่าให้องกฤษที่มาใหม่อยู่ในประเทศนี้ยังไม่ถึงสิบปี ซื้อที่ตกเปนของตัว
เปนแต่จะเช่าอยู่นั้นได้ ที่ห่างกรุงฯ กว่าสองร้อยเส้นออกไป
ภายใน ๒๔ ชั่วโมงเข้ามานั้นแห่งใดแห่งหนึ่ง องกฤษจะเช่าก็ได้
จะซื้อที่ นา สวน ที่ บ้าน เรือน ตกเปนของตัวก็ได้ ท่านเสนาบดี
จึ่งได้เชิญพระราชดำริห์นี้ ไปพูดปฤกษากับทูตองกฤษซึ่งเข้ามาขอทำ

Extract from Mongkut's 1856 proclamation on English people buying and leasing land.

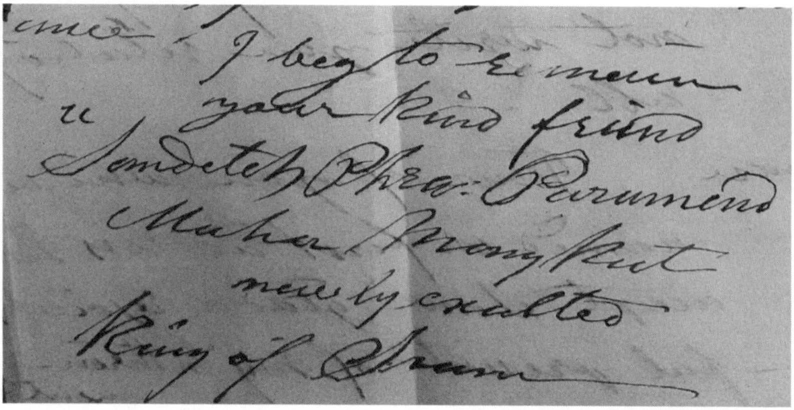

came — I beg to remain
your kind friend
Somdetch Phra: Paramendr
Maha Mongkut
newly exalted
King of Siam

Mongkut's signature in English extracted from his letter to Hamilton Grey, 24 May 1851.

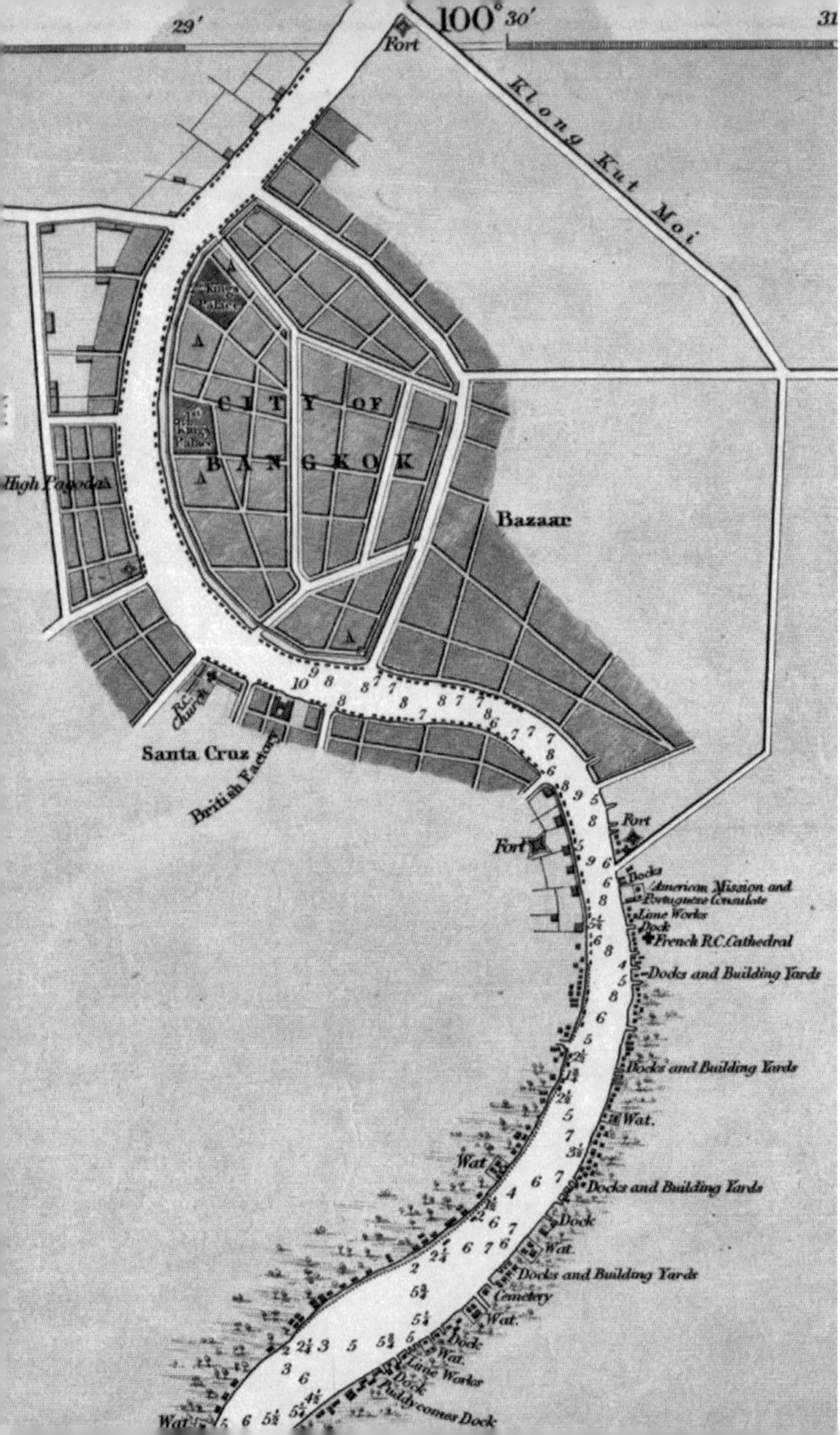
29'
100° 30'
31
Fort
Klong Kut Moi
CITY OF BANGKOK
High Pagoda
Bazaar
R.C. Church
Santa Cruz
British Factory
Fort
Fort
Docks
American Mission and Portuguese Consulate
Lime Works
Dock
French R.C. Cathedral
Docks and Building Yards
Docks and Building Yards
Wat.
Wat
Docks and Building Yards
Dock
Wat.
Docks and Building Yards
Cemetery
Wat.
Dock
Wat.
Lime Works
Dock
Puddy comes Dock
Wat

Chapter 5

A "paroxysm of passion"

HILLIER GETS A CHANGE OF AIR

British consulate, 4-23 September 1856

The curt tone of Hillier's letter to the Phraklang in early September, though reflecting his indignation, could be attributed in part to the effects of his deteriorating physical condition. The first days of September saw Hillier afflicted with a severe attack of constipation followed a few days later by symptoms of dysentery. By mid-month he was confined to his bed for several days with an "internal inflammation" and was forced to write his letters "in a recumbent posture".[1] His symptoms then began to ease and he was able to resume work, but only for a few days.

Hillier initially sought medical treatment from the American missionary, Dr Bradley, believing him to be "the only professionally medical man in the place".[2] In fact, Bradley's missionary colleague, Dr Samuel House, was also a qualified medical practitioner, but he had resolved not to provide medical services, partly to devote himself fully to his missionary work and partly, it was suggested, due to a constitutional aversion to gore. Hillier found Bradley's insistence on the virtues of homeopathic remedies "peculiar", yet nevertheless he did submit himself to Bradley's methods for a while. However, he soon tired of Bradley's conviction that "hydropathy and homeopathy can effect nearly all the good to be accomplished by human means in the present state of medical science" and his refusal "on conscientious grounds to attempt the cure of

Opposite page: Map of Chaophraya river, surveyed by John Richards in1856. (© The British Library Board, Maps SEC. 13 [999])

his patients by those ordinary remedies, which the majority of persons in the East deem the most effectual".

Feeling "threatened with rheumatism on the one hand, and attacked, on the other, by a painful inflammatory disease with the rapid ravages, the serious consequences and often fatal results of which I am but too well acquainted", Hillier appealed to Clarendon for a solution to the lack of decent medical support at the consulate, eventually leading to the appointment of Dr James Campbell, who arrived in May 1857. For more immediate relief, Hillier turned to the more conventional treatment of Dr George Hill, the assistant surgeon on board the surveying ship HMS *Saracen*, which "happened fortunately to be on the spot".[3] In fact, since helping Harry Parkes delineate the four-mile circuit around the city in April, the *Saracen* had been engaged in surveying the Gulf of Siam and had arrived back in Bangkok where it had been anchored in the Chaophraya river, close to the British consulate, since 8 September.[4]

However, the ministrations of neither Dr Bradley nor Dr Hill provided sustained relief. Hill considered his condition dangerous enough for him to suggest Hillier's "immediate removal from Bangkok to Singapore at least if not to England" if there were no improvement.[5] Unwilling to abandon his post, and no longer in a fit state for a lengthy voyage, the best course of action appeared to be a temporary escape from Bangkok in search of sea air. As the *Saracen* was now located in the city and would not provide the required change of air, it was agreed that Hillier's convalescence should take place on board the American ship, *Don Quixote*, that was then anchored outside the bar. With his condition once again deteriorating, Hillier himself begged to be taken to the Gulf. Hillier reported to Clarendon that he had left his post "under the advice of Dr Hill",[6] although later Eliza wrote that Dr Hill was reluctant for Hillier to make the long journey and only agreed on Hillier's insistence.

Charles Bell and Captain Richards of the *Saracen* helped arrange matters with a boat borrowed from the Kalahom on the evening of 23 September. According to Eliza's account, Charles was moved on Monday 20 September, but that date was actually a Saturday. (The remainder of Eliza's account of events in September wrongly attributed dates to days, although from Wednesday 15 October dates and days correspond.) Charles' dates appear more reliable and are in line with other accounts. Transporting Hillier to the Gulf was not a simple nor painless matter.

A cot was installed in the boat and Dr Hill gave Hillier "a large dose of morphia to quiet him and enable him to bear his pain and the fatigue of removal". The party took nine hours to reach the *Don Quixote*.[7] Once on board, Hillier's health began to improve and Dr Hill, promising to visit every third day, left encouraged.

But three days later on Friday 26 September (not Monday 27 September as erroneously reported by Eliza) Dr Hill arrived with a letter to Hillier from Bell. There had been a serious violation of the Bowring treaty and the inexperienced assistant left in charge of the consulate felt unable to handle it on his own. In fact, the issue was so serious and his own diplomatic skills so inadequate that Bell requested Hillier to curtail his much-needed convalescence and return immediately to Bangkok. Hillier felt compelled to acquiesce.

THE ARREST OF AI-FUNG

Bangkok, 24-29 September 1856

When Hillier removed himself to the *Don Quixote* he left his young first assistant, Charles Bell, in charge of the consulate. The day after Hillier left, Christopher Puddicombe, a British ship-builder based in Bangkok, had turned up at the consulate to lodge a complaint. He asserted that his foreman, Ai-fung, "had been seized by the Siamese Authorities and arrested and that the rest of his workmen and servants had fled and left his premises totally unprotected".[8] The reason for Ai-fung's arrest was not made explicit, but it was understood to be "in consequence of some transactions in which he had been engaged with reference to that ground" on which Puddicombe had built his home and business.[9]

Whatever his offence, Bell immediately realised that Ai-fung's arrest constituted a violation of Article III of the Bowring treaty, which stated that:

> If Siamese, in the employ of British subjects, offend against the laws of their country, or if any Siamese having so offended or desiring to desert, take refuge with a British subject in Siam, they shall be searched for and, upon proof of their guilt or desertion, shall be delivered up by the Consul to the Siamese authorities.[10]

The Siamese authorities had made no application to the British consul in regard to a case against Ai-fung. However, of greater concern to Hillier than the arrest of a Siamese employee was the wider threat he perceived to British interests. He saw the arrest of Ai-fung as "a repetition of those cruel practices towards foreigners, which it was hoped the Treaty had forever terminated".[11] He was later to elaborate on this point:

> A mere message to the servants of a foreign resident that their remaining longer in his employ will be followed by unpleasant consequences is sufficient to disperse every domestic in the establishment in half an hour, and a similar notice to the market stalls will prevent the sale to foreigners of every necessary of life. This power before the treaty came into operation was exercised on several occasions causing much hardship and privation to the foreign residents then consisting almost entirely of American missionaries.[12]

Ensuring the protection of both the consulate and Puddicombe's property was therefore his main priority. As he was "quite unable to write or move",[13] he dictated a letter to Eliza, which Bell received in the afternoon of Saturday the 27th. Despite his debilitating illness, Hillier's rational processes were functioning well, and he was able to give Bell detailed instructions on how to proceed: first see Captain Richards and tell him to prepare an armed guard to protect Puddicombe's family and property from "violence and plunder"; next see Puddicombe and get him to sign a letter explaining what happened and claiming protection from the British government; then take the document to Richards who should at once assemble the guard at Puddicombe's property "but to give the strictest caution respecting the use of their fire arms"; and finally try to obtain an audience with the Phraklang, or failing that the highest ranking officer available, to convey Hillier's strong complaint.

The complaint was to be accompanied by a thinly veiled threat that "a continuance of such conduct must render the constant presence of a British ship of war in the neighbourhood of Bangkok absolutely necessary for the safety of the lives and property not only of British traders, but also of Consular officers themselves." In this light, Bell was told to report to the Siamese authorities that Hillier was asking the *Saracen* not to leave the river and an armed guard was being placed at Puddicombe's premises, with Hillier holding the Siamese "accountable for any loss" suffered by Puddicombe or expense to the British government.

Bell was also instructed to make two specific demands to the Siamese authorities: that all Puddicombe's workers should "be sent back and allowed to remain" at Puddicombe's property; and that Ai-fung be handed over to the British consul's custody. If these demands were met, Bell was to withdraw the armed guard from Puddicombe's property and indicate that Hillier would be open to discussing any "ambiguity in the Treaty respecting the acquisition of land on lease" once matters were settled.[14]

Bell tried his best to follow Hillier's instructions. On 28 September, he called on Captain Richards who told him he would be prepared to provide an armed guard for Puddicombe's property, but only if he could have first a statement from Puddicombe that there was an immediate danger to his family and property. But Puddicombe was unwilling to make such a statement as his servants and some of his workmen had already returned; instead, Puddicombe wanted to ease tensions and only "wished much for a public notification to the effect that his servants should not be molested by the Authorities".[15] Richards did, however, provide an armed guard of three marines and one bluejacket for the consulate,[16] and, believing "it right to be prepared for the worst", he also mounted the guns on the *Saracen* and confined his officers and crew to the ship.[17]

Bell also tried his best to meet the Phraklang but found him "evidently desirous of avoiding me".[18] As Hillier reported to Clarendon:

> During what remained of Saturday, and the whole of Sunday, he [Bell] endeavored in vain to procure a moments conversation with any one of the Siamese officials; all were either asleep or sick or absent from home.

Bell was finally able to track down the Phraklang as he was on his way to the king's palace on Monday morning at seven o'clock. Accompanied by young Robert Hunter as interpreter, Bell had a two-hour long meeting with the Phraklang in which he delivered Hillier's two demands for "the delivery over of Mr. Puddicombe's foreman and a public notification to the workmen". The Phraklang agreed immediately to the latter but declined to give a clear answer on Ai-fung's release as "the matter had been referred to the Senaputi" who had yet to make a decision.[19]

Bell and Hillier understood that Ai-fung had been arrested for the actions he had taken in support of Puddicombe's land lease, and the Siamese were not prepared at this stage to overlook what they considered a serious crime.

CAPTAIN PUDDICOMBE

The son of a master mariner originally from Poole, Dorset, who became a Devon squire, Christopher Puddicombe was born in 1807 and ran away to sea in his boyhood.[20] As Captain Puddicombe he had settled in Bombay with his wife (Margaret Elizabeth, née Baker) and their four young children around 1842. The family remained based in Bombay for the next thirteen years where another five children were born, despite the fact that Puddicombe spent much of his time away as captain of the British brig, *Mayaram Dayaram*. The ship was mainly plying the Bombay-Singapore route with occasional visits to Siam and Chinese ports, among others. His association with the *Mayaram Dayaram* ended in 1850 when the ship was sold at auction in Singapore.

By 1851, he had established a business in Bombay, Puddicombe & Co, which was engaged as merchants and auctioneers, buying ships and organising sales in Bombay's wharves and godowns, as well as handling estate and relocation sales. But Puddicombe soon resumed his nomadic life as captain of another British ship, the *Prince of Wales*, essentially trading on the same routes as the *Mayaram Dayaram*, but with more frequent visits to Siam.

Towards the end of 1851, Puddicombe took his wife and at least seven children on the *Prince of* Wales to visit Siam, with the family becoming house guests of the Bradleys who became friends. Two years later, the family were again lodging at the Bradleys, this time for several weeks from 3 November 1853.[21] Bangkok's Protestant cemetery contains a gravestone for two young Puddicombe children: Richard, who died aged five on 6 April 1842 and was buried in Batavia, and Emily, who died aged four and a half, on 1 December 1853, two days before Puddicombe left Bangkok for Singapore as captain of the *Prince of Wales*. There is no reference to Emily's death in *Bradleys' Journal*, nor is it known whether Puddicombe took his family to Singapore on 3 December or left them a little longer in Bangkok. However, it is clear that the Puddicombe family were no strangers to Bangkok even before the 1850s. Bradley mentions

Puddicombe with his wife and children attending one of the mission's services in Bangkok in January 1844.[22]

These and other visits would have made him aware of the emerging business opportunity created in the wake of the Bowring treaty, and he was the right man in the right place at the right time to take advantage of it. He could bring the expertise he had acquired running merchant ships on the main trading routes in the region and as a trader in ships and other goods to a fresh market where there was as yet little competition.

For merchant mariners such as Puddicombe viewing the landscape in 1855, the greater access to the Siam trade for European merchants brought in by the Bowring treaty made the country an interesting proposition. To tap into the new market opportunities, more ships would be needed, and Puddicombe set about establishing a dock yard in Bangkok for shipbuilding, possibly in collaboration with Captain Phillips, the commander of King Mongkut's ship, *Bangkok Mark*, which brought Puddicombe to Bangkok in March 1856. In fact, Bradley ascribed the lease that had got Ai-fung into trouble to Captain Phillips, rather than Puddicombe although all other evidence supports it being Puddicombe's.[23] Bradley's error is curious as the Bradleys had entertained the Puddicombes at their house on several occasions and were close. Bradley also knew Phillips: Phillips and the Puddicombe children had attended services at Bradley's mission with Harry Parkes and Townsend Harris.[24] If not an error of transcription or in information received at the time, Bradley's journal entry could suggest a business relationship between Phillips and Puddicombe.

The provisions of the treaty explicitly supported Puddicombe's new career, with Article VIII stating: "British subjects will be allowed to build ships in Siam on obtaining permission to do so from the Siamese authorities."[25] It is clear from a letter to Puddicombe from Mongkut that Puddicombe had not only obtained this permission before the Bowring treaty, but had formed a strong relationship with the king dating back over a decade, to the time when the king was abbot at Wat Bowonniwet:

> Are you not my old friend long has been my very intimate more than ten years? did you not request me formerly my pectuliar [*sic*] permission for building your vessel here before coming of the mission of Sir John Bowring.[26]

Such strong connections no doubt further encouraged Puddicombe to take the plunge and relocate his family (including now seven children, two having died young) to Bangkok. Two months after Bowring had completed his mission to Bangkok, Charles Bell reported to him that "an Englishman has been sent up from Singapore to superintend the building of several vessels for merchants here."[27] No name is given, but Bell was probably referring to Puddicombe. Nevertheless, Puddicombe continued to captain the *Prince of Wales* until March 1856, when his last voyage from Bangkok to Singapore proved quite eventful, with the ship rescuing the crew and passengers of a stranded Chinese junk bound for Chin Chew (now, Quanzhou) on the way to Singapore. Puddicombe then left the *Prince of Wales* in Singapore, ending a five-year association with that ship, departing Singapore on 17 March for Bangkok on the *Bangkok Mark*, a new 700-ton ship built in Bangkok in 1855 and owned by Mongkut.[28]

Within a few months of the new British consulate being established in June 1856, Puddicombe had made significant progress in developing his new business. He was the third "European Britisher" to register his residency at the new British consulate on 30 June 1956[29] and had probably been resident in the city from the first quarter of that year.[30] He had identified land on the east bank of the river, some three miles south of the city in Ḅangkholaem, for his home and dock yard and appeared to have carefully complied with the new rules laid out in the treaty at every step. The price of timber in Bangkok being hugely inflated, he decided to travel outside the city to buy supplies. For this, under the treaty, he needed a permit from the British consul, which he obtained. But his timber-buying expedition required a certain amount of guile as well as regulatory compliance.

Consul Hillier acknowledged this in what he discerned as "sagacity" in the way the entrepreneurial Puddicombe obtained the timber for his shipbuilding:

> To obtain the necessary timber at a cheaper rate than was possible at Bangkok (the price of wood having risen to a height of 250 percent above its former level) he obtained through the Consul, with some difficulty, a pass to proceed towards the course of the Menam, beyond the 24 hours boundary, and his journey seems to have been tolerably successful. But success

> was owing, it seems, to his own sagacity in not delivering to the Governor of that district, until he had concluded his purchases, a letter from the Kings brother which professing to facilitate his journey in reality gave precise directions to defeat its object.[31]

Hillier's tacit support of Puddicombe's tactics reflected the strong suspicion common in the foreign community that some of the nobles of the land, while demonstrating overt support of their treaty obligations, would do all they could short of outright defiance to preserve their prior business interests and monopolies.

Buying wood was one thing, but when Puddicombe applied his entrepreneurial "sagacity" to making a clever deal on the land he had identified for his business, this proved to be a step too far for the Siamese.

PUDDICOMBE'S LAND LEASE

As we have seen, Article IV of the Bowing treaty was designed to ensure that valuable land near the city centre remained in the ownership of the Siamese or long-term foreign residents, while giving other foreign residents a path to occupation (through leasehold rights) and the right to purchase outright land more than four miles, or 200 *sen*, from the city walls.

Puddicombe's land being three miles from the city was well within the four-mile boundary within which foreign ownership was prohibited. This would have been evident from the posts erected in the river to delineate the boundary during Parkes' visit and corroborated by being "opposite the lot of Mr. King" which had already proven to be inside the restricted zone. On this land, Puddicombe had "located his family and constructed a dock for a ship which he is about to build".

Knowing that he could not legally own the land, yet wanting to secure a long-term possessory right, he had arranged for his foreman, Ai-fung, to act as his nominee in the transaction by buying the land (funded by Puddicombe) and then leasing it back to Puddicombe for ninety-nine years. From Puddicombe's point of view, none of these details contravened the provisions of Article IV. Hillier may have concurred, although his comments to Clarendon on the lease arrangement show that he was well aware of its deviousness and that the Siamese authorities would likely see it in a very different light to Puddicombe:

> I anticipated some difficulty, on the part of the Siamese, concerning the land on which Mr. Puddicombe has settled; the lease being effected with a view to evade the prohibition in the Treaty, against the purchase of land within four miles of the city except under certain conditions and for the purpose of effecting the transfer of possession without the intervention of the Authorities, which in case of an absolute purchase is necessary, and which is likely to enhance the price and to cause inconvenient delay.

Despite viewing the deal as at best controversial, it appears that Hillier did not raise any real objection to the questionable tactics employed by Puddicombe. He acknowledged that "as no limit is set as to the number of years which the agreement to rent is to cover, the clause is clearly most easy of evasion, and in this case the ground was purchased by Mr. Puddicombe's own servant (a Siamese) from the actual occupant, and then leased with a deposit of the title deeds."[32]

With the support of the consul, Puddicombe's "lease was drawn out and duly registered at the British Consulate, the money paid over, and the purchaser took possession of the property, no one supposing that anything wrong had been done".[33] This somewhat disingenuous assumption was supported by the fact that Puddicombe had been "for some time in possession without interference or objection from the Siamese Authorities".[34]

But as it turned out, Hillier's earlier concerns were well founded. Two months after the signing of the lease, the king became aware of the transaction and was "much annoyed" by it, which led to the arrest and imprisonment of Ai-fung and his family. The Siamese considered the acquisition to be a breach of Article IV because the transaction was "a virtual purchase under the name of a lease" and "it was done without the knowledge and consent of the Authorities".[35] Article IV was silent on maximum lease terms, but the limited Siamese experience of leasehold interests had not prepared them for anything like the Puddicombe lease. According to Bell, the longest lease in Siam was for three years,[36] while an article in the *Singapore Free Press* stated that it was ten.[37] Whichever was the case, the Siamese authorities had some justification in considering the ninety-nine years of Puddicombe's lease an egregious violation of the spirit of the treaty, if not of the treaty itself.

THE ARREST OF SENG

Phraklang's residence and British consulate, 29 September 1856

The arrest of Ai-fung was bad enough, but worse was to follow. After concluding his unsatisfactory meeting with the Phraklang on the morning of 29 September, Bell was returning home when he met the wife of the Siamese writer attached to the consulate, Kru (Teacher) Seng, and learnt that Seng had been summoned by the king at around six o'clock the previous evening and "no sooner was he in the Kings presence than, by His Majesty's direction, he was thrown, on his face, to the floor and (His Majesty being present the whole time) received 99 blows of the rattan; for what crime neither she nor her husband were aware."[38] The *Straits Times* description was particularly graphic:

> The poor victim of this absolute sovereign, it is said, was placed over a bar of wood; his legs were lashed to his neck, so as to make the back nearly round, and in this position, the flogging was inflicted by right and left handed men alternately, with green Bamboos of the thickness of a man's finger.[39]

Bell tried his best to investigate. He rushed to the Phraklang's residence, but the Phraklang "assured me of his total ignorance of the whole matter. He then left for the palace and Mr. Hunter and myself were completely nonplussed." Bell resolved to go to the palace to interview the prisoner, but was delayed for want of boatmen, as they were too afraid to service the consulate. While waiting, the teacher's wife arrived and told him that she had been allowed into the prison briefly to talk to her husband. From that, she was able to confirm the story of his punishment and told Bell "that the alleged reason was his having copied the lease of Mr. Puddicombe".[40] The authorities considered Seng's crime to be that he had drawn up Puddicombe's lease and witnessed it at the consulate.[41]

Bell finally was able to get a boat to the palace, once again accompanied by Hunter, but on the way they passed Prince Wongsa's palace:

> I saw the P'ra Klang's boat waiting there & I determined to see him first. On entering we found HRH [Prince Wongsa] in deep consultation with the P'ra Klang & the Yommarat. I asked the P'ra Klang whether he had found K'ru Sen's case as I had reported it in the morning. He replied that he was sorry to say he had. Both the Prince & the Yommarat declared that until a few minutes previously they had heard nothing of the affair.

During the hour-long meeting, Bell asked to be admitted to the prison to talk to Seng directly. This request was turned down, with the officials professing ignorance of "the cause and the author of the punishment". Bell demanded the instant release of the prisoner, "the P'ra Klang replied that he dare not for his life do such a thing".[42]

When he arrived back at the consulate, Seng's wife confirmed that the king had been present during his punishment and that the flogging was scheduled to be repeated the next day, 30 September.

HILLIER RETURNS TO BANGKOK

Don Quixote and the British consulate, 29 September-1 October 1856

Hillier received the news of Seng's flogging on the *Don Quixote* in a second dispatch from Bell brought to him by Dr Hill and resolved to return immediately to Bangkok. There had now been "two open infractions" of the Bowring treaty committed by the Siamese authorities during Hillier's absence.[43] This arrest of Seng was an even more flagrant breach of Article III of the treaty as it concerned a direct employee of the British consulate. Hillier saw events spiralling out of control and suspected that the authorities or some evil-minded advisors were "taking advantage apparently of my sickness and absence" to cause trouble.

At the same time, Hillier had little confidence in Bell's ability to deal effectively with the crisis. After the arrest of Ai-fung, Hillier had reprimanded Bell for issuing two official letters to the Siamese authorities on the issue and told him he should if possible "get these letters cancelled", in future only communicating verbally with the authorities while taking accurate notes which he must sign and file in the consulate's archives. In terms intriguingly reminiscent of Bowring's instructions to himself – in substance if not in tone – Hillier gave the following guidance to Bell:

> I cannot too strongly impress upon you the necessity for proceeding to the accomplishment of such part of the delicate task of settling this difficulty as may be entrusted to you, in a calm and dispassionable temper. Nothing like turbulence or violence must be exhibited, but your proceedings should be marked by courtesy, yet by quiet and unwavering determination.[44]

To handle the escalation brought about by Seng's arrest and punishment would require more experience and skill than could be imparted to Bell through long-distance guidance. The situation now constituted the most serious threat to Anglo-Siamese relations since Sir James Brooke had been rebuffed by the king's half-brother and predecessor some six years earlier. The *Singapore Free Press* was not exaggerating when it later claimed that the situation "threatened the peaceful relations existing between the Kingdom of Siam and Her Majesty's Government".[45]

Hillier knew that he risked his health worsening once again should be return to Bangkok, but he could see no alternative. Dr Hill initially voiced strong objections, "but seeing that the irritation caused by anxiety was doing him harm, he at last yielded, believing that moderate action on the spot would be less prejudicial than the anxiety and care consequent upon absence from his post at a critical juncture".[46]

The Hilliers started out from the *Don Quixote* at three o'clock in the morning of 1 October in order "to take advantage of a good tide". For the first half of the journey, they were in a cramped, open man-of-war boat, with Hillier in constant pain or fear of pain despite being "under the influence of morphia". At Paknam, the party transferred to a covered boat provided by the governor and Hillier was then able to lie down and get some relief, finally arriving at the consulate in the afternoon.[47]

Hillier got to work immediately to determine what had happened and what action should be taken. His initial concern for the security of the consulate appeared well founded as he found that "all the Consular servants, public and private, had absconded". He naturally appreciated Captain Richards' decision to post an armed guard at the premises.

The actions against Ai-fung and Seng had not only scared away the consular staff, they had also caused more widespread alarm:

> The whole of the community foreign and native were in a state of great excitement, several of the servants of the former were leaving them through fear, and the latter to whom, in accordance with Siamese custom, the flogging of the writer appeared one of the grossest insults capable of being offered to the Consul himself, and the Monarch whose Commission he holds, were doubtful into what further act of violence the King, by evil advice, or the impetuosity of his own passions, might be betrayed.[48]

Bell's own enquiries having made little progress, Hillier resolved to gather support from the other foreign consuls – Mattoon and Moor – as well as Captain Richards and submit a formal protest to the Siamese authorities. He invited the three men to the consulate the next day to agree the text of the letter and then go together to meet the Phraklang. The meeting at the consulate was set up for early the next morning, but by then events had developed further: overnight, Seng had died.

THE DEATH OF SENG

Prince Wongsa's palace, 30 September-1 October 1856

After his severe flogging, Seng was in dire need of medical care, which he was to receive with unexpected consequences. A lashing of one hundred strokes could be viewed as a death sentence, so he was lucky to still be alive. If he had to endure the same punishment again the next day, it would almost certainly have been fatal for him.

Wongsa was not only one of Mongkut's most trusted advisors who had been heavily involved as one of the five commissioners negotiating the Bowring and other foreign treaties, a major trader and owner of several ships, he had also served the king as a military commander in a failed attack on Kengtung in 1854. Apart from these activities, the prince was, according to Bradley, "the most learned and skillful physician in the land".[49] He was the king's chief physician and the head of the department of royal physicians, wrote the first textbook on Thai herbal medicines and had not only a life-long interest in western medicine, but also held a certificate from the New York Academy of Medicine.[50]

When Wongsa heard of the treatment of Seng, he was dismayed on both medical and political grounds. According to Bradley, "he had become very alarmed at the indignation expressed by the British Consul for the atrocious act of the King" of seizing and flogging the writer "for what the Consul had told him to do". As the action would be interpreted as an insult both to the consul and Queen Victoria, the government – including the prince – "had become terrified of the appearances". Bradley speculated:

> It seems that the officer and princes had not been consulted in the matter, that the King had done it in a paroxysm of passion.[51]

The prince therefore begged the king to allow him to give Seng medical treatment. The request was granted and so on 30 September, rather than being inflicted with another ninety-nine blows of the rattan, Seng found himself released from prison and taken to the prince's palace across the river from the king's palace. Wongsa treated him immediately by having an opium plaster applied to the open wounds on his back to ease the pain. Bradley was called in to assist, but by the time he got there "these wounds had imbibed the narcotic of the opium which had put the patient into a deep sleep from which he could not be awakened" and was showing other critical symptoms, including a very weak pulse.[52]

Bell visited the prince's palace to look in on Seng and confirmed Bradley's account that "a large quantity of opium had been introduced into the raw sores of the back, causing the patient to be quite insensible" with the result that Bell was not able to question him on the incident and his treatment by the king.[53]

The next day, Bradley reported no improvement in Seng's condition. In the evening of that day, Dr Hill was called in to look at the patient, but the damage had already been done and on the following day Bradley reported that "Teacher Seng died last night about midnight."

The immediate cause of Seng's death was attributed to an overdose of opium. However, the severe flogging had contributed by putting him in a seriously weakened and susceptible state. Bradley reported Hill's conclusion on the cause of death:

> Dr. Hill examined the body and found strong congestion in the brain with the inflammation predisposed by the whipping and made fatal by the opium plaster to the wounds.[54]

MEETING OF THE CONSULS

British consulate and Phraklang's residence, 2 October 1856

A sick and exhausted Charles Hillier rose early to the news of Seng's death. What was the day before a grievous breach of the treaty provisions had now escalated into a potentially catastrophic diplomatic crisis involving the death of a British consular official at the hands of the Siamese state. The onerous task facing the three consuls and Captain Richards was how best to respond to the actions against Ai-fung and Seng, which they viewed as a "flagrant violation of a Treaty right"[55] that threatened "the welfare and safety of the whole foreign community".[56]

At the meeting, "the Consuls agreed to present at once to the King a strong and earnest protest" in the form of a letter.[57] That letter contained two key complaints. First, the arrest of a Siamese employee of the British consulate constituted an "illegal seizure" under the treaty. The consuls considered Article III "the foundation of our liberties" which had been "utterly ignored and set at nought" by the actions of the authorities. Second, the "cruel punishment" meted out by the authorities resulting in his death would be seen by the Siamese people as "one of the greatest insults that could be offered to the Consul personally, to the office which he fills, and to the monarch whose Commission he holds".

Although official information had been impossible to obtain, there had been attempts to justify the actions of the Siamese authorities by a "profession of ignorance" that the writer was employed at the British consulate and that "the British Treaty was intended to bear such a construction as that to which foreigners up to this moment have unhesitatingly assigned to it". On the first point, the letter argued that Seng's employment was "notorious among Your Majesty's officers of State, and every Siamese connected with them"; and, on the second, "the doubt" on the treaty's intentions "must be astonishing to every foreigner, and the Treaty is worth but little indeed if the plainest rules of verbal construction and facts which are patent to the senses of all, are to be disregarded at the will of either of the contracting parties".

The writers appealed to the good sense of the king while, at the same time, making an indirect threat:

> Our present object is to entreat Your Majesty to stop short in a course which sooner or later must put an end to all the earnest hopes of benefit to this country, of glory to Your Majesty, of happiness to the Siamese people, in which the faithful and noble adherents to Your Majesty's engagements with foreign powers will, we doubt not result; and to replace these by a miserable view of discord and war, and all their attendant horrors.

The letter concluded with a request which reflected Hillier's suspicion – or possibly conviction – that the conservative forces that had tried to undermine the Bowring treaty from its inception were still lobbying the king and may have been responsible for the actions against the incarcerated Ai-fung and the deceased Seng. Hillier was equally convinced that when the king allowed common sense to prevail over impassioned rhetoric, he would be inclined to reject these negative elements:

> We would entreat Your Majesty to banish from your presence all councillors who would make light of the sacred obligations of the Royal word, and to choose those only who shall seek to build up Your Majesty's Kingdom upon the sure foundations of truth, justice and mercy.[58]

After agreeing on the text of the letter, the group went to meet the Phraklang who was waiting with the Yommarat (the minister of the capital). As with Bell earlier on, the consuls were unable to extract much information from the Phraklang. When asked what crime Ai-fung had committed and why he had been seized by the Siamese authorities instead of going through the consul, the foreign minister could only respond that "he 'knew nothing whatever about it'" and told Hillier to ask the Yommarat. As this minister was also present, Hillier repeated the question for his benefit and received the response that "Ai-fung was questioned concerning a certain purchase of land, and his answers being unsatisfactory he was detained." Turning to the case of Seng, the Phraklang merely informed Hillier that "he could say nothing" on this subject.

With no progress to show from his efforts to obtain information, Hillier moved on to his main demand, which was that Ai-fung be delivered into his custody within the next twelve hours, failing which Hillier would demand an official audience with the king. Here, he achieved his objective as "Ai-fung was within two hours, sent down to the British Consulate."[59] Bradley reported that Hillier had also demanded that Seng's body be handed over to him, and that this demand was also quickly granted. The alacrity with which these demands were met reflected the ministers' regret over the actions that had been taken, but Hillier's strong tone was also a factor. Perhaps not wishing to risk being accused of stepping over a line, he failed to report to Clarendon that in the event of non-compliance with his demands he had threatened not only an audience with the king, but that he would attend that audience "with an armed guard at the Royal Palace".[60]

As the person of Ai-fung and the body of Seng had already been delivered to the consul, there was not much more Hillier could do except deliver the consuls' letter to the king, which was done the next day. Having completed these tasks, his attention turned once more to his health.

THE DEATH OF HILLIER

British consulate and Don Quixote, 3-20 October 1856

The strain of the events in Bangkok had taken a heavy toll on Hillier's health. The day after the meeting of the consuls, "diarrhoea returned" with "extreme pain in the bowels". He struggled to complete his report on the tumultuous events in Bangkok to Clarendon, relying once again on dictation through Eliza until the pain became too strong and he took his morphine. After a night of suffering on 4 October, the next morning he told Eliza that "he must be taken to sea again, or he should never recover, but out at sea he felt sure with God's blessing he should recover, as he had before done." Dr Hill was alarmed at Hillier's worsening dysentery and agreed that he should be moved as soon as possible.[61]

A gig from the *Saracen* was arranged for his second and final arduous journey along Bangkok's Chaophraya river on 5 October.[62] Back on board the *Don Quixote*, his disease appeared to be "increasing in violence" until after a few days "it moderated and at noon a large substance was passed which proved to be a tumour which had formed in the stomach." Over the next week, his condition seemed to improve, but then he suffered a relapse on Saturday 18 October, with Eliza mournfully describing his last moments:

> At last his poor glazed eyes turned to me, he heard my voice, and I felt there was hope again. He fixed his eyes on me and his lips moved with the effort to speak, but no sound came. I prayed him to say one word, and at last said "kiss me to show that you know me" the poor white lips were immediately put together, and I kissed them frantically, but they were icy cold, and I was kissing and embracing cold clay – this I did not know, but persisted in fanning and bathing his temples. It was two hours before I knew or could believe that I was a widow, and alone in the world. The Doctor did not arrive till four pm and by that time my dear one had been laid out ready for his last home.[63]

Dr Hill examined the body and concluded "though dysentery was the approximate cause of death that Mr Hillier must for some time past have been labouring under Cartifaginication of the deep-seated glands of the abdomen".[64] However, he was quite clear that the events in Bangkok hastened his end, telling Captain Richards that "the violent excitement [the Seng affair] occasioned brought on the relapse in [Hillier's] sickness that led to his untimely end."[65] Charles Bell, the erstwhile student-interpreter, now first assistant in charge, concurred:

> That the melancholy event was greatly accelerated by his precipitate return to Bangkok . . . none of his medical attendants have the slightest doubt.[66]

Hillier's body was transported back to Bangkok on 20 October for the funeral which accorded "every mark of respect for his rank and private character".[67] Captain Richards elaborated on the great efforts made by both the Siamese and foreign communities to pay their last respects to the first British consul to Siam:

> I made as much display of respect at his funeral as possible; firing minute guns &c., and attending with my whole ship's company. The funeral procession of boats extended about three quarters of a mile on the river. The boats of the *Saracen* headed the centre line, consisting entirely of European and American residents and Masters of Merchant Ships in port. The native boats formed in lines on each side the boat containing the body. They were headed on one side by the First King's representative in the person of the Prince his youngest brother, and on the other by Prince George, the Second King's eldest son, and heir apparent.[68]

Hillier was buried at the new Protestant cemetery on the east bank of the Chaophraya river. Nothing is known of the funeral arrangements and the subsequent life of Seng's family. One British newspaper reported that the king made provision for Seng's family[69] and one historian speculated that the king would have helped the family judging by his prior actions,[70] but no independent evidence has been found to confirm or disprove such assistance.

Eliza's immediate prospects were also dim. Even though Hillier had paid some £600 into a superannuation fund, the foreign office made no provision for widows to claim a husband's pension. Eliza claimed that she and her children had been "left almost wholly destitute". Appeals to the treasury that special consideration be given to Eliza's case came from numerous sources, including Eliza herself, Charles' brother Edward, a group of Singapore merchants and newspapers, Sir John Davis, Bowring and even Clarendon.[71] But the treasury blithely declared that they had

Hillier's grave (© Hillier Collection, by courtesy of Andrew Hillier and Historical Photographs of China, University of Bristol)

"no funds at their disposal applicable to the payment of Pensions to Widows of Consuls".[72] Eventually, after the intercession of Prime Minister Palmerston and Clarendon, a pension of £50 a year from the Civil List was found for Eliza.[73] Eliza also claimed that she was due payment of Charles' outstanding salary of some £324. Bowring concurred and advanced £150 of this amount to her. But Eliza's appeal for the balance was again rejected by the British government, in part because the Bangkok accounts had been left in such a mess by Hillier. The consequent reconstruction of the 1856 accounts by the audit office (necessarily based on imperfect information) indicated that Bowring's advance had more than covered any possible salary shortfall.[74]

In the meantime, the only realistic option for Eliza was to return to England. On 3 November, just two weeks after Charles' funeral, she and Maud boarded the *Auckland*, the same ship that had brought them to

Siam only five months earlier, for Singapore. Arriving in England on 1 January 1857, she first went to her sister-in-law's in Cambridge to break the news to her three sons. There, on 11 March, she gave birth to Charles' fourth son, Edward Guy (known as Guy).[75]

The eminent missionary, the Reverend Walter Medhurst, Eliza's father, had decided to retire from his mission in China and return to England in 1856, leaving his son, also Walter, British consul at Foochow (Fuzhou), as the only family member remaining in China. The elder Medhurst arrived in England three weeks after his daughter, not yet knowing of Charles' death. "Overwhelmed by the news and already in poor health", Walter was to die just two days after landing in England.[76] Eliza, having lost both her husband and her father within the space of three months and with limited financial resources, moved into the home of Charles' brother, Edward, but would relocate with her children to Devon in 1862 where she remained until her death in 1886. Eliza was to marry a local town clerk, Charles Marshall Hole, in 1864, a relationship that would give her financial security at last, as well as two more children.

Three of her sons from Hillier were to retrace their father's journey to China, each having distinguished careers there and, like their father, acquiring Chinese language skills. The eldest, Walter, rose to be Chinese secretary (1885-89) and consul-general in Seoul (1889-96), having accompanied by then Sir Harry Parkes to Korea to negotiate the 1883 treaty that gave Britain some of the same privileges as Bowring and Parkes had negotiated in Siam in 1855; Harry, the second son, became commissioner of the Chinese customs service in several Chinese treaty ports; and Guy, the youngest, was Peking agent of The Hongkong and Shanghai Banking Corporation for over thirty years until his death in 1924. None of the family, however, would follow their father's fateful journey to Siam.

Chapter 6

The king manages the consequences

NAI KHAM'S REPORT

Hong Kong, I November 1856

King Mongkut had sent his emissary, Nai Kham of the *mahatlek* (royal pages department), to Hong Kong in May 1856 on his ship, the *Siamese Crown*. Kham's instructions were to serve as supercargo, supervising the sale of six ship loads of Siamese produce (such as pepper, ivory, birds' nests and nutmeg) that were bound for Canton and purchase with the proceeds a range of luxury goods (such as writing cases, gold betel-nut boxes and jade tea cups) for the king. Kham was to disembark and complete the king's business in Hong Kong.

In the royal pages department Kham was in one of the four groups of private ministers reporting to Chao Muen Sanphet Phakdi, one of the king's two favourites sent daily to look after Bowring during his 1855 mission[1] and later appointed second ambassador in the embassy sent by Mongkut to Britain in 1857. Mongkut referred to Chao Muen Sanphet Phakdi as the "adopted son of the first King of Siam & his household" in a note to Bowring.[2] Kham had also met Bowring during the 1855 mission as he was one of the three "private ministers" first sent by Mongkut to the *Rattler* to welcome Bowring to Bangkok.[3] The king had asked Bowring to provide assistance and instruction to Kham in Hong Kong until the *Siamese Crown* returned from Canton for the onward journey to Bangkok in October or November.[4]

Opposite page: King Mongkut, photographed by John Thomson in 1865.

The timing was unfortunate. On 23 October, British forces commenced a bombardment of Canton that constituted the first campaign in the Second Opium War. Damages were extensive. Mongkut estimated his own losses through fire and theft of his goods at over $2,000. He asked Bowring to help him gain restitution and instructed Kham to stay in Hong Kong to try to recover what he could by appealing to the British authorities.[5] The strategy was to prove unsuccessful, with Clarendon finally ruling that he could not include the Siamese claim in the British claim "without claiming also for those of other Powers".[6]

The two British officials most directly engaged in Britain's Canton policy were Harry Parkes, who had been stationed as acting consul at Canton since his return from Bangkok earlier in the year, and Sir John Bowring, his immediate superior in Hong Kong. While Parkes was temperamentally the more prone to belligerence, Bowring had let his frustrations with his Chinese counterparts outweigh his liberal inclinations. His brinkmanship brought about the conflict with China that would be strongly criticised in London and eventuate the termination of his role as plenipotentiary to China.

The bombardment of Canton was still in progress at the beginning of November when Kham came to meet Bowring. It was to be expected that Bowring would have little time for him. Instead, he first sent one of his men to talk to Kham. Bowring's man was more interested to discuss recent developments in Bangkok involving the British consulate than China. Bowring and his team had already received reports on the events leading up to the death of Seng, although they had yet to hear about the death of Hillier. But Kham had no knowledge of these events and was not prepared for the direction the conversation took, as suggested by his opening remarks in his report of the meeting to Chao Muen Sanphet Phakdi in early December 1856:

> Please inform the king that I did not know that Nai Seng was punished to death.
>
> On the 4th of the 12th month of the waxing moon [1 November] I went to see Sir John Bowring, but he had not yet come out as he was talking to other British people. Another person came to talk to me, though I'm not sure if Sir John Bowring told him to ask me certain questions or if they were his own questions. He asked me if I worked for the king in Bangkok, how the

system worked, are there titles, what do I do, how much I get paid and if I knew Nai Seng, a teacher at Bell's house? He said that Nai Seng had said that he was a royal page with a title and got paid by King Rama IV. Is it true that King Rama IV knows Seng well?

I said that it is true. He asked if they had known each other long. I said, yes. Since when? Since Nai Seng was a *parian* [scholar] monk. He translated religious works when the king was also a monk, so he saw the king regularly. Once he left the monkhood, he became a royal page and worked for the king in the palace printing house. How much was his pay? I didn't know. Did you know that Nai Seng was a teacher at Bell's house?[7] I said that he hadn't told me.

After that, he was quiet for a while and asked me: is it true that Siamese people really cheat a lot? So I asked him back: is every Englishman a good man? He said that some are good. I said that England has good and bad people and Siam has good and bad people, like every nation. Then he asked about the government. I said that I didn't know much.

At that moment, Sir John Bowring came out and we talked, but he didn't say anything at all about Nai Seng. . .[8]

The identity of Kham's interlocuter is not given. However, the abrupt shift in his questioning from details of Seng's background to a contemptuous smear on the character of the Siamese people suggests a perception among at least some of Bowring's men that the events in Bangkok risked damaging Siam's reputation among the British.

This extraordinary report contains the only reference to Seng thus far found in the Siamese archives. It gives important information on Seng's background, but significantly it also provides more context to the king's actions. Seng, the Siamese writer at the consulate, was unsurprisingly also working as language teacher to Charles Bell, with the lessons taking place on Bell's rented floating house, presumably with Edward Forrest also attending. Seng had been known to the king since their days as monks. As a *parian*, or scholar, monk, Seng would have been a significant member of Mongkut's reformist Thammayut sect and, with his English skills, may have benefited from English lessons given by the missionaries to Mongkut and selected monks. Given the timing and the tiny coterie of people capable of translating Christian literature, it is quite likely, but unproven, that the Seng employed by Bradley in 1844 as a writer to help translate his old testament history was the same person.[9]

The report also suggests that Seng was one of the cohort of religious officials who had left the monkhood in the early years of King Mongkut's reign to enter government service. In 1854, the king had been so concerned that this trend would lead to a deterioration in religious instruction in the royal monasteries that he issued two decrees to restrain it. In these, the king complained that over sixty ecclesiastical officials and learned monks had left the monkhood for government service in the first three years of his reign and decreed that such people would not be allowed to join the senior ministries, instead being required to work shifts in the royal printing house, as Seng had done. A breach of this decree carried a penalty of fifty strokes of the rattan.[10] In short, Seng was not a random civil servant, but like Chao Muen Sanphet Phakdi, was a *khaluang doem*; that is, one of the king's close associates from his days in the monkhood.

This information does not of course justify the king's treatment of Seng, but it does corroborate the claim that Seng was – or at least had been – his subordinate and well known to him. It also suggests that the king's rage might have been exacerbated by his sense of betrayal by a trusted acolyte. Whether he knew that Seng had also taken up employment at the British consulate and was therefore entitled to Article III protection remains a moot point.

THE KING'S ATONEMENT

King Mongkut's palace, 3-6 October 1856

Well before Kham's meeting in Hong Kong, Mongkut had taken action to defuse the crisis. The consuls' protest letter needed to be addressed quickly, especially the claim that the king's actions constituted an insult to Queen Victoria. As well as feeling remorseful for his impetuous actions, he would do everything he could to avoid undermining his own efforts to build a strong, friendly and mutually respectful relationship with the western powers, especially Britain.

However, his conciliatory measures were not solely a reaction to the consuls' protest. King Mongkut was also responding to the strong condemnation of his behaviour by the principal officers of state who, according to Bradley, were "much displeased with the late shameful conduct of his Majesty" and were prepared "to show their disapprobation of it by unmistakable signs, even to demand of him a promise that he will henceforward take counsel with them on all matters concerning their relations with the English". Despite the evident reticence of senior officials to repudiate the king's actions displayed to Bell and Hillier, Bradley believed that "it is quite evident that the King fears their power to depose him and has humbled himself before them."[11]

Bradley may well have overstated the threat from the senior officers; it is unlikely that they would have made such direct demands of the king. Nevertheless, the king was well aware that a collapse in relations with the British would not only attenuate his political strategy and its potential economic benefits, it could also weaken his own position in the eyes of his senior officials, many of whom had opposed the strategy.

The key officers involved, however, were primarily his supporters: the Phraklang, the Yommarat and Wongsa. The Kalahom was not mentioned as having attended any of the meetings on this issue. Whether this was because he was physically absent from Bangkok at the time or he wished to distance himself from the affair, we do not know. Nevertheless, the show of unanimity by the other officials suggests that Hillier's suspicion of a conservative conspiracy may have been overblown. On the other hand, the king's abrupt adoption of a conciliatory tone supports Hillier's supposition that all should return to normal if the king were to take an unimpassioned view of events.

In order to placate both the foreign community and his own nobles, the king decided that a gesture was required which would signal his recognition that his actions were an error of judgement and not an indication of hostility to Britain. US Consul Mattoon was probably the first in the foreign community to be apprised of the king's proposed act of atonement:

> The King upon receiving the Protest immediately sent for me and I have had two or three interviews with his Majesty since. He has given no written reply to the Protest though he promises to do so, and gave me permission to read a partial reply which he had prepared. He acknowledges his fault and offers to make satisfaction, proposing to give ground for the English Consulate the reason for such gift to be made known to his subjects.[12]

Not only was the land to be gifted to the British government, but the king was to pay out of his own resources, "by expending the amount from my own chamber (not from Treasure of Siamese Governments)".[13] Furthermore, in addition to buying the land, he would place on the land "a perpetual monument stating his offense and that he had given the plot of ground for the Consulate as a lasting memorial of his crime", according to Bradley.[14] The king also informed Bell of his proposed gift of land, although the nature of the "perpetual monument" appears to have changed in form from "a flagstaff bearing upon its base an inscription to the effect that the ground and flagstaff have been presented to the British Government as an atonement for the insult offered by his seizing and putting to death a servant in the employ of HBM's Consul" to "a proclamation" stating the reason for the atonement.[15]

To deal with the immediate consequences of his actions, the king put in place three measures. First, in order to address the fear of working for foreigners, he "issued proclamations under the Royal Seal to quiet the fears of the Siamese assuring them that they were permitted to engage freely in the employ of foreigners and that they would not be exposed to punishment therefore".[16] Second, not long after Hillier's death, he issued another proclamation "to the effect that no obstacles would be placed in the way of foreigners wishing to buy or rent land, so long as they conformed to Treaty regulations".[17] Third, although he still considered a lease of ninety-nine years to be "contrary to Siamese law and usage", he nevertheless resolved the unsettled status of Puddicombe's land by agreeing "as a personal favour to leave the Lessee in quiet possession of his land and promise the owner of the land exemption from all punishment on account of the lease".[18] Confirming this to his "old friend" Puddicombe a few days later, the king wrote "to assure you peclutiar [*sic*] permission to purchase that piece of ground freely in part of my power".[19]

In his desire to demonstrate his affection for Puddicombe in particular, the king was venturing beyond the provisions of Article IV by allowing Puddicombe to purchase land within the four-mile boundary. He no doubt wished to avoid the precedent of a long lease term that he had argued was illegal, but by doing so he had set another precedent. Within three weeks of allowing Puddicombe to buy his land, the former American missionary, John Hassett Chandler, who had run into serious opposition from the Siamese authorities over his land deal in 1854, was able to buy his intended plot next door to Puddicombe. Mattoon was also allowed to buy the controversial land at Samrae. As Bradley noted, "the Government now seem wonderfully gracious and anxious to make ample reparation for the late disgraceful violation of the Treaties with the three western powers by the King."[20]

Puddicombe, however, never availed himself of the king's magnanimity. When he returned to Bombay in 1859, he asked for permission to sell his land to a Mr Foreman who would take over the business. The Siamese initially refused permission, in part because Mr Foreman was not entitled to purchase land not having been resident for ten years, but also because Puddicombe, having failed to execute the purchase agreement, was in reality still a tenant and so had no right to sell the freehold. Eventually, Wongsa relented and permitted the sale, although it is not known whether the deal was consummated.[21]

Over the next year, King Mongkut continued to use his discretionary power over land to benefit foreign, especially British, investors. Some decisions merely delivered rights enshrined in Article IV, such as granting permission to Robert Hunter and the missionary Samuel Smith to buy land in Bangkholaem, within the four-mile circuit, because they had been resident for more than ten years; and to Charles Bell and a Mr Christy to buy between the four-mile and twenty-four-hour circuits, as the treaty allowed,[22] although Bell's deal did not materialise as he decided the land plot was too small while his preferred plot, which was owned by the king, could not be bought because it was "in the line of a fort". But when Mongkut received applications to buy land from Samuel Gilfillan (the first Siam representative of the Borneo Company) and C. H. H. Wilsone (from Hamilton, Grey & Company), whom he regarded as friends who had been "of much service to His Majesty" in helping him acquire goods from abroad, he was prepared to be more generous than the treaty required. In both these cases the king instructed the authorities to buy 3.3 acres of land on either side of the new Thanon Trong road and canal in Bangna (again, outside the city) and present it to the British businessmen. He also allowed them to purchase adjacent land of at least the same size again. However, D. K. Mason, another British businessmen who, like Gilfillan and Wilsone, had been posted from Singapore, was not yet as well known to the king and was not granted land, although he too was allowed to purchase – in this case some 6.6 acres next door to Wilsone's land.[23]

These permissions accompanied the king's acquiescence to the request of the foreign community to build the Thanon Trong to Bangna. British business leaders had appealed to the king for this new infrastructure as it would enable the western community to create their own community away from the multi-ethnic, crowded and conflict-prone Bangrak area, as well as providing less competitive mooring facilities for western shipping. The British contingent provided satisfactory engineering solutions to overcome the king's reservations that the new community would suffer from a lack of fresh water and the new canal could lead to salt water flooding upstream rice fields, and the construction was completed at the considerable cost to the king of some 16,633 baht for the Chinese labour alone. Another 400-600 baht was spent by the king on the land to be presented to Gilfillan and Wilsone. Eventually, the king came to consider his generosity a waste of money as it achieved neither the desired removal of the foreign community from Bangrak (even Gilfillan and Wilsone failed to develop their new land), nor did it lead to the hoped-for increase in tax collection from shipping. Instead, as he was to note ruefully, the only people who appreciated the new road and canal appeared to be criminals who found the deserted area suitable for ambushing people and those who benefitted from the construction works.[24]

For Seng's family, there were no "acts of atonement". It is, of course, conceivable that the king provided financial or other assistance to Seng's family, but no reference has been found to suggest this or any other expression of regret for Seng's fate. Indeed, the Siamese authorities continued to regard the actions of Seng as illegal and his punishment in accordance with Siamese law and custom. As Bradley saw it, the cruel fate of Seng was not a subject that the king dwelt upon:

> Still he does not appear to feel that he has been unjust and unmerciful to one of his subjects. He fears the displeasure of Queen Victoria. His sin he thinks is against her and not against any other creature nor against God.[25]

There is similarly no evidence that the punishment and death of one of the consulate's local hires for undertaking consular work much exercised the thoughts of senior British officials, nor – with the exception of Bradley and possibly some of his colleagues – of others among the foreign community in Siam.

MANAGING THE NARRATIVE

For Bowring, the success of the Anglo-Siamese relationship had become a cornerstone of his own reputation. He could not afford to let the Seng affair derail it, especially as the impact of the new war in China on his own position and reputation could not be foreseen. Fortunately, King Mongkut, out of both political necessity and personal desire, was equally dedicated to the task of papering over the cracks and restoring good relations. His swift atonement had made the path to the resumption of friendly relations possible, but there remained another step that needed to be taken but which was proving difficult to finesse. That was the need to explain to the British, not only his friend Bowring but the authorities in London, what had happened, and why. Gifting land, exempting Puddicombe's transaction from Siamese laws and customs and assuring his people that they were free to work for foreigners and sell or rent them land would all be seen as unequivocal actions in support of the Anglo-Siamese friendship. But any written explanation admitting the king's fault could be misconstrued, either intentionally or otherwise, and have unintended consequences.

It is therefore not surprising that he laboured over his reply, and would appear to have decided, in the end, not to send it. He had shown a draft to Mattoon the day after the consuls' protest letter. A month later the draft was six-sheets long, but had still not been sent:

> Nothing has occurred in reference to the late disturbances. No written reply has been received to the Protest though I had been led to believe that one would have been given long since. Repeated verbal assurances have been given of the regret of His Majesty and the principal nobles at the late unfortunate occurrences. Whether His Majesty's written reply is only delayed on account of Mr. Hillier's death or other cause given up entirely I know not.

Mattoon's frustration led him to suspect that "with the usual fickleness of the Siamese it will remain unfinished".[26] But Mattoon's conclusion was only partially correct: the king's failure to reply directly was not due to fickleness but rather to his preference for a more subtle, and more effective, two-pronged strategy. The first approach was to use the good offices of another British friend, Captain John Richards, to deliver a direct yet non-official message accepting his own guilt. The second approach was to delegate responsibility for delivering an official explanation to the Phraklang which would emphasise regret rather than guilt.

Bangkok, 29 October 1856

John Richards had played an important supporting role throughout the events of 1856, popping up as a *deus ex machina* to resolve thorny issues thrown up by events from time to time: the captain of the *Saracen* was on hand to survey the four-mile limit to unblock the impasse that threatened to scupper the signing of Harry Parkes' agreement in April; at the end of September he provided an armed guard and military heft to Hillier in the wake of the king's treaty violations; he assisted the Hilliers in providing medical support (Dr Hill) and transport for some of the journeys to and from the *Don Quixote* necessitated by Hillier's illness; he was a co-signatory to the consuls' letter of protest; and he had finally provided the organisational and logistical support that ensured an appropriate funeral for Hillier. At one point only did he emerge as an active protagonist himself, when his decision in August to sail the *Saracen* upriver to anchor outside the British consulate without first seeking the permission of the Siamese authorities was deemed the very first treaty violation and required Hillier's new-found diplomatic skills to smooth the flurry of protest from the Siamese authorities.

Nothing attests to his importance as a behind-the-scenes influencer more than his use as a channel for Mongkut's expression of remorse and guilt to Bowring. Since first arriving in Bangkok in February 1856 and impressing King Mongkut with his plans for a survey of the Gulf of Siam,[27] Richards had evidently developed a close relationship with the king. After the deaths of Seng and Hillier, the king felt sufficiently confident in their relationship to use him as a conduit to Bowring, a role he was better positioned to fill than Mattoon.

The king first sought Richards' advice shortly after Seng's demise. Not long after Hillier's funeral, the king sent Richards a letter on which he had obviously spent a great deal of effort.[28] The letter's tone of informality was deliberate. It implied that the contents were not a final statement, thus leaving the door open for denial or a change of direction. On the one hand, the king admitted his fault ("I am sincerely confessing of my own fault"), repeated his commitment to acts of compensation and requested

Richards to forward the letter to Bowring as his "testimony of my true and sincere statement". On the other hand, the king presented the letter to Richards as a draft and even asked him to rewrite it for him:

> I shall be very glad to have from you a draft from which I should write to [Bowring] and you will oblige me much for your kindness in verbal or written declaration and I am not standing in opposition merely.

While the king did not provide any reasons for his actions against Seng in the letter to Richards, he did explain why he was reluctant to send a more definitive letter to Bowring. Not knowing how Hillier and Bell had presented the incident to Bowring, he feared that if his own account contradicted theirs Bowring "may think me in opposition or consider me unsincere". He also worried that his draft letter to Bowring (presumably the same six-page document he had shown Mattoon) was too long and may lead Bowring to think that the king was trying "to defend or plead with unsincerity". Instead, he wanted Richards to help compose a concise summary, "enough for shewing my being remaining his true friend waiting to hear his kind advice".

In the end, what at first appears to be a rather rambling letter, a stream-of-consciousness outpouring of disparate thoughts, could be construed as an unconventional mechanism for delivering the king's sincere apology and measures of atonement to the British government. By this interpretation, the king's avoidance of official channels limited the risk of aggravating potential enemies he suspected may be opposed to him in Britain and its territories.

If that was indeed the king's intention, he could be well satisfied that it achieved the desired outcome. Bowring willingly accepted his apology and friendly relations were restored. Bowring understood that the king's letter to Richards was to be as close as he would get to a direct, official apology from the king. He accepted it as such, replying that "I most willingly accept Your Majesty's assurance that in future no such grounds for anxiety shall be permitted to interrupt for a moment our relations." He also expressed appreciation for the offer to buy land "as a reparation for the error committed", but expected the British government to consider any future "avoidance of any similar cause for solicitude" to be "the most acceptable method of burying the past in oblivion".[29]

Bangkok, 6 November 1856

The job of explaining the king's actions was assigned to the Phraklang, who wrote to Bowring just one week after the king's letter to Richards. There are two English-language versions of this letter: one Mattoon sent to US Secretary of State Marcy and the other – the final version – was sent by the Phraklang to Bowring.[30] The letter contained a vigorous defence of the king based on his "ignorance" of Seng's employment at the British consulate; the king's actions were a rational response to an illegal incident. There was no acknowledgement of the "paroxysm of passion" that dominated western accounts.

The letter explained that since the Bowring treaty had come into force, some minor officials had been working for both the Siamese government and Europeans. Such officials were not necessarily known to the senior nobles. Seng was identified as one of this cohort, his government job being as a scribe in the royal printing office, "employed by the King to write the Laws and Royal proclamations".

The letter provides the only narrative of the Seng affair from a Siamese source. The details do not differ from other accounts, but the viewpoint is unique. The Phraklang's account highlighted the king's investigation of the Puddicombe lease. It argued that the lease was clearly illegal under Siamese laws and that Seng, as someone responsible for drafting laws, would have known that. Before having Seng arrested, the king had verified that Seng was still working at the royal printing office. Seng acknowledged that he had drafted the lease, but when asked for a reason by the king could only respond that "Ai-Fung was the owner of the land" and "he had written as Ai-Fung directed". Apart from drafting an illegal lease, Seng had "taken business not belonging to his department". The king therefore sentenced him to "the full punishment of one hundred blows according to the law", with one deducted to accord with the number of years on the lease. The senior ministers were not aware of these events until informed by Bell the next day and then immediately took action to have him removed to Wongsa's palace for treatment. Seng's death was attributed to his being administered "the wrong medicine" by the Siamese doctors, rather than to the flogging.

The letter also included one material fact that had not appeared in any of the consular reports: Puddicombe's ninety-nine-year lease contained a renewal clause of an additional ninety-nine years to be triggered "by the payment of an additional sum of five Ticals". By any modern standard, such a lease would be deemed a virtual freehold.

The Phraklang pointed out that it was understood "that the parties being all Siamese there was no interference with the English Treaty". Nevertheless, fearing that it would be reported that Seng had been "whipped to death", the Phraklang said that the king had decided to assure Bowring that there was no design to insult the English nor any displeasure at Seng's work for the consul. Instead, the king's displeasure was over "matters wholly Siamese". Thus, any violation of the treaty was unintentional and had "arisen from ignorance". Bowring was asked to help quash "false rumors" which could affect trade and profits. The sincere admission of guilt that had been central in the king's letter to Richards was now relegated to an admission of "an apparent fault" over a "comparatively small matter" in Mattoon's version or a "fault committed through neglect" over "a trifle" in the final version.

While the very different translation styles of the two versions make comparisons speculative, a few additional paragraphs were clearly inserted in the final version. The new content suggests an alternative explanation for the king's actions, namely that the king had not realised Siamese subjects could be subject to British protection under the extraterritorial provisions of the treaty. This reasoning had first been suggested in the consuls' protest letter of 3 October and was now evoked by the Phraklang: "there are certain portions of the Treaty still needing explanation, for example as to British subjects purchasing slaves, and in regard to occasionally not permanently in the employ of the English, these points are not yet clear". The new text was probably added by the king as the language is similar to that used a few months later in the king's letter to Clarendon, informing him that the Siamese ambassadors to London had been ordered to seek "some explanation and some instruction" from the British government on the treaty because:

> There are many things which were not well understood by us regarding several clauses in the Treaty & its explanatory or commentary agreement & more over in code of International laws, which we have just tested by partly audience from conversation of certain bodies came from enlightened nations.[31]

Throughout the hostile reaction from the western residents and press to the Seng affair, little credence was given to the possibility that the king's "profession of ignorance" was real. It may seem unlikely (though not impossible) that Seng's employment at the British consulate remained unknown to the king throughout the interrogation, but it is surely conceivable that the king had not realised that Siamese subjects could be entitled to British protection. Although Article III clearly states that its provisions apply to Siamese "in the employ of British subjects", the main thrust of the article was to provide consular jurisdiction to British subjects, not their employees. It is therefore quite possible that in the heat of the moment this subordinate meaning had been either overlooked or forgotten by the king and some of his officers. In that case, the king would have understood Seng to be his subject and could have viewed Seng's assistance to Puddicombe as not only illegal but also a betrayal of trust.

GINGELL BUILDS THE CONSULATE

Providing a convincing and acceptable narrative of the Seng affair was the first step to rehabilitating the relationship with Britain. Delivery on the king's promise should bring closure. It was therefore important for the British to take up the offer and build their new consulate on the land allocated. This should not have been difficult to ensure, but the path to completion of the consulate was strewn with obstacles, some of which could not be overcome without the king's intervention.

The British were not averse to accepting the free gift of land. Clarendon diplomatically neither explicitly accepted nor rejected the offer, but strongly implied acceptance, noting that the king's "communication has been received with much satisfaction" by the British government.[32] The new acting consul, W. Raymond Gingell, duly passed on the message verbatim to King Mongkut on 13 May 1857[33] and was tasked with bringing the project to completion.

The first obstacle faced by Gingell could not be resolved by the king as it concerned his unfriendly reception at Bangkok by his own compatriots. Gingell arrived on the king's ship, the *Siamese Crown*, the same vessel that Nai Kham had taken to Hong Kong. However, he was not afforded the expected convenience and courtesy of being met by a boat from the consulate. Charles Bell, Gingell grumbled, "appeared inclined to dispute my authority". Bell believed that Bowring lacked the authority to appoint the new consul and had persuaded the leading British merchants to submit a letter to the Phraklang refusing to recognise him. The letter was signed by Wilsone, Gilfillan, Baxter, Hunter and Mason; wisely or fortuitously, Puddicombe had avoided involvement in this new controversy. When Bowring heard about it, he was furious, suspecting Bell "had been concocting with the merchants this strange scheme for retaining Consular Power in his own hands".[34] Gingell defused the situation by showing evidence of Bowring's plenipotentiary status in Siam. The British merchants were duly placated and sent another letter to the Phraklang reversing their original position but complaining of Bowring's failure to inform them of his diplomatic powers.

While Bell's actions were clearly insubordinate, he nevertheless had a point. Bowring had overstepped his authority and Clarendon was unforgiving. Appointing consuls was the remit of the secretary of state, and Clarendon had appointed Sir Robert Schomburgk to replace Hillier even before Gingell had reached Bangkok. Clarendon considered Bell to be acting consul and expected Schomburgk to take over directly from him, a position that would be validated by the British government's law office.[35] Bowring had appointed Gingell at the end of January 1857, telling him that he expected Clarendon to confirm him as full consul. Clarendon was forced to acknowledge Gingell's temporary appointment "until the arrival of Mr. Hillier's successor" but was furious with Bowring. He stripped him of his oversight role in Siam, informing him that his "interference" with Siam would cease on Schomburgk's arrival,[36] thus supplementing Bowring's *annus horribilis*. Clarendon was also to strip him of his role as plenipotentiary to China and his authority to lead a mission to Japan. As his descendent Philip Bowring noted, if 1855 marked the zenith of Bowring's career in government, largely due to the Siam treaty, 1856 marked the nadir, largely due to the China war: "Perhaps success in Siam had made Bowring overconfident."[37]

Clarendon did not seem to blame Bell for his insubordination. When Bell, realising his position had become untenable, submitted his resignation, just three days after Gingell's arrival from Hong Kong,[38] Clarendon accepted it "with regret as your good conduct and ability would have ensured your advancement in your profession".[39] Gingell was to be sent back to China as vice-consul to Amoy, complaining to Clarendon of his bitter disappointment and of being misled by Bowring.[40] Nevertheless, he proved an efficient manager during his ten months in Bangkok. He improved the running of the consulate, especially the "confused state of

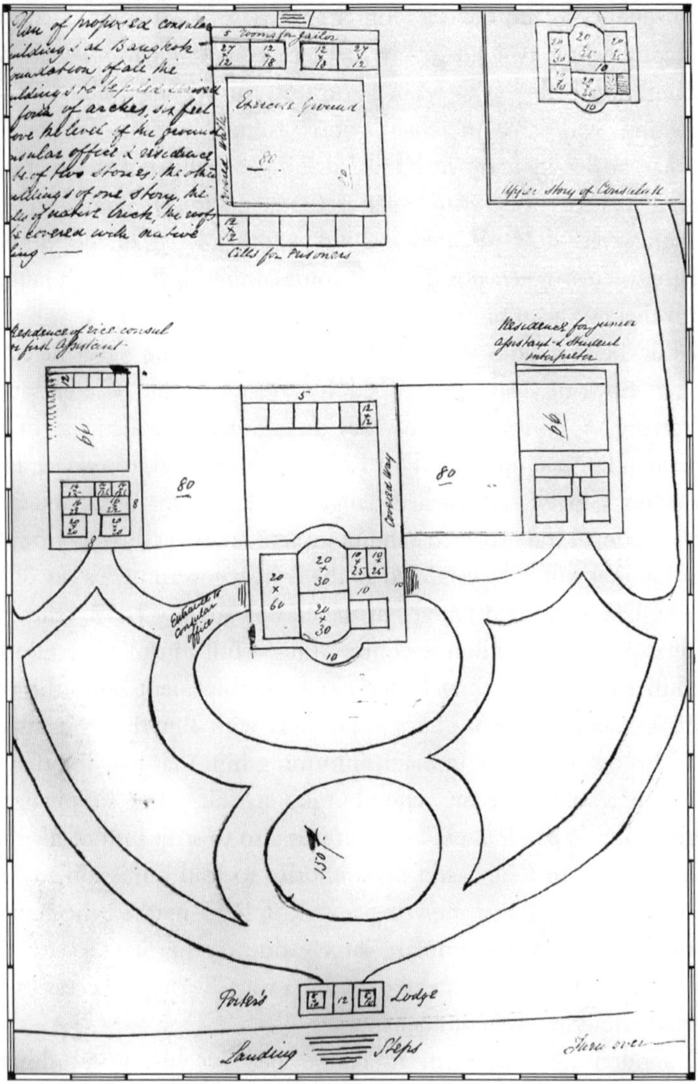

Hillier's original layout for the British consulate, Bangrak, in 1856.

the Archives"[41] and the "utter state of complexity" of the accounts that he inherited from Hillier.[42]

He also made a better impression on the Siamese authorities than had Hillier. The Phraklang went to the trouble of writing a glowing account of Gingell's performance during his stay in Bangkok, informing Bowring that

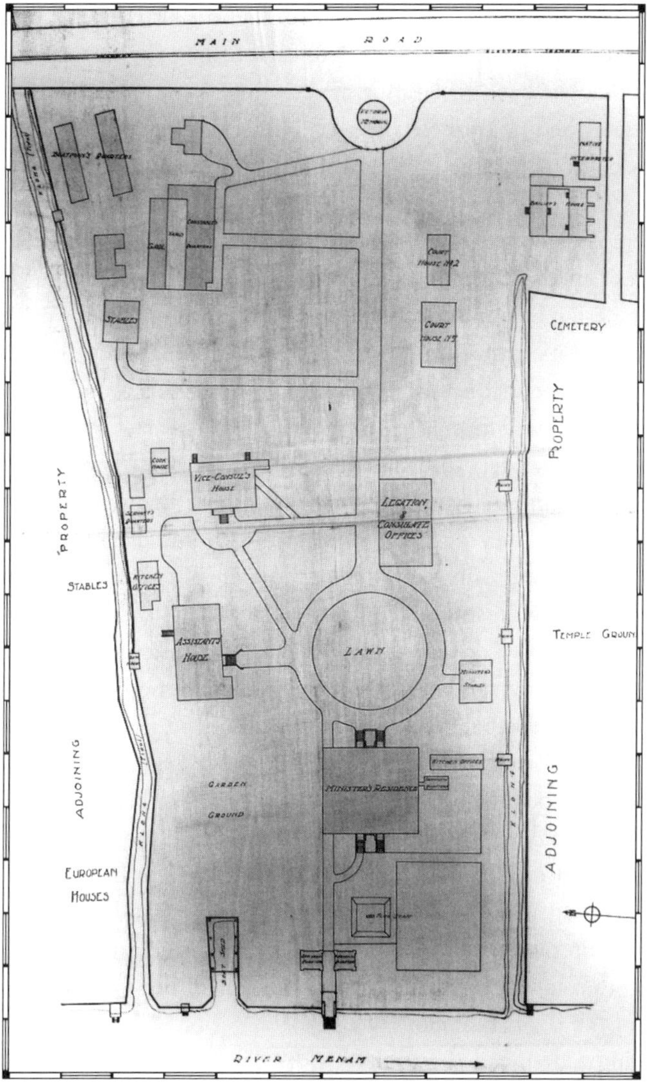

Actual layout of the British consulate/legation, Bangrak, in 1895.

the two kings and Wongsa "have a very great affection for Mr Gingell", while all the senior officials were "highly pleased and praise him much" for his impartiality and sense of justice.[43] Nevertheless, he was not always an easy person to deal with. To his own officials, the king observed that Gingell was "melancholy, anxious, sickly and not in good spirits".[44]

Whatever his personal feelings towards Gingell, King Mongkut was determined that he should succeed in establishing the new consulate on the land that had been gifted. But, again, Gingell was to face unanticipated difficulties. The first of these was that Hillier's original plans as approved by London were nowhere to be found. Gingell undertook a redesign, reducing the buildings' footprint on the site because, he argued, Hillier had overestimated the river frontage and he believed the planned single-storey residences would be unhealthy due to poor ventilation. The new building design had a similar internal area but was now two storeys raised nine feet (2.7 metres) from the ground with verandahs on all sides, while the consul's residence would have eight rooms with an additional four rooms on the foundation level for offices and ancillary functions.

Gingell also made improvements to the site layout. He was very critical of Bell for digging a new canal along one side of the site, viewing it as a waste of both money and of "some four fathoms of land": it "neither serves to drain the ground, nor does it meet the purposes of a fence" and a wall or paling would still be required. In fact, Bell's canal was worse than useless as it was a muddy, swampy ditch at low tide and provided an inlet for the rapid current to encroach and wash away good land at high tide, which would exacerbate the site's susceptibility to flooding in the rainy season. But the canal had already been dredged.

Instead Gingell focused on value enhancements. He proposed buying an additional plot of waste land to make the site shape more regular. The additional cost of 824 ticals (about £100) would not breach the £6,000 approved budget and on that basis was approved by London. He also, with the approval of Moor, the Portuguese consul, relocated a public pathway that ran through the land to the rear of the site and behind the houses of the Baptist mission.

Having redesigned the project to his satisfaction, Gingell faced two more problems that could have put paid to the execution of his plans. There was "no money in the consular chest" and he had almost "despaired of meeting with anyone who would contract" to build the consulate for him. Gingell understood that both stumbling blocks could be removed with the help of the king, and Gingell's appeals to the king were answered quickly and effectively.

Hillier had failed to sort out the funding for the new British consulate and consequently some staff salaries had not been paid. Gingell had to pay

Bell and Forrest over a year's salary in mid-1857, as they had not received any since Hillier's arrival. Gingell was embarrassed to ask for a loan from the Siamese government, but not enough to deter him. The king obliged with two loans of 8,000 ticals each and requested repayment be made to the Siamese ambassadors who would soon be going to London.

Failing to find a contractor, Gingell was considering either turning down the loan or resorting to purchasing material and paying daily labour to get the job done. Again, he asked for help from the king. The king "immediately took an active interest in the building, and issued, under the Royal Seal, proclamations calling upon the people to contract and work for me" and instructed Wongsa to assist Gingell. By the end of April, he was thus able to find a Chinese contractor and a supervisor.

The two loans were applied for in March and May, giving Gingell sufficient funds to pay for three contracts: for the consulate in late April at a cost of 8,000 ticals, with a five-month build period from the date of commencing foundation work; for the two assistants' houses in early June at a cost of 7,500 ticals, excluding hardware and paint; and for construction of the jail and rooms for the jailor and boatmen at the same time for 1,000 ticals.

In the end, Gingell committed to spend a total of £5,500 (44,000 ticals) on the project: £500 to cover land clearing costs in late April; £2,000 for construction of the consulate in late May; and £3,000 for consular buildings, servants' offices, the prison, a river wall and a perimeter fence in late July.[45] As requested by the Siamese authorities, the Siamese loan was repaid to Ambassador Montri Suriyawong (a brother of the Kalahom) when the first Siamese embassy arrived in England in late 1857.[46]

By early July, Gingell was able to report that good progress was being made. But the king's desire to regain possession of the British factory at expiry of the one-year lease term on 10 June, as negotiated by Harry Parkes, had been frustrated. When Schomburgk was in Singapore waiting for a man-of-war to take him to Siam, he was worried that he would be forced to find a floating house to stay in when he got to Bangkok. Schomburgk finally arrived in Bangkok on 8 December. Gingell handed over "the public property and archives of the consulate and money" to him two days later and left Bangkok to report to Bowring in Hong Kong. Even though the Siamese had the right to take back the British factory from June 1857, Schomburgk was allowed to occupy it on his arrival. Nevertheless,

Photographs of the British consulate/legation, Bangrak.

he was asked several times by the Phraklang and both kings when he would be moving. The new urgency arose because the British merchant, D. K. Mason, had agreed to pay the "enormous rate" of 250 ticals a month for the building (which Schomburgk now referred to as "the King's Factory") as soon as the consulate moved out. Schomburgk set himself the deadline of year-end 1857 to relocate, but the consulate was still "far from completion", not least because the Chinese contractor was facing financial problems of his own. Schomburgk decided to take possession of the new first assistant's house, which was structurally complete. It only lacked hardware which had been sent in eighteen crates from London by ship in October, despite Gingell's request to use the quicker overland route. To avoid what he felt to be a moral obligation to start paying 250 ticals a month in the new year, Schomburgk resolved to buy hinges and locks locally and sell off the now surplus hardware once it arrived from England.[47] The new assistant, John Markham, was away on leave at the time, but when he returned with his family he was forced to find alternative accommodation with the American missionaries.

Schomburgk took possession of the first assistant's house on the last day of 1857, announcing that all consular business would be transacted from that building from 1 January 1858. By the end of that month, the contractor had become bankrupt, "running away and leaving the works unaccomplished". Schomburgk delegated the task of supervising the remaining construction work to Thomas Knox, who had joined the consular staff as interpreter.[48] The opening of the new consulate signified the fulfilment of Mongkut's core promise to the British government. By that time, the circumstances that lay behind the king's gift of land had been largely forgotten and would no longer disturb the trajectory of the Anglo-Siamese relationship. Nevertheless, the decisions of Mongkut in 1856 and the attitudes they embodied have continued to resonate implicitly through to the present day.

The British legation, Ploenchit.

Chapter 7

Legacies

THE SENG AFFAIR IN HISTORY

A measure of the Siamese success in managing the ramifications of the Seng affair is the lack of attention paid to the crisis by history. Granted, the Bowring treaty violations pale into insignificance when juxtaposed with some British colonial crises occurring around the same time – events that led to war with China (1856-60) and the Indian rebellion (1857), for instance. Yet the mishandling of such seemingly minor issues often leads to an escalation, as the *Arrow* incident that precipitated the Anglo-Chinese conflict in Canton attests, and different responses or different leadership could easily have led to far greater disruption to Anglo-Siamese relations.

Even at the time, the incident did not leave a deep impression. Apart from the three Siamese documents discussed in Chapter 6 (Kham's report, King Mongkut's letter to Richards and the Phraklang's to Bowring), other contemporary accounts are all from western observers. These include the diplomatic dispatches of Bell, Bowring, Hillier, Mattoon and Moor; Bradley's journal entries; and a handful of newspaper articles in Singapore and England, all of which were based on information from the western community in Bangkok. The historical record is thereafter largely silent on the episode until rediscovered by a handful of twentieth-century historians who mostly relied on information contained in Hillier's dispatches from Bangkok or Bradley's journal.[1]

As a result, the western contemporary and historians' accounts agree on the unlawfulness and brutality of Seng's arrest and punishment. Some stress Seng's innocence, some the king's temper, while others dwell on the perceived insult to Britain and the queen, with one newspaper contributing the most alarmist statement: "England has nearly been at war with the kingdom of Siam."[2] Most accounts, however, recognise that once the king's quick temper had cooled, his remorse was genuine and his act of expiation confirmed his "sound sense and friendly disposition".[3]

Most contemporary accounts did not delve deeply into the motivation for the king's initial reaction. It was known that the *casus belli* was the king's displeasure at the length of Puddicombe's land lease and that Seng had been "an old servant" of the king. One account suggested that the Siamese officials failed "to inform His Majesty that the culprit had been decoyed to the British Consulate".[4] These reasons, it was recognised, may have inflamed the king's rage, but a few also pointed to the influence of the king's advisors: Hillier suggested that the king had been influenced by an anti-English lobby of "evil advisors". Both Hillier and Bradley recognised that the king's more liberal advisors had played a decisive role in pulling the king back from the brink, but both suspected that the king's readiness to follow this lead suggested he feared their "power to depose him"[5] or even the "dread of poison or the knife, which is ever present to the mind of the generality of Eastern Potentates".[6]

Such views appear overly melodramatic and improbable, although one historian – Constance M. Wilson – more convincingly developed the idea of a power struggle, wondering if the incident could have resulted "from a conflict between the king and some of his officials or whether they indicated strife within the elite circle". On balance, she concluded that if such a conflict existed, it was most likely between the Bunnag family and those families that felt excluded by the Bunnags from power circles. The latter may have attempted "to discredit the favored few by making an issue out of certain of the provisions of the treaty, especially the special privileges granted to the western community" and, as a consequence, Mongkut, being "uniquely sensitive to any innuendo which would denote weakness or cast reflections on his honor" might react "by inhumane or arbitrary decrees".[7]

Wilson concluded that under this scenario, the swift action taken by the Bunnags and Wongsa enabled them to silence the anti-Bunnag or anti-treaty factions. Terwiel picked up this idea, suggesting that if that was indeed the Bunnag's plan, it was "quite successful": "The anti-treaty party became silent . . . Henceforth there was no high-level obstruction against the treaties, the various foreign groups acquired the right to trade under more favorable conditions than before, and the consuls were granted the power to protect the interests of those who wanted to take advantage of Siam's 'opening up'."[8] Similarly, Wilson was surely right in pointing out the beneficial effects of the incident on the British position:

> The British did not make a major issue out of Consul Hillier's death. . . . The British, as a result of the incident, were now able to persuade the Thai to do whatever they desired to improve the terms of trade and the treatment of British subjects.

Such benefits extended to the whole western community. After the Seng affair "there are no further reports of arbitrary arrests of servants of European and American residents."[9]

A more elaborate theory on the legacy of the Seng affair was constructed by Khachon Sukphanich in "The Death of Nai Insen". Hillier for unknown reasons had referred to Seng as "Ing Sen" in his dispatches. Khachon's account, based solely on Hillier's, translated the name back into Thai as นายอินเสน (*Nai Insen*).

Khachon saw the event as "giving birth to the freedom of commoners by enabling them to make a living through earning wages".[10] Khachon explained that as a *phrai* (commoner) working for a government department, Seng would be subject to strict leave regulations: he would need to be on duty three times a year, each time for a month. Although he would be free to work elsewhere including for foreigners when not on official duty, the demands of his official work would make it difficult to hold down a regular job. Such constraints on the freedom of commoners limited the development of skills and perpetuated poverty. The manner of the death of Seng, according to Khachon, "played a part in the issuing of the king's proclamation of 17 April 2400 [1857] that permitted Siamese people to work for the British consul". And that decree was an important landmark on the path to freedom culminating in 1905 with the abolition of slavery,[11] "within fifty years of the death of Nai Insen". The traditional ways of life thus eventually gave way to modern society with its stronger foundations, international standards of justice and friendlier relations with foreign powers:

> The world of Nai Insen is a different world, but the death of Nai Insen helped those of us in later generations to experience the modern world with prosperity, happiness and the freedom to lead our lives the way we want to.[12]

While the theories of Wilson and Khachon undoubtedly have merit, they are ultimately speculative. As such, they lie within the bounds of possibility but cannot be verified by internal records. One historian put his finger on a reason for the king's actions which accords with that declared by the king in the subsequently discovered correspondence. Manich Jumsai concluded that the dispute arose "due to the king's understanding that all Thai subjects came under his bidding" and the Seng affair was thus "the first case when it was shown to him that Thai subjects employed by the British consul no longer came under his sway".[13]

THE SENG AFFAIR AND FOREIGN PROPERTY RIGHTS

As we have seen in Chapter 2, property rights were not well developed in nineteenth century Siam; usufruct rights under which the occupier could make use for profit of someone else's land, either documented or not, were the best that most land occupiers could hope for. Similarly, the king's nominal status as owner of all land, the *chao phaendin*, was far from absolute, although when he decided to exercise his authority over particular land plots there was little either Siamese or foreign subjects could do about it.

Article IV of the Bowring treaty changed that dynamic for foreign residents only, giving them legal protection and recourse against arbitrary state action on their property. The impact is neatly illustrated by the contrasting fortunes of the land deals organised by John Hassett Chandler in 1854 and Christopher Puddicombe in 1856 – one either side of the Bowring treaty. Both transactions infuriated the king and led to the arrest of Siamese (or, quite likely, Chinese) facilitators (Nang Chang in Chandler's case; Ai-fung in Puddicombe's), while the more culpable foreigners who had devised the schemes in the first place were left unmolested. But whereas in 1854 the king's command effectively terminated Chandler's deal, in 1856 the new constraint on his authority soon became evident.

The Bowring treaty continued to frame the debate on foreign property rights well into the twentieth century, and in some ways still does.[14] In the late nineteenth and early twentieth centuries, the twenty-four-hour boundary became a fraught topic in Anglo-Siamese negotiations as many British subjects found their ownership of land, particularly in the north of the country, called into question for lying outside the permitted zone. However, by then the issue had become entangled with that of extraterritorial rights.[15]

During the Bowring treaty negotiations in 1855, both the king and the Kalahom raised concerns about the potential abuse of consular authority. The king sought an assurance from Bowring that consuls would not charge extortionate fees for services, while the Kalahom was worried that Burmese and Chinese subjects of the British might take advantage of extraterritorial provisions. Bowring was able to reassure the king that the consuls would be well paid and of good character and persuaded the Kalahom that his concern was a political issue that had no place in a purely commercial treaty.[16] But it didn't take long for the Kalahom's concerns to be realised. In early 1858, dubious claims to British protection from a Chinese man induced Schomburgk to voice his own concerns:

> I fear . . . that there are many, who not born as British Subjects, become such by naturalisation, only for the purpose or under the hope of thereby profiting themselves. If a large number of Chinese, who, for such aim become British naturalised Subjects, were to arrive at Bangkok and settle here, the whole of the Commerce would soon be in their hands and as their manner of dealing is so different from that of the upright British merchant, the latter could not contend with them. The Chinese would ultimately rule the Country, and as the Siamese Government already entertain such apprehensions, they would form the focus to which every Chinese inclined to Rebellion would resort to.[17]

But it took the British annexation of Upper Burma in 1886 and the French creation of Indochina in 1887 for the issue to become acute. Many more Asian subjects of the western powers were now entitled to claim protection under treaty provisions. The confusion over Seng's position as a Siamese subject employed by the British was largely forgotten and replaced by the much broader controversy over the status of Siamese residents of Asian descent claiming the right to be treated as subjects of the western powers, particularly Britain and France:

> As a result, Siam was deprived of jurisdiction over hosts of Cambodians, Annamites and Laos from Indo-China, Javanese, Malayans, Burmese, Chinese born in Macao or Hong Kong, and East Indians, even though residing permanently and perhaps doing an extensive business in Siam. Whatever violations of Siamese law they might commit, Siam was powerless to touch them or their property.[18]

Extraterritorial rights were originally intended to apply to the "white western races of the world, between whom and the Siamese a great gulf was fixed from a religious, ethical, social and moral standpoint", not to people of the same "race-stock" with similar "creeds and modes of life and thought" as the Siamese.[19] The problem was compounded by the growing practice of some western consuls to view the issuing of protection documents to non-Siamese Asians in Siam as a fee-earning business. The practice had acquired a financial motive as early as the 1860s when American consul James Hood faced criticism from his government for registering hundreds of Chinese protégés.[20] Apart from containing a growing population that was not subject to its jurisdiction, the danger to Siam was the potential alienation of large parts of its territory – outside the remit of both the legal system and its traditional owner, the king as *chao phaendin*; essentially threatening a form of piecemeal colonisation.

One solution, applied to Lao war captives and other communities who could claim to be French subjects, was to "suppress the ethnic origins of the enslaved Lao communities and treat them as ordinary 'Thai citizens'". This approach culminated in the 1913 Nationality Act which granted citizenship to all those born in Siam.[21] An alternative solution, first proposed by King Chulalongkorn's minister of foreign affairs, Prince Devavongse, then by the king's American advisor, Edward Henry Strobel, was to abrogate extraterritorial rights in exchange for a bundle of rights and privileges that included the right to own property, even outside the twenty-four-hour boundary.[22] Siam's ceding of Cambodian provinces to France in 1907 and Malay states to Britain in 1909 was, in one sense, an extreme manifestation of this policy.

The 1901 Land Title Deed Act had stipulated that owners of land in Siam must be subjects of the Siamese state. As Larsson pointed out, the distinction between Siamese and non-Siamese was "not based on origin or ethnicity but on jurisdiction". Thus, after the 1907 French treaty and the

1909 British treaty, certain French and British residents who no longer had extraterritorial rights would be considered Siamese to the extent that they were subject to Siamese laws.[23]

Extraterritorial rights were not fully rescinded until after the Second World War. Once they had been dealt with, the property rights that had been conceded in exchange for extraterritoriality were also soon rescinded. The new reality was enshrined in the 1954 Land Act which explicitly tied foreign property rights to the provisions in the international treaties. The process of revoking or replacing those treaties began with the US-Thailand Treaty of Amity in 1966 and was followed by eighteen more international agreements that effectively prohibited foreign land ownership, a prohibition that still remains in place.

However, as in the 1850s, there are today various exceptions to the blanket prohibition. Just as Mongkut was prepared to override the restrictions of the Bowring treaty to grant foreigners permission to purchase restricted land, more recently Thai governments have allowed the exclusion of foreigners from land ownership in the 1954 Land Act to be set aside. In both cases, the allowance has been based on the desire to facilitate foreign investors. In the modern age, these exemptions are encapsulated principally in the provisions of the 1971 Petroleum Act, the 1977 Investment Promotion Act and the 1979 Industrial Estate Authority of Thailand Act, which allow foreign companies investing substantial amounts in targeted sectors to acquire freehold land.[24]

In the 1850s, a merchant's residence was often also his place of business, which made distinctions between residential and commercial premises unhelpful. Today, the exemptions from the 1954 Land Act apply almost exclusively to commercial uses, the exception being a 1999 amendment that allows foreigners to own up to one *rai* for their own residence in certain areas and subject to strict rules, provided they also invest more than forty million baht in Thailand in assets beneficial to the country and receive ministerial approval. Foreigners are also entitled to purchase freehold units in a condominium building, but only up to a maximum of forty-nine per cent of the saleable area to ensure that effective control of the land remains in Thai hands.

Although the property provisions of the Bowring treaty and its zones have now passed into history, the terms of the debate that underlay Article IV are still relevant today. From the Siamese/Thai perspective, the dilemma was and is how to ensure the kingdom is as attractive as possible to foreign capital while at the same time protecting the land market from too much of that same foreign capital. The latter concern is regularly recited to justify the kingdom's strict restrictions on foreign ownership as well as its reluctance to consider applying the international legal principle of reciprocal rights.

In this context, the Seng affair offered a stark warning of how legal property rights, once promulgated, could be exploited and of how the authorities' scope to counter unforeseen problems would be henceforth limited by the treaty. It also offered a case study on how leasehold rights could be used as a vehicle for undermining the principles of the treaty. The incident engendered deep suspicion of long leasehold interests in the king, a suspicion that remains a core component of Siamese land policy to this day.

At the time of the Puddicombe controversy there was no official guidance on an acceptable lease length. The Phraklang was to comment later that Puddicombe's ninety-nine-year lease was excessive because it exceeded a normal lifespan and that it was "the custom of Siam" for such deeds to be limited to ten years.[25] Although the Bowring treaty was silent on this topic, the king obviously considered Puddicombe's ninety-nine years a circumvention of the freehold prohibition. Rather than endorse Puddicombe's lease, the king's response was to outflank it. He used his royal prerogative to grant land ownership to Puddicombe and went on to demonstrate his magnanimity to the foreign community by acquiescing to their requests for new roads and canals. Chandler's earlier deal was also ushered through. It is open to debate whether the king's intention was simply to make generous concessions in the spirit of his act of atonement to the British government or, more circuitously, to demonstrate his authority as the *chao phaendin* with the power to decide on who should have access to land; a show of his unlimited *sakdina* in the literal sense of "power over the fields".

Whatever the applicability of such traditional concepts, the king's opposition to Puddicombe's long lease was surprisingly contemporary. In modern property terms, the length of the lease determines its value; in theory, the longer it is, the more it resembles a freehold property with a perpetual ownership right. The value of a ten-year lease would generally be a fraction of its freehold value, but at ninety-nine years the discount from freehold value would be minimal. While the discrepancy is explained today through the exposition of discounted cash flows, the king and Puddicombe were able to reach the same conclusion by common sense.

There are few records of long leaseholds in the nineteenth century after Puddicombe. However, Mongkut's road- and canal-building policy unwittingly – and somewhat ironically – would create a wider market for leaseholds. To finance the new infrastructure, he developed the practice of granting land on both sides of new routes to noblemen who would take on the task. These nobles would recoup their investment by subdividing the newly-acquired land and renting out plots of land to rice farmers, thus becoming Siam's first professional landlords.[26] This market would continue to grow throughout the nineteenth century and take unexpected forms. A case in point was the 1889 contract with the Siam Canals, Lands and Irrigation Company to develop the Rangsit canal system. The German enterprise was granted a twenty-five-year concession to develop irrigation canals on 240,000 hectares of land in Rangsit. However, rather than subdivide the land and issue leases as the noblemen funding canal construction had done earlier in the century, the owning company decided to issue title deeds on its concession and facilitated the acquisition of these deeds by foreigners assuming a false Siamese identity.[27] As such, it was using its concession to circumvent restrictions on foreign land ownership, just as had Puddicombe some thirty years earlier. The company's monopoly position on a large land tract also allowed it to develop other income streams to the detriment of both farmers and the state, according to the irrigation engineer van der Heide. Rather than an agricultural development project, the Rangsit concession had become "a real estate business in disguise".[28] As rice exports grew, land values followed and wealthy Siamese became increasingly involved in land speculation and sub-letting to tenant farmers. Typical leases for farmers, even in Rangsit, were only for a single year. But a one-year lease offered no incentive for farmers to make long-term improvements either to the land or farming techniques, leading inevitably to deterioriating productivity and widespread suffering among tenant farming families.[29]

Codification of lease length was finally embodied in the country's 1935 Civil and Commercial Code, which limits property rental contracts to a term of thirty years with the possibility of one renewal of another thirty years. However, lawyers tend to regard such renewals as unsafe because the obligation to renew may not be enforceable on successors to the freehold title. Therefore, leases are often limited to only thirty years, especially when the freeholder is in the private sector.

While many countries limit foreign access to freehold land, Thailand is unusual in combining an effective prohibition on most foreign freeholds with one of the shortest leasehold terms. Even in its immediate region, Thailand is something of an outlier. With the possible exception of Indonesia, it has the shortest maximum leasehold period of all ten nations in its regional grouping, the Association of Southeast Asian Nations. Two of its main regional competitors, Singapore and Malaysia, allow for ninety-nine years leases, while Vietnam permits up to seventy years.[30]

While unusually limited in length, Thai leaseholds are nevertheless non-discriminatory, at least superficially. Under the Civil and Commercial Code both Thai and non-Thai citizens have an equal right to buy, sell and occupy leasehold properties. However, this is subject to the not insignificant proviso that the underlying freehold is owned by Thai interests. This discrepancy has encouraged some contemporary, creative lawyers and property developers to construct "workarounds" by developing legal structures for leases that have many of the characteristics of freehold ownership. Such structures are sometimes referred to as perpetual leasehold interests. To work effectively, the freehold needs to be owned by Thai nominee shareholders controlled by the foreign lessee. As the foreigner retains control of the structure, he is assured that the lease can be renewed repeatedly into perpetuity. Puddicombe did not need to resort to a perpetual leasehold structure, but his "workaround" was equally dependent on the co-operation of a Thai nominee owning the freehold interest.

Apart from being against the spirit of the Civil and Commercial Code, the use of nominees for holding land title is itself illegal in Thailand today. Property developments that have been sold on the basis of such leases have therefore often attracted controversy. The repercussions for the lawyers who drafted these agreements have naturally been far less dire than those that befell Seng in 1856, but the consequences for modern nominee shareholders who act as proxies for foreign money can be a longer prison term than that experienced by Ai-fung. Modern drafters have shown more sophistication and awareness of the legal issues and risks than Seng, but the mechanics of an illegal circumvention of the land law have not fundamentally altered since the days of King Mongkut.

In the wake of the 1997 Asian financial crisis, the Thai government promulgated several emergency laws designed to encourage foreign investment. Among these was an act that was designed to offer leases for an initial period of up to fifty years (with an option to renew for another fifty) for investors in commercial and industrial properties.[31] However, the new leasehold law proved to be cumbersome to implement and had limited take-up as it contained a number of requirements that were difficult to meet. More recently, the government has considered putting in place a leasehold law with an initial fifty-year term and a renewal term of forty-nine years (giving a potential total term of ninety-nine years) as a vehicle to encourage investment on government property in the Eastern Economic Corridor provinces of Chonburi, Rayong and Chachoengsao, although it is unclear whether the provisions would be substantially less burdensome. It is interesting to note the persistence of the ninety-nine-year benchmark as a targeted leasehold length from the 1850s to the present day.

Another recent proposal to liberalise the leasehold regulations – this time emanating from the Thai, not foreign, business community – also envisioned a ninety-nine-year lease. In 2016, leading Thai property developers submitted a proposal through the Thai Chamber of Commerce to the government to amend the maximum leasehold term under the Civil and Commercial Code to ninety-nine years to bring it into line with Singapore and Malaysia. The ministry of the interior rejected the proposal on the grounds that the Civil and Commercial Code was designed to protect the rights of individuals – and individuals have a limited lifespan (though, presumably, most can expect to live longer than thirty years, the current maximum lease term) – and suggested that other countries may allow longer leases to compensate for the fact that all land is nominally owned by the state, unlike in Thailand where private land ownership is permitted. The latter point may be relevant to the longer leases available in countries such as Vietnam and China, but not to Singapore and Malaysia.

If official reasons for opposing the lengthening of leasehold rights ring hollow, a more likely explanation can be inferred from the reaction of Mongkut to the Puddicombe lease in 1856. The core issue for both Mongkut and the Thai authorities today is that a long leasehold interest blurs the distinction between freehold and leasehold rights and thus creates a level playing field for foreign investors. Today, some would consider this undesirable because of a perception that the weight of foreign capital could deprive local citizens of the ability to purchase land in their own country. This is often expressed questionably as a concern that smallholder farmers will lose their land to foreign capitalists. A more significant threat is arguably to large local landowners, developers and investors, who control the most valuable land in the country.

It is probable that Mongkut held similar concerns. At one level, he took Puddicombe's lease as a personal affront. He considered Puddicombe a friend who had gone behind his back. He was to tell Puddicombe that if he had requested permission to buy the land, it would have been granted. Yet within the context of the Bowring treaty, the king did clearly view the full opening up of the land market to foreigners as an undesirable outcome. As land was still abundant, the threat to smallholder farmers was not a major concern; rather, foreigners should be prohibited from buying land in remote places, because they might be attacked by ignorant locals which could lead to conflict with the foreign powers. The purpose of creating a zone restricted to leaseholds in Bangkok, however, had more in common with modern concerns. The principal landowners were concerned for their competitive position in this zone and the ten-year residential qualification was imposed to ensure that only a limited number of localised foreigners would be enabled to compete for freehold land.

The fallout of the Seng affair brought home to the Siamese that the old way of doing things had changed. First, certain Siamese subjects were now entitled to the protection of foreign governments. Second, the king's already-compromised status as *chao phaendin* could be subject to further diminution in the face of western demands. As a response to these new threats, the king's approach was to accede to the new limits while simultaneously affirming his continuing authority over the land. Today, it is remarkable to observe that while the Thai economy and social attitudes have developed in many different respects, the official attitude to, and policy direction of, foreign property rights has changed so little over the last 165 years. Other than through the foreign ownership quota of the Condominium Act, the only avenues to property ownership for foreigners remain limited leasehold rights, special-purpose laws, the discretionary powers of a minister and, illegally, the use of nominee Thai shareholders.

MOVING WITH THE TIMES

There was no exemption from the Article IV provisions of the Bowring treaty for diplomatic use. So even without the Seng affair the British would have needed the king to exercise his discretionary authority in 1856 to allow them to acquire land for the consulate. Nevertheless, the Seng affair not only expedited the process, it also brought about a windfall gain that has continued to benefit the British government right up to the present day.

The British government was to remain the beneficiary of the king's land grant for some seventy years, first as a consulate and from 1895 as a legation, before relocating in the 1920s. By then, the riverside was no longer the prime residential location it once was. The compounds of the past were being replaced with commercial properties. The location was no longer peaceful, with noise and sometimes noxious fumes emanating from trams and traffic on the main and access roads, steamers on the river, a nearby temple and a bar on the other side of the road. Moreover:

> Apart from the adverse surroundings the houses are crude in construction and finish; the contrast between them and the modern residences, native and foreign, in the suburbs, is now very marked, gives rise to unfavourable comment, and is probably not without some effect on our national prestige. In the legation house the accommodation too is limited and inconveniently arranged for family purposes and there is little privacy in the bathroom and W.C. arrangements.[32]

Given such constraints, the building was considered unsuitable for a married minister, and it was recommended that until a new house was ready, only bachelors should be appointed.

Timing the land market was also an issue. A British government report noted that land prices in the new residential areas had quadrupled between 1907 and 1921, with further increases anticipated. On the other hand, the value of the riverside location had depreciated substantially from over 300 to around 125 ticals per square *wah*, the main causes being new roads opening up new sites at prices under 100 ticals per square *wah* and increased motor traffic making distance less of an obstacle. River frontage still commanded some premium, but the market was weak: "there is no money and no market for land at present." Yet waiting for a stronger market was not a good option because the price differential between the current and proposed locations would only increase.

The British treasury in 1908 had insisted that any move would have to be self-financed. The initial target was a site first proposed in 1908/09: King's College in Sapathum district, which contained a palace built by Chulalongkorn for the crown prince and known as Windsor Palace due to some physical similarities with England's Windsor Castle. At the

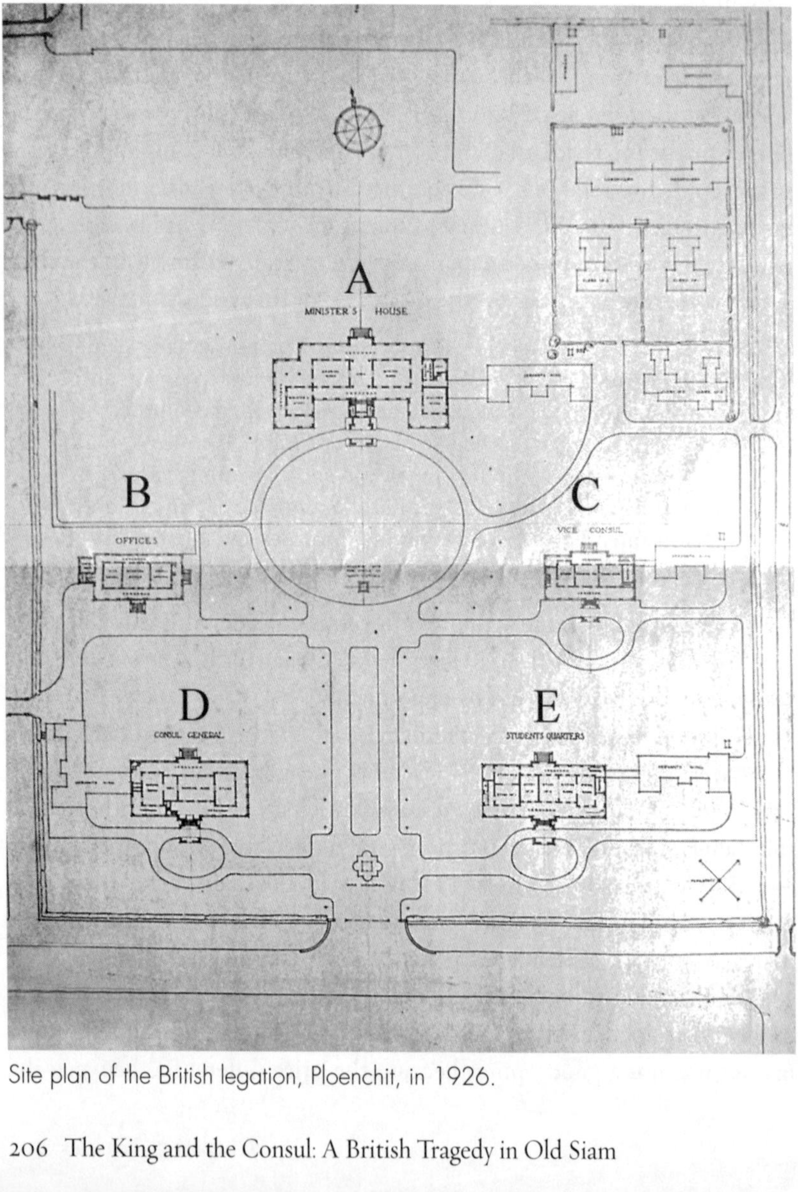

Site plan of the British legation, Ploenchit, in 1926.

time, the property was occupied by the royal pages department and used as an agricultural college. But the price tag at 40 ticals per square *wah* was considered "outrageous" by the British, while there was also doubt the deal could be consummated as the land had been presented to the royal pages department by the king. The exchange rate had also moved against the British, from 13 ticals to the pound before the First World War to 9.4 ticals in the early 1920s. As a result, the redevelopment of the King's College site would cost one-third more in pounds than the pre-war estimate, resulting in a net new cost to the British government of some £50,000. The British considered waiting a couple of years in the hope that the exchange rate would revert to the pre-war "norm" but finding a cheaper deal would be preferable.[33] The opportunity passed and the land was later used to found Chulalongkorn University. The palace was demolished in the 1930s for the construction of the National Stadium, now on Rama I Road.

A local businessman came to the rescue. Nai Lert Sreshthaputra, or Phra Bhakdi, adjudged "one of the few enterprising Siamese that exist", first proposed a slightly less expensive option, but finally came up with an alternative at the much cheaper price of eight ticals per square wah. This was the site on Ploenchit Road, also in Sapathum, that was to become the home of the British government for over ninety years. The deal eventually struck was even sweeter for the British: Phra Bhakdi agreed to give them some eleven acres (11,000 square *wah*) of land at no cost at all in exchange for a two-year option to buy the riverside land at 1,100,000 ticals (estimated at £117,021 at the time) less 250 square *wah* to be retained by the British for a shipping office. Moreover, Phra Bhakdi agreed to transfer the freehold at Ploenchit to the British government immediately and would allow the British to occupy the Bangrak site rent free for twelve months after he exercised his option.

For Phra Bhakdi, the deal had significant benefits. Though he would not achieve his asking price in selling to the British government, he retained possession of some sixteen acres adjacent to the new legation site, which he anticipated would increase in value more quickly with the British next door. The land retained by Phra Bhakdi would eventually be developed into a luxury hotel and mostly sold by his descendants to BDMS, a Thai hospital group in 2016 for 10.8 billion Thai baht, with the family retaining part of the land containing the historic family residence.

The British legation, Ploenchit, in the 1920s.

Phra Bhakdi would also gain a much more immediate benefit from the deal as he had arranged to flip the Bangrak land to the Siamese government for use as the new general post office. At the time the deal was being finalised, the British understood that Phra Bhakdi would deliver the Bangrak land to the Siamese government at the option price of 1,100,00 ticals in exchange for a grant of government land elsewhere.[34] However, the price to be paid to him would amount to some 1,800,000 ticals, giving him an immediate return of over 60 per cent.[35] Unsurprisingly, he quickly exercised his option, paying the Treasury in full within three months of signing the agreement on 23 March 1922.

While the British may not have known the pricing in Phra Bhakdi's back-to-back deal, from their point of view his offer was virtually risk-free and met all their requirements. Even though they had not maximised their selling price, at 140 ticals per square *wah* they had achieved a price some twelve per cent higher than their estimate. Moreover, the potential problem of disposing of the old site in a weak market was averted. It was also important that the British should not be seen to make a large profit from the sale. There was pressure from the Siamese government for the British not to remit the sale proceeds oversees as that would make a bad impression: "as the funds were provided by them [the Siamese government], they expect the money to remain in the country". There was another sensitivity that the British may well have considered, namely "the old question of the claim of the Siamese Government" to the riverside property. Before the First World War, there had been discussion within the foreign office that if the Siamese authorities wanted the property returned, they should be prepared to pay full market value for it, unless they were to provide a new site in exchange (which was considered unlikely). In the end, no serious consideration was given to returning the land granted by Mongkut to the Siamese state.[36]

The British could also be satisfied with the new site. It was almost half as large again as the riverside property and judged "the best available", as it came equipped with connections to roads, canals, electricity and water. It was also partially filled, which would reduce development costs. In the worst case, if Phra Bhakdi failed to exercise his option, they would still be able to develop or sell the land, which was estimated to be worth £11,000 – a conservative estimate compared to Phra Bhakdi's no doubt excessive valuation of around £40,000. More importantly, the estimated cost of developing the new site at £116,000 meant that the new purchase could be fully funded from the sale of the old property, thus adhering to the treasury guideline for self-funding. Indeed, the transaction should result in a net gain of almost £1,000. A proforma statement amended on 5 March 1929 indicates that the margin was maintained despite the British deciding to purchase a large pond next to the site for 40,000 ticals.[37] The additional cost was covered by the 50,000 ticals earned by selling the shipping office site that was originally to be retained, but eventually deemed surplus to requirements.

However, the move in the 1920s was not without controversy. Sir Robert Greg, who served as envoy extraordinary and minister plenipotentiary during the development of the new premises had at first doubted the wisdom of the move. Apart from regret at giving up the "charm and picturesqueness" of the river front site, the move also removed the British flag from a prominent position on the river. According to Greg's successor, Sir Sydney Waterlow, "The Siamese were glad to see it go; its position there was a symbol of a state of things which is dead and buried." Waterlow was the first ambassador to reside in the new premises, moving in on 22 September 1926. Both he and Greg were to overcome their reservations and come to see the merits of the move. The new compound was "spacious", "admirably planned and furnished with every modern device for comfort and coolness". Being "on the edge of open country" made it a healthier environment than the river front site increasingly surrounded by commercial developments. The minister's house was "spacious, dignified and comfortable", "delightful to live in" and "well calculated to enhance the prestige of His Majesty's Government in this country"; a welcome contrast to the riverside residence which was "insanitary, small, inconvenient, tumble-down, noisy, dirty and hot".[38]

As had been expected, over the course of the twentieth century the city of Bangkok radiated further out from its original focus around the royal quarter, Samphaeng and Bangrak, developing to the north and east. When a decision was made in the mid-2000s to sell the Ploenchit site, which had been upgraded to an embassy property in 1947, the location was now at the heart of the country's prime commercial district, surrounded by retail complexes, hotels, office buildings and residential towers. Financial pressure on the foreign and commonwealth office had led to a review of global holdings. The Bangkok property stood out as one of the most valuable in the portfolio and considered an unwarranted luxury, especially as funding was now needed to build or repair a number of other properties around the world.

The sale was bifurcated. A plot of slightly less than nine rai (14,400 square metres) fronting Ploenchit Road was sold first for 3.4 billion baht (£50 million) in 2006 to the Central Group, Thailand's largest retailer, which developed a luxury retail mall and five-star hotel on the site. The remaining 23 rai was sold in 2018 to the same group, this time in partnership with Hongkong Land, a unit of Jardine Matheson Group, for around 18 billion baht (£425 million).[39] Some of the proceeds of each sale were retained in Thailand for either improvements to existing buildings (£11 million budgeted in 2006) or acquiring new properties after the 2018 sale. Nevertheless, each sale was FCO's largest ever disposal

The British legation, Ploenchit, minister's residence in the 1920s.

when they occurred, the second sale also being reported as the largest ever property transaction in Thailand. The embassy moved into rented office space on Sathorn Road and the ambassador's residence was housed on the 66th floor of a brand-new luxury condominium project on Charoenkrung Road. Ironically, the residence was now back on the same road as the original Bangrak property, fronting the Chaophraya river. The location is some two kilometres south of the property opened by Schomburgk in 1858, close to the site of the original offices of Samuel Gilfillan and the Borneo Company.

Queen Victoria statue at the entrance to the British legation, Bangrak, in 1907.

HILLIER'S SHADOW

British embassy compound, Bangkok, 2020

The sale of the Ploenchit embassy site reflected a trend among foreign governments to dispose of the legacy properties in Bangkok they had acquired in the nineteenth and twentieth centuries. While some foreign governments still retain their historic properties and freehold ownership in Bangkok, others, such as the Japanese and Australian governments, have also recently sold prime land to move into leasehold properties, albeit in purpose-built dedicated buildings rather than within a multi-tenanted office building. Such moves constitute a tacit realisation that the exemption of foreign governments from the kingdom's strict land ownership laws no longer holds value commensurate with the opportunity cost of retaining landed assets.

For the British government, the opportunity cost was just too large to overlook. The chain of events set in motion by Hillier's negotiation to buy a plot of land in 1856 had led to the British government being granted free land that was later transformed into a larger site at no new net cost in the 1920s and would finally be monetised into a value of some £475 million in the first two decades of the twenty-first century. The *quid pro quo* in the nineteenth century had been to relinquish extraterritorial rights for property rights. In the more transactional contemporary era, the *quid pro quo* has been to relinquish property rights for cash.

The British government's financial calculation failed to factor in the accumulated soft power and prestige that had become associated with the Ploenchit site over the years. The extensive embassy grounds formed a green oasis in the heart of Bangkok's urban sprawl, with mature trees and gardens surrounding the elegant ambassador's residence, fronted by the war memorial and backed by the imposing bronze statue of Queen Victoria, both monuments funded by British residents over a hundred years previously. The residence had become a popular location for social and business events, with the most senior Thai and expatriate dignitaries attracted in part by the charm of its unique physical attributes. It had also provided a spectacular venue for annual ceremonial events, such as Armistice Day, and highlights of the social calendar, such as the popular Ploenchit Fair. But most of all it was seen as a symbol of Britain's continued commitment to Thailand. Its sale, coinciding with Britain's exit from the European Union, was viewed by some as a sign of the United Kingdom's retreat from the unique position of global influence and importance that it had enjoyed in the kingdom since the 1850s.

Much of the prestige of the Ploenchit site was bound up in its historic assets. Their fate reflected the new reality. The war memorial to commemorate British servicemen in Siam who had died in the First World War, the first structure erected on the Ploenchit land when it was unveiled on 10 January 1923, was relocated in 2019 to the British Club between Silom and Surawongse Roads where it could retain some connection with its heritage. The ambassador's residence would have come under increasing pressure to be preserved as a heritage building as it reached the age of one hundred some six years later. Under Thailand's 1961 Ancient Monument Act, the registration of historic or heritage buildings is at the discretion of the director-general of the department of fine arts. However, the process can be influenced by civil society. Instead, the residence was demolished by the new owners with a promise to rebuild it or something similar on part of the site. Most incongruously of all, the statue of Queen Victoria was to be handed over to the new owners of the property.

The fate of the queen's statue inevitably carried singular symbolic resonance: the embodiment of Britain's imperial grandeur celebrated at the 1851 Great Exhibition was to become an ornament for a commercial development one hundred and seventy years later. The statue was a reproduction of an original in Winchester by Alfred Gilbert and showed the monarch "seated upon a throne, crowned, bearing sceptre and orb, and arrayed in the robes of State".[40] Bangkok's British residents – incidentally, mostly Chinese British subjects – had raised 20,000 ticals (£1,275) for it in 1901 and saw it unveiled on 23 March 1905 by Siam's crown prince with four of his senior ministers in attendance. It was then located on and facing Charoenkrung Road, outside the compound fence. On moving to the Ploenchit site, the statue was placed in front of the ambassador's residence within the site, facing out to Ploenchit Road. Local women came to think of the statue as a symbol of fecundity and were known to pray to it for the gift of children (as well as guidance in buying lottery tickets). During the Second World War, the occupying Japanese reportedly bricked in the statue, but still showed a modicum of respect by leaving "a slit opposite Queen Victoria's eyes so that she could see out".[41] In 2006, after the first tranche of the Ploenchit sale was completed, the statue was moved to the rear of the residence, now facing the building's back door, attracting unflattering comments at the time that it represented a turning inwards and away from the former greatness of Britain.

Although we are yet to see how the new owners of the Ploenchit land will dispose of the statue, its assumed incorporation into a commercial property project horrified those who fretted about the potential Disneyfication of the queen. The prospect amplified concerns at what appeared to be the British government's indifference to non-financial assets and lack of respect for history and the bilateral relationship. Proponents of the deal were equally disdainful of what they viewed as sentimental nostalgia for the emblems of empire. From this perspective, the statue's fate could be seen as representing the democratisation of public assets. It would allow a new generation of locals and tourists at all levels of society to appreciate Britain's most powerful queen, although modern pilgrims would be more likely to value her contribution to their photographs, rather than to the size of their households, as perhaps had some of their grandmothers. Indeed, it could be argued, the sale signalled Britain's post-EU opening up to a new world of opportunities, or in the words of Boris Johnson, the man destined to be prime minister the following year: "Recalibrating the relationship for the twenty-first century! Onwards and upwards!"

Glossary

Brief explanations of Thai terms that appear in the book. Quotations may contain variant spellings.

angrit: English or British.

biawat: annual gift of money from the king.

chamnam: to pledge.

Chakri: the royal family or dynasty that has reigned in Siam/Thailand since 1782.

chanode tra daeng: a title deed with a red seal that was used to designate rights to paddy fields. Other types of title deeds available included ***chanode suan*** (garden title deeds) for orchards, ***chanode paa*** (jungle title deeds) for perennial cash crops such as vegetables and sugar cane, ***bai yeab yam*** (title deeds to trample on) largely for short-term use and ***tra jong*** (reserved title deeds) for longer-term use.[1]

chao phaendin: lord of the land, used to refer to the king.

Chao Muen: a title for a nobleman below Phraya and above Phra.

Chaophraya: a royally-conferred senior title for a nobleman, sometimes equated with "duke".

Chaosua: a wealthy Chinese man.

farang: a foreigner from a western country.

hang: store or shop.

Kalahom: the ministry responsible for military affairs (see also: Cast of characters).

khaluang duem: a person who was formally in the service of the king.

khai fak: to sell with conditions, including the right to redeem.

Khun: a title for a nobleman ranked below Luang.

khun nang: a nobleman or the nobility.

krom: a government department.

kru: teacher.

Krungthep: The Thai name for Bangkok, with the literal meaning of city of angels. It is a shortened form of the extraordinarily long full formal name: Krung Thep Mahanakhon Amon Rattanakosin Mahinthara

Ayutthaya Mahadilok Phop Noppharat Ratchathani Burirom Udomratchaniwet Mahasathan Amon Piman Awatan Sathit Sakkathattiya Witsanukam Prasit.

Luang: a title for a nobleman ranked below Phra, sometimes equated with "baron".

mahatlek: the royal pages department.

Mahatthai: the ministry responsible for civilian affairs.

mueang: a town or city.

Muen: a title for a nobleman ranked below Luang, sometimes equated with "baronet".

Nai: a title for low-ranking officials.

Nang: the wife of an official.

Phraklang: the ministry responsible for foreign trade (see also: Cast of characters).

Phra: a title for a senior nobleman ranked below Phraya, sometimes equated with "viscount".

phrai: a commoner obliged to work for the government for part of the year.

Phraya: a title for a senior nobleman ranked below Chaophraya, sometimes equated with "earl".

picul: a unit of weight equivalent to around 60 kilogrammes.

parian: a learned monk, a degree-holder with knowledge of the Pali language.

rai: a land measurement equivalent to around 0.4 acres or 1,600 square metres.

Rattanakosin: the royal city area of Bangkok; also refers to the period of the Chakri dynasty.

sakdina: system of ranking the population.

salung: one quarter of a tical.

sen: a land measurement equivalent to around 40 metres, or 20 *wah*.

senabodi or ***senaputi***: a senior minister or council of senior ministers.

sok: a land measurement equivalent to around 50 centimetres, or one quarter of a *wah*. The *sok* was originally based on the length of the forearm to the tip of the middle finger, like the cubit (generally, 18 inches).

Somdet Chaophraya: highest royally-conferred title for a nobleman with only four recipients in history.

thamboon: to do good deeds, make merit.

Thammayut: a Buddhist reform sect formed by Mongkut before he became king.

Than Phuying: a title for the wife of a senior nobleman.

tical: baht.

tuk: a building.

uparat: the second or vice king, sometimes translated as "viceroy".

wah or ***wa***: a land measurement equivalent to 2 metres. It is also still used colloquially to mean "square *wah*" (4 square metres). The *wah* originally denoted the length between the extreme points of the middle fingers of both hands of a man with outstretched arms, like the fathom (6 feet).

wat: A Buddhist temple.

Yommarat: the ministry responsible for the capital city.

Source notes

Cast of characters

1 Nattawut, *Srisuriyawong*, vol. 2, p. 976.

Introduction

1 Thongchai, "The Quest for '*Siwilai*'", p. 541.

2 Martin, "Staging China, Japan, and Siam", p. 139.

3 From British consular reports summarised in Peter Sek, "Anglo-Siamese Economic Relations", p. 46.

4 See, for instance, Hong, "Stranger Within the Gates" and Thongchai, *Siam Mapped.*

5 Bowring's account is mostly found in *Kingdom and People of Siam*, vol. 2, pp. 248-337; Parkes' is in NA (UK), FO 17/229, Parkes & Bowring Jnr to Bowring, 1 April 1855 and "Bowring's Embassy: Journal" by Parkes, enclosures 2 and 15 in Bowring to Clarendon, 28 April 1855, pp. 167-183 and pp. 224-279.

Chapter 1: Bowring's 'total revolution'

1 NA (UK): FO 17/229, "Bowring's Embassy: Journal", enclosure 15, Bowring to Clarendon, 28 April 1855, p. 274; Bowring, *Kingdom and People of Siam*, vol. 2, p. 327.

2 NA (UK): FO 17/229, "Bowring's Embassy: Journal", enclosure 15, Bowring to Clarendon, 28 April 1855, pp. 274-275.

3 Vella, *Siam Under Rama III*, p. 23.

4 NA (UK): FO 97/268, Hammond to Clarendon, 21 February 1853, pp. 51.

5 For first-hand accounts of Brooke's failed mission, see Brooke's own extensive notes in NA (UK): FO 69/1, Brooke to Palmerston, 5 October 1850, pp. 67 ff. and FO 69/2, pp. 114 ff, and the account given by his secretary and amanuensis, Spenser St John, in *Life of Sir James Brooke*, pp. 217-225. For a more recent analysis, see Tarling, "Siam and Sir James Brooke", pp. 43-72.

6 NA (UK): FO 69/1, Brooke to Palmerston, 5 October 1850, pp. 69-70.

7 NA (UK): FO 69/1, Prince Mongkut to Messrs. Hamilton, Grey & Co., undated, p. 166.

8 *Phraratchalekha phrachomklaochaoyuhua*, p. 57. Also see NL (Th): 1218/137.

9 NA (UK): FO 69/3, Phraya Si Suriyawong to Brooke, 23 April 1851, p. 91.

10 NA (UK): FO 69/1, Mongkut to Messrs. Hamilton, Grey & Co., Singapore, p. 166.

11 P. Bowring, *Free Trade's First Missionary*, p. 229.

12 Bowring, *Kingdom and People of Siam*, vol. 2, pp. 260, 269, 286

13 Winai and Theera, *Writings of Mongkut to Bowring*, 31 July 1857, p. 60.

14 NA (UK): FO 17/211, Clarendon to Bowring, 25 November 1854, pp. 209-210.

15 NA (UK): FO 17/210, Clarendon to Bowring, 13 February 1854, p. 69.

16 NA (UK): FO 17/210, Clarendon to Bowring, 8 June 1854, pp. 235-239.

17 NA (UK): FO 17/217, Bowring to Clarendon, 27 November 1854, p. 248. For unfavourable comparisons of Stirling's convention with the US treaty with Japan, see FO 17/217, Bowring to Clarendon, 29 November 1854, p. 315 and FO 17/225 Clarendon to Bowring, 27 July 1855, pp. 65-70.

18 NA (UK): FO 17/215, Bowring to Clarendon, 22 August 1854, p. 212.

19 NA (UK): FO 17/214 Bowring to Clarendon, 15 June 1854; FO 17/226 Bowring to Clarendon, 6 January 1855, pp. 84-85; and FO 17/228, Bowring to Clarendon, 5 March 1855, pp. 144-145.

20 NA (UK): FO 17/229, Phraklang to Bowring, February 1855, enclosure in Bowring to Clarendon, 28 April 1855, pp. 122-128.

21 P. Bowring, *Free Trade's First Missionary*, p. 115.

22 NA (UK): FO 17/226, Phraklang to Bowring, 20 November 1854, enclosure in Bowring to Clarendon, 6 January 1855, pp. 88-89.

23 NA (UK): FO 17/229, 'Bowring's Embassy: Journal,' enclosure 15, Bowring to Clarendon, 28 April 1855, pp. 233-234.

24 Bowring, *Kingdom and People of Siam*, vol. 2, pp. 282-283.

25 Ibid., p. 287.

26 Both quoted in Cosenza, *Journal of Townsend Harris*, p. 113n.

27 Bowring, *Kingdom and People of Siam*, vol. 2, p. 304.

28 As reported to Parkes by Bell and quoted in NA (UK): FO 17/236, Parkes to Hammond, 10 September 1855, p. 114.

29 Quoted in Bell's report to Bowring, 1 September 1855, enclosure 2 in NA (UK): FO 17/234, Bowring to Clarendon, 18 October 1855, pp. 80-83.

30 NA (UK): FO 17/229, "Bowring's Embassy: Journal", enclosure 15, Bowring to Clarendon, 28 April 1855, pp. 239-240.

31 Bowring, *Kingdom and People of Siam*, vol. 2, p. 278.

32 Vella, *Siam Under Rama III*, pp. 135, 140.

33 Bowring, *Kingdom and People of Siam*, vol. 2, p. 277-278.

34 NA (UK): FO 17/229, 'Bowring's Embassy: Journal', enclosure 15, Bowring to Clarendon, 28 April 1855, p. 236.

35 Bowring, *Kingdom and People of Siam*, vol. 2, p. 289.

36 Ibid., p. 294.

37 NA (UK): FO 17/229, "Bowring's Embassy: Journal", enclosure 15, Bowring to Clarendon, 28 April 1855, p. 238.

38 Ibid., p. 246.

39 Ibid., p. 247.

40 Ibid, p. 254.

41 Bowring, *Kingdom and People of Siam*, vol. 2, p. 289.

42 NA (UK): FO 17/229, "Bowring's Embassy: Journal", enclosure 15, Bowring to Clarendon, 28 April 1855, p. 246.

43 Sng and Pimpraphai, *History of the Thai-Chinese*, p. 159.

44 Khun Pimpraphai has suggested that 'Chay Sootsun' may more probably be read as "Chaosua Sun", though his background remains unclear.

45 According to Bell in his report dated 1 August 1855, enclosure 1 in NA (UK): FO 17/234 Bowring to Clarendon, 18 October 1855, p. 73.

46 NA (UK): FO 17/229, "Bowring's Embassy: Journal", enclosure 15, Bowring to Clarendon, 28 April 1855, p. 258.

47 Ibid., p. 238.

48 Ibid., pp. 265-266.

49 Bowring, *Kingdom and People of Siam*, vol. 2, p. 226.

50 NA (UK): FO 17/229, Bowring to Clarendon, 25 April 1855, p. 95.

51 Terwiel, "The Bowring Treaty", p. 45.

52 Hong, *Thailand in the Nineteenth Century*, p. 68.

53 Kullada, *Thai Absolutism*, pp. 32-33.

54 NA (UK): FO 17/216, Bowring to Mongkut, 15 September 1854, p. 82.

55 Bowring, *Kingdom and People of Siam*, vol. 2, p. 183n.

56 Neon, "Siamese Relations with Britain and France", pp. 20-21.

57 NA (UK): FO 17/229, "Bowring's Embassy: Journal", enclosure 15, Bowring to Clarendon, 28 April 1855, p. 248.

58 Lord, "Missionaries, Thai, and Diplomats", p. 418.

59 Bowring, *Kingdom and People of Siam*, vol. 2, p. 286.

60 NA (UK): FO 17/229, "Bowring's Embassy: Journal", enclosure 15, Bowring to Clarendon, 28 April 1855, pp. 245-246.

61 Larsson, *Land and Loyalty*, p. 35.

Chapter 2: Parkes and property rights and wrongs

1 Translatated by Edward Forrest in NA (UK): FO 69/5, Parkes to Clarendon, 23 May 1856, enclosure 7, p. 112.

2 P. Bowring, *Free Trade's First Missionary*, p. 131.

3 Lane-Poole, *Life of Harry Parkes*, vol. 1, p. vi.

4 NA (UK): FO 228/207, Parkes to Clarendon, 5 March 1856, pp. 4-9.

5 For a detailed statement on the intended and eventual distribution of presents, see NA (UK): FO 17/265, Parkes to Bowring, 12 March 1857, pp. 205-213

6 NA (UK): FO 69/5, Parkes to Clarendon, 23 May 1856, 86 and enclosure 10, Drought to Parkes, 1 May 1856, p. 123.

7 Feltus, *Bradley's Journal*, 29 May 1856, p. 189.

8 Bowring, *Kingdom and People of Siam*, vol. 2, pp. 275, 278; NA (UK): FO 69/5, Parkes to Clarendon, 23 May 1856, pp. 42-43; NL (Th): R4, 1227/117.

9 Kullada, *Thai Absolutism*, pp. 33-34.

10 NA (UK): FO 69/5, Parkes to Clarendon, 23 May 1856, pp. 44-46.

11 Ibid., p. 80.

12 NA (UK): FO 17/236, Parkes to Wodehouse, 7 December 1855, pp. 188-190.

13 Tarling, "Harry Parkes' Negotiations", pp. 172-174.

14 NA (UK): FO 69/5, Parkes to Hammond, 10 June 1856, p. 185.

15 NA (UK): FO 69/5, Parkes to Clarendon, 23 May 1856, pp. 65, 67.

16 Ibid., p. 36.

17 Baker and Pasuk, *History of Ayutthaya*, p. 181.

18 Low, "Laws of Mu'ung Thai", pp. 336-337.

19 Lingat, *Prawatisat kotmai thai*, pp. 36-37.

20 Feeny, "Decline of Property Rights", p. 290.

21 Thanyaporn and Jessica, *Economic History of Land Rights*, p. 84.

22 "Prakat rang phraratchahatlekha phraratchathan na phra chao luk thoe", 1223 (1861), in Charnvit, *Prachum prakat ratchakan thi 4*, pp. 295-296, translated in Chatthip and Suthy, *Political Economy 1851-1910*, pp. 231-232.

23 "Phra borom ratchaongan rueang phra ratchakamnot wa doi phra ratchathan thi ban ruen na suan", 1222 (1860), translated in Chatthip and Suthy, *Political Economy 1851-1910*, pp. 226-230, and in *Socio-Economic Institutions*, pp. 1-3.

24 Quaritch Wales, *Ancient Siamese Government*, p. 30.

25 Akin, *Organization of Thai Society*, p. 28.

26 Jit, "The Real Face of Thai Saktina Today", p. 140.

27 Quaritch Wales, *Ancient Siamese Government*, p. 35.

28 For more on the *sakdina* system, see Akin, *Organization of Thai Society*, especially chs 2.2, 6, 7.3; Brummelhuis, *King of the Waters*, ch. 2.2; Chai-anan, *Sakdina*; Jit, "Real Face of Thai Saktina", pp. 88-95; Damrong, "Laksana Kanphokhrong", p. 19; Quaritch Wales, *Ancient Siamese Government*, especially ch. 3; Tanabe, "Land Reclamation", pp. 70-71 and 73n; and Terwiel, *Thailand's Political History*, pp. 20-25.

29 Sng and Pimpraphai, *History of the Thai-Chinese*, pp. 132, 136.

30 La Loubère, *Kingdom of Siam*, p. 11.

31 Baker and Pasuk, *History of Ayutthaya*, p. 203.

32 Van Roy, *Siamese Melting Pot*, p. 4.

33 Sng and Pimpraphai, *History of the Thai-Chinese*, p. 107.

34 Van Roy, *Siamese Melting Pot*, map on p. 26 and *passim*.

35 Ibid., p. 61.

36 Pallegoix, *Description of the Thai Kingdom*, pp. 386, 407.

37 Van Roy, *Siamese Melting Pot*, pp. 62, 65.

38 Van Roy, *Siamese Melting Pot*, pp. 210-211; Pallegoix, *Description of the Thai Kingdom*, pp. 400, 407.

39 See Chatthip, *Thai Village Economy*, pp. 9-15, for a succinct summary of pre-Bowring property rights.

40 "Phra borom ratchaongan rueang phra ratchakamnot wa doi phra ratchathan thi ban ruen na suan", 1222 (1860), translated in Chatthip and Suthy, *Political Economy 1851-1910*, pp. 226-230, and in *Socio-Economic Institutions*, pp. 1-3.

41 Lingat, *Prawatisat kotmai thai*, p. 41.

42 Damrong, "Introduction of Western Culture", p. 94.

43 Translated from the Letter of Concession dated 9 November 1820 in Portuguese in Cunha, "1820 Land Concession", p. 148.

44 Adey Moore, "An Early Merchant in Bangkok", p. 46.

45 Neale, *Narrative of a Residence*, p. 46.

46 Crawfurd, *Journal of an Embassy*, vol. 1, p. 187.

47 *The Crawfurd Papers*, Crawfurd to Swinton, 3 April 1823, pp. 161, 163.

48 *The Burney Papers*, vol. 1.1, 15 February 1826, pp. 160, 178.

49 Wood, *Fankwei*, p. 230.

50 Bowring, *Kingdom and People of Siam*, vol. 2, pp. 61-62.

51 Burney treaty, Article VII.

52 *The Burney Papers*, vol. 2.5, Burney's mission to Siam, p. 144; vol. 2.4, Malloch's journal, p. 230.

53 Adey Moore, "An Early Merchant in Bangkok", pp. 34-35.

54 *The Burney Papers*, vol. 4.3, Butterworth to W. Edwards, 13 February 1845, p. 161.

55 Adey Moore, "An Early Merchant in Bangkok", p. 22.

56 Ibid., pp. 24, 21.

57 Earl, *Eastern Seas*, pp. 175-176, 162.

58 Neale, *Narrative of a Residence*, pp. 32-33

59 Earl, *Eastern Seas*, pp. 161-162.

60 Earl provided a first-hand account of witnessing Hunter's efforts to dispose of his 'contraband' opium, *Eastern Seas*, pp. 156, 178, 180.

61 *The Burney Papers*, vol. 4.3, Hayes to Butterworth, 1 November 1843, pp. 92-94.

62 *The Burney Papers*, vol. 4.3, Butterworth to Edwards, 13 February 1845, pp. 162-163, 165; Butterworth to Hunter, 19 March 1844, p. 169.

63 Ibid.

64 *The Burney Papers*, vol. 4.3, Hunter to Butterworth, 6 February 1845, pp. 175-176.

65 NA (UK): FO 69/2, "Extracts from the Correspondence of Hunter & Hayes", undated, enclosure 19 in Brooke to Palmerston, 5 October 1850, p. 133. The consideration of the extra payment as "ground-rent for the buildings &c." is from the complaint of James Hayes dated 7 October 1850, enclosure 27 in the same dispatch, p. 140.

66 Roberts treaty, Article VII.

67 Charles Robinson, "Protestant Missions of Siam: A Sketch of the origin of the first Protestant Mission to Siam, with an account of the first Missionaries, their reception by the Siamese labors &c." in Bradley, *Bangkok Calendar, 1866*, p. 69.

68 Neale, *Narrative of a Residence*, p. 46.

69 Described as six square rods in Bradley, *Bangkok Calendar, 1870*, p. 91 and McFarland, *Historical Sketches*, p. 11.

70 Bradley, *Bangkok Calendar, 1870*, p. 91.

71 Feltus, *Bradley's Journal*, 5 September 1835, p. 11.

72 McFarland, *Historical Sketches*, pp. 13-14.

73 Feltus, *Bradley's Journal*, 6 September, 12 September and 1 October 1835, pp. 11-12.

74 Bradley, *Bangkok Calendar, 1870*, pp. 100-101.

75 Ruschenberger, *Voyage Round the World*, p. 336.

76 McFarland, *Historical Sketches*, p. 15.

77 Feltus, *Bradley's Journal*, 26 February and 8 April 1838, pp. 50.

78 McFarland, *Historical Sketches*, p. 41.

79 Mattoon, "Life of Mattoon", pp. 13-14.

80 Quoted in Feltus, *Samuel Reynolds House*, p. 103.

81 McFarland, *Historical Sketches*, p. 31.

82 Feltus, *Bradley's Journal*, 5 January 1851, p. 133.

83 McDonald, *A Missionary in Siam*, p. 95.

84 Feltus, *Samuel Reynolds House*, p. 102.

85 From information in Hills, "King Mongkut's Interactions with Christianity", pp. 140-147.

86 Quoted in Feltus, *Samuel Reynolds House*, pp. 108-109.

87 Feltus, *Bradley's Journal*, 5 and 6 February 1852, p. 148; 20 February 1852, p. 149; and 19 April 1852, p. 151.

88 Feltus, *Bradley's Journal*, 30 July 1853, p. 163.

89 Bowring, *Kingdom and People of Siam*, 10 April 1855, vol. 2, p. 293.

90 Feltus, *Bradley's Journal*, 28 September 1854, p. 173.

91 *Straits Times*, 12 September 1854.

92 NA (UK): FO 17/228, Mongkut to Bowring, 27 December 1854, p. 148.

93 Feltus, *Bradley's Journal*, 14 October 1854, p. 173.

94 Quoted in Feltus, *Samuel Reynolds House*, p. 130.

95 Feltus, *Bradley's Journal*, 18, 21 and 25 December 1854, p. 175.

96 Feltus, *Bradley's Journal*, 28 and 30 December 1854, p. 176; 6 January 1855, p. 177; and 27 March 1855, p. 180.

97 Bowring, *Kingdom and People of Siam*, vol. 2, p. 323.

98 Feltus, *Bradley's Journal*, 31 May 1855, p. 183; 22 September 1855, p. 185; and 24 October 1856, p. 192.

99 *Singapore Free Press*, 30 October 1856.

100 Quoted in Tarling, "The Bowring Mission", p. 121.

101 NA (UK): FO 69/1, Brooke to Palmerston, 5 October 1850, p. 75; FO 69/2, Brooke to Phraklang, 11 March 1850, enclosure 1 in Brooke to Palmerston, 5 October 1850, pp. 120-121.

102 NA (UK): FO 69/2, Phraklang to Brooke, 24 September 1850, enclosure 12 in Brooke to Palmerston, 5 October 1850, p. 127.

103 NL (Th): R4, 1218/86. Similar language is included in the "Proclamation Concerning Treaty Farangs" that explained the rights of English, French and American residents under the new treaties (Seni and Kukrit, *King of Siam Speaks*, p. 47).

104 Bowring treaty, Article IV.

105 NA (UK): FO 17/229, Bowring to Clarendon, 25 April 1855, p. 97.

106 NA (UK): FO 69/5, Parkes to Clarendon, 23 May 1856, pp. 69-70, 74.

107 Bowring treaty, Article IV.

108 Sunthari, *Panha kan thuekhrong kammasit thidin*, pp. 3-4.

109 Tarling, "Harry Parkes' Negotiations", p. 175n.

110 Chaiyan, *Thai Absolute Monarchy*, p. 3.

111 Perhaps an example of the "epistemological hybrid" of Mongkut's indigenous and western worldview, Thongchai, *Siam Mapped*, p. 57.

112 Seni and Kukrit, *King of Siam Speaks*, Mongkut to Siamese Ambassador to Paris, 1864, p. 187.

113 See Chapter 7.

114 Cosenza, *Journal of Townsend Harris*, 21 April 1856, p. 102n.

115 Wood, *Fankwei*, p. 160.

116 Cosenza, *Journal of Townsend Harris*, 21 April 1856, p. 102n.

117 NA (UK): FO 69/5, Parkes to Clarendon, 23 May 1856, pp. 67-68.

118 NL (Th): R4, 1218/86.

119 NA (UK): FO 69/5, Parkes to Clarendon, 23 May 1856, pp. 71, 73-74.

120 NA (UK), FO 17/248, "Government Notification, Articles of Agreement entered into between the Siamese and Mr. Parkes", 18 June 1856, p. 88.

121 Ibid., p. 89. The Thai version is in NL (Th): R4, 1218/86.

Chapter 3: The Hilliers in Bangkok

1 NA (UK): FO 69/4, Hillier to Clarendon, 11 June 1856, p. 79.

2 NA (UK): FO 69/1, Logan to Brooke, 14 June 1850, p. 57.

3 NA (UK): FO 69/4, Hillier to Clarendon, 11 June 1856, p. 79.

4 *Hillier Papers*: Eliza Hillier to Martha Saul, 26 May 1856.

5 NA (UK): FO 69/4, Hillier to Clarendon, 11 June 1856, pp. 80, 93, 84.

6 E. Hillier, "At Home in Siam", p. 481; *Hillier Papers*: Eliza Hillier to Martha Saul, 11 June 1856.

7 Charles Hillier wrote of "two boats each pulling 30 oars" (NA (UK): FO 69/4, Hillier to Clarendon, 11 June 1856, p. 85).

8 E. Hillier, "At Home in Siam", pp. 481-482; *Hillier Papers*: Eliza Hillier to Martha Saul, 11 June 1856.

9 NA (UK): FO 628/1/2, Hillier to Bowring, 17 June 1856, p. 22.

10 *Hillier Papers*: Eliza Hillier to Martha Saul, 11 June 1856.

11 NA (UK): FO 69/4, Hillier to Clarendon, 18 July 1856, p. 138.

12 NA (UK): FO 69/5, Parkes to Hammond, 10 June 1856, p. 185.

13 *Hillier Papers*: Eliza Hillier to Martha Saul, 11 June 1856.

14 NA (UK): FO 69/5, Parkes to Clarendon, 23 May 1856, p. 48.

15 *Hillier Papers*: Eliza Hillier to Martha Saul, 29 April 1856: "we have every reasonable prospect, please God, of going home in three years."

16 *Hillier Papers*: Eliza Hillier to Martha Saul, 29 April and 26 May 1856.

17 See A. Hillier, "Mediating Empire", ch. 3. For Hillier's time in Hong Kong, also Endacott, *Biographical Sketch-Book*, pp. 84-88.

18 Endacott, *Biographical Sketch-Book*, pp. 86, 88.

19 NA (UK): CO 129/45, Caine to the Duke of Newcastle, 5 and 18 April 1854, pp. 300, 303; Hillier to Caine, 14 October 1851, pp. 109-110.

20 NA (UK): CO 129/45, Bowring to the Duke of Newcastle, 17 and 21 April 1854, pp. 338, 340; Hillier to Viscount Palmerston, 18 February 1854, p. 129.

21 Quoted in Norton-Kyshe, *Hong Kong Laws and Courts*, vol. 1, pp. 378-380.

22 Ibid., vol. 2, pp. 517-518.

23 Ibid., vol. 2, p. 517.

24 Endacott, *Biographical Sketch-Book*, p. 85.

25 *Hansard*, col. 88, 4 August 1846, pp. 340-341.

26 NA (UK): FO 230/56, Clarendon to Bowring, 6 March 1856.

27 NA (UK): FO 17/235, Bowring to Clarendon, 4 December 1855, p. 115.

28 Charles Robinson, "Protestant Missions of Siam: A Sketch of the origin of the first Protestant Mission to Siam, with an account of the first Missionaries, their reception by the Siamese labors &c." in Bradley, *Bangkok Calendar, 1866*, p. 64.

29 Biblioasia, "A Missionary's Guide".

30 Lane-Poole, *Life of Harry Parkes*, p. 192.

31 Terwiel, *Through Travellers' Eyes*, p. 232.

32 Pallegoix, *Description of the Thai Kingdom*, p. 29.

33 Van Roy, *Siamese Melting Pot*, p. 22.

34 Pallegoix, *Description of the Thai Kingdom*, p. 153; Hallett, *A Thousand Miles*, pp. 446-447 reported receiving this information from Henry Alabaster, formerly of the British consulate, in the 1880s when Alabaster was said to be "the confidential advisor to the king".

35 Skinner, *Chinese Society in Thailand*, p. 83.

36 Van Roy, *Siamese Melting Pot*, pp. 6-8.

37 The location of these residences was pinpointed on a map entitled "Plan of the City of Bangkok" by Bradley in his *Bangkok Calendar, 1860*.

38 Ibid.

39 NA (UK): FO 17/236, Parkes to Hammond, 3 August 1855, p. 54.

40 Bradley, *Bangkok Calendar, 1860* included a map of Bangkok (reproduced in Landy, "Maps of Bangkok", pp. 88-89) which showed the riverside residences of thirty-three prominent Chinese merchants.

41 Seni and Kukrit, *King of Siam Speaks*, p. 228.

42 Cosenza, *Journal of Townsend Harris*, 29 April 1856, p. 129.

43 Van Roy, *Siamese Melting Pot*, p. 30.

44 Pallegoix, *Description of the Thai Kingdom*, p. 405.

45 Damrong, "Introduction of Western Culture", p. 90.

46 Cosenza, *Journal of Townsend Harris*, 27 April 1856, p. 122.

47 Feltus, *Bradley's Journal*, 26 April 1856, p. 190.

48 *The Burney Papers*, vol. 4.3, Hunter to Ellenborough, 24 April 1844, p. 130.

49 These were James Hayes and Daniel Brown (From J.H. Chandler's *Bangkok Calendar, 1847-1850*, reprinted in Smith, *Siam Repository, 1869*, pp. 324, 329).

50 Bradley, *Bangkok Calendar, 1859-1873, passim*; Falkus, "Early British business", pp. 129, 131-132; Longhurst, *The Borneo Story*, p. 41; Wright and Breakspear, *Twentieth Century Impressions of Siam*, pp. 152, 175.

51 Bradley, *Bangkok Calendar, 1859*, pp. 60-62.

52 Bradley, *Bangkok Calendar, 1873*, "Directory", pp. 29-35.

53 NA (UK): FO 69/4, Hillier to Clarendon, 12 September 1856, p. 278.

54 W. Bradley, *Siam Then*, p. 105.

55 Cosenza, *Journal of Townsend Harris*, 24 and 14 May 1856, pp. 153, 145.

56 Feltus, *Bradley's Journal*, 29 May 1856, p. 189.

57 Cosenza, *Journal of Townsend Harris*, 26 April 1856, p. 121.

58 From Stephen Mattoon letter of 14 June 1856 quoted in Mattoon, "Life of Mattoon", p. 32.

59 NA (UK): FO 69/7, Gingell to Clarendon, 1 June 1857.

60 Ibid.

61 Neon, "Siamese Relations with Britain and France", p. 466. The background to the dispute is on pp. 461-466.

62 Ibid., pp. 433-434.

63 NA (UK): FO 17/223, Neff to Hammond, 10 October 1854, p. 22.

64 NA (UK): FO 17/211, Clarendon to Bowring, 24 October 1854, p. 145.

65 NA (UK): FO 17/228, Bowring to Clarendon, 6 March 1855, p. 161.

66 Feltus, *Bradley's Journal*, 1 June 1856, p. 190.

67 FO 69/4 Hillier to Clarendon, 3 September 1856, p. 245.

68 E. Hillier, "At Home in Siam", pp. 482, 484-485.

69 *Hillier Papers*: Eliza Hillier to Martha Saul, 29 April 1856.

70 *Hillier Papers*: Eliza Hillier to Martha Saul, 1 August 1856.

71 E. Hillier, "At Home in Siam", p. 484.

72 Lane-Poole, *Life of Harry Parkes*, vol. 1, p. 209.

73 E. Hillier, "Siamese Kings", pp. 448, 450.

74 E. Hillier, "Siamese Women", p. 41.

75 *Hillier Papers*: Eliza Hillier to Martha Saul, 1 August 1856.

76 Information from Andrew Hillier.

77 A. Hillier, "Mediating Empire" ch. 3.

78 *Hillier Papers*: Eliza Hillier to Martha Saul, 1 August 1856.

79 NA (UK): FO 69/4, Hillier to Clarendon, 18 July 1856, p. 146.

80 *Hillier Papers*: Eliza Hillier to Martha Saul, 1 August 1856.

81 Pallegoix, *Description of the Thai Kingdom*, p. 30.

82 Bradley, *Bangkok Calendar, 1871*, p. 133.

83 *Hillier Papers*: Eliza Hillier to Martha Saul, 1 August 1856.

84 Terwiel, *Through Travellers' Eyes*, p. 211.

85 *Hillier Papers*: Eliza Hillier to Martha Saul, 1 August 1856.

Chapter 4: Hillier gets to work

1 Bowring, *Kingdom and People of Siam*, vol. 2, pp. 321, 322, 327-328.

2 Norton-Kyshe, *Hong Kong Laws and Courts*, vol. 1, p. 383.

3 Endacott, *Biographical Sketch-Book*, pp. 84.

4 NA (UK): FO 628/1/6, Bowring to Hillier, 5 May 1856.

5 Coates, *China Consuls*, p. 70.

6 NA (UK): FO 230/56, Bowring to Hillier, 10 July and 28 August 1856.

7 NA (UK): FO 69/4, Hillier to Clarendon, 11 June 1856, p. 86 and 12 September 1856, pp. 271-272; FO 69/5, Parkes to Hammond, 8 August 1856, p. 21.

8 NA (UK): FO 69/4, Bell's "Memorandum", enclosure in Hillier to Clarendon, 11 June 1856, p. 114.

9 Cosenza, *Journal of Townsend Harris*, 5, 16 and 21 May 1856, pp. 139, 147, 151.

10 NA (UK): FO 69/4, Hillier to Clarendon, 3 and 12 September 1856, pp. 244-247, 273-276.

11 NA (UK): FO 69/4, Hillier to Clarendon, 18 July 1856, p. 160; 3 September 1856, p. 245; 22 August 1856, pp. 237-239; 12 September 1856, pp. 271-274; FO 628/1/2, Hillier to Bowring, 16 June 1856, p. 20.

12 Bradley, *Dictionary of the Siamese Language*, p. 318.

13 NL (Th): R4, 1219/63.

14 NA (UK) FO 69/4, Clarendon to Hillier, 7 July 1856, pp. 3-5; 28 August 1856, pp. 29-30.

15 NA (UK): FO 69/7, Gingell to Clarendon, 10 June 1857.

16 NA (UK): FO 628/1/6, Bowring to Hillier, 5 May 1856.

17 NA (UK): FO 17/249, Hillier to Bowring, 28 June 1856, p. 40; FO 69/4, Hillier to Clarendon, 18 July 1856, p. 141.

18 NA (UK): FO 69/4, Hillier to Clarendon, 18 July 1856, p. 141.

19 Bowring, *Kingdom and People of Siam,* vol. 2, pp. 268-269.

20 NA (UK): FO 17/229, Parkes and Bowring Jr to Bowring, 1 April 1855, enclosure 2 in Bowring to Clarendon, 28 April 1855, p. 176.

21 NA (UK): FO 228/207, Parkes to Clarendon, 23 May 1856, p. 48.

22 Consenza, *Journal of Townsend Harris*, pp. 83-84, 89.

23 NA (UK): FO 69/4, Hillier to Clarendon, 6 August 1856, p. 178.

24 Bowring, *Kingdom and People of Siam*, vol. 2, p. 259.

25 NA (UK): FO 69/4, Hillier to Clarendon, 6 August 1856, p. 180.

26 NA (UK): FO 69/4, Phraklang to Hillier, 7 June 1856, p. 90.

27 NA (UK): FO 228/221, Hillier to Bowring, 16 June 1856, p. 27.

28 NA (UK): FO 628/1/4, Hillier to Phraklang, 9 July 1856.

29 NA (UK): FO 17/249, Hillier to Bowring, 28 June 1856, pp. 38-39, 41.

30 NA (UK): FO 69/4, Hillier to Clarendon, 18 July 1856, pp. 142, 145, 146.

31 NA (UK): FO 17/249, Hillier to Bowring, 28 June 1856, p. 40.

32 NA (UK): FO 69/4, Hillier to Clarendon, 18 July 1856, p. 147.

33 NA (UK): FO 17/249, Bowring to Clarendon, 19 July 1856, p. 35.

34 Mattoon, "Life of Mattoon", p. 36.

35 NA (UK): FO 69/4, Hillier to Clarendon, 18 July 1856, p. 142.

36 See Chapter 2.

37 Wood, *Fankwei*, p. 230.

38 NA (UK): FO 69/4, Hillier to Clarendon, 18 July 1856, p. 146.

39 Ibid., pp. 142, 146.

40 NA (UK): FO 628/1/4, Hillier to Mongkut, 7 July 1856.

41 NA (UK): FO 69/4, Hillier to Clarendon, 18 July 1856, pp. 144-145.

42 NA (UK): FO 17/249, Hillier to Bowring, 28 June 1856, p. 38.

43 NA (UK): FO 628/1/4, Hillier to Mongkut, 7 July 1856.

44 Baker and Pasuk, *History of Ayutthaya*, p. 152.

45 NA (UK): FO 628/1/4, Hillier to Mongkut, 9 July 1856.

46 *Singapore Free Press,* 30 October 1856.

47 NA (UK): FO 628/1/2, Hillier to Bowring, 16 June 1856, p. 20.

48 NA (UK): FO 628/1/4, Hillier to Phraklang, 9 July 1856.

49 NA (UK): FO 628/1/4, Hillier to Mongkut, 7 July 1856.

50 NA (UK): FO 69/4, Hillier to Clarendon, 18 July 1856, p. 141.

51 NA (UK): FO 628/1/4, Hillier to Mongkut, 9 July 1856,

52 NA (UK): FO 69/4, Mongkut to Hillier, 17 July 1856, pp. 153-154.

53 NA (UK): FO 69/4, Hillier to Clarendon, 18 July 1856, p. 141.

54 Ibid., pp. 138-139, 141.

55 NA (UK): FO 628/1/4, Hillier to Mongkut, 29 July 1856.

56 NA (UK): FO 69/4, Phraklang to Hillier, 21 August 1856, pp. 250-253.

57 Ibid., p. 252.

58 NA (UK): FO 69/4, Hillier to Clarendon, 18 July 1856, p. 141.

59 NA (UK): FO 628/1/4, Hillier to Phraklang, 3 September 1856.

60 NA (UK): FO 69/4, Clarendon to Hillier, 9 October 1856, p. 41.

61 NA (UK): FO 69/5, Parkes to Hammond, 8 August 1856, p. 23; FO 17/235, Bowring to Clarendon, 4 December 1855, p. 115.

62 NA (UK): FO 69/4, Hillier to Clarendon, 12 September 1856, pp. 279-280.

Chapter 5: A 'paroxysm of passion'

1 NA (UK): FO 69/4, Hillier to Clarendon, 12 September 1856, p. 287.

2 *Hillier Papers*: "Memorandum".

3 NA (UK): FO 69/4, Hillier to Clarendon, 12 September 1856, p. 265.

4 NA (UK): ADM 53/6092: Ship's Log: H.M. Ship: *Saracen*, 20 April 1855 to 20 November 1856.

5 NA (UK): FO 69/4, Hillier to Clarendon, 12 September 1856, p. 287.

6 NA (UK): FO 69/4, Hillier to Clarendon, 4 October 1856, p. 290.

7 *Hillier Papers*: "Memorandum".

8 NA (UK): FO 628/1/1, Bell to Bowring, 6 October 1856.

9 NA (UK): FO 69/4, Hillier to Clarendon, 4 October 1856, p. 290.

10 Bowring treaty, Article III.

11 NA (UK): FO 69/4, Hillier to Bell, 27 September 1856, p. 300.

12 NA (UK): FO 628/1/4, Hillier to Senior Naval Officer, 2 October 1856.

13 NA (UK): FO 69/4, Hillier to Clarendon, 4 October 1856, p. 292.

14 NA (UK): FO 69/4, Hillier to Bell, 27 September 1856, pp. 299-302.

15 NA (UK): FO 628/1/6, Bell to Hillier, 29 September 1856.

16 NA (UK): ADM 53/6092: Ship's Log: H.M. Ship: *Saracen*, 1 October 1856.

17 NA (UK): FO 17/252, Richards to Bowring, 21 October 1856, p. 363.

18 NA (UK): FO 628/1/6, Bell to Hillier, 29 September 1856.

19 NA (UK): FO 69/4, Hillier to Clarendon, 4 October 1856, pp. 292-293.

20 Information from Puddicombe family descendant Robin Phillips and from the short biography of grandson Alfred William Alcock at

https://royalsocietypublishing.org/doi/10.1098/rsbm.1933.0008.

21 Feltus, *Bradley's Journal*, 17 November 1851 and 5 November 1853, pp. 145, 166.

22 Feltus, *Bradley's Journal*, 21 January 1844, p. 92.

23 Feltus, *Bradley's Journal*, 29 September 1856, p. 191.

24 Feltus, *Bradley's Journal*, 26 April 1856, p. 190.

25 Bowring treaty, Article VIII.

26 NA (UK): FO 628/1/6, Mongkut to Puddicombe, 8 October 1856.

27 NA (UK): FO 17/233, Bell to Bowring, 1 July 1855, p. 49.

28 Bradley, *Bangkok Calendar, 1860*, p. 79.

29 Robin Phillips' papers, Bangkok Times Office to D. A. Kelson Ford, 27 May 1939.

30 Based on information in NA (UK): FO 228/244, "Foreign Residents at the Port of Bangkok", 29 May 1857, p. 103.

31 NA (UK): FO 69/4, Hillier to Clarendon, 12 September 1856, pp. 282-283.

32 Ibid., pp. 282-284.

33 *Singapore Free Press*, 30 October 1856.

34 NA (UK): FO 69/4, Hillier to Clarendon, 12 September 1856, p. 284.

35 NA (US): Mattoon to Marcy, 3 October 1856.

36 NA (UK): FO 228/221, Bell to Bowring, 4 October 1856, p. 97.

37 *Singapore Free Press*, 30 October 1856.

38 NA (UK): FO 69/4, Hillier to Clarendon, 4 October 1856, p. 294.

39 *Straits Times*, 11 November 1856.

40 NA (UK): FO 628/1/6, Bell to Hillier, 29 September 1856.

41 *Singapore Free Press*, 30 October 1856.

42 NA (UK): FO 628/1/6, Bell to Hillier, 29 September 1856.

43 NA (UK): FO 69/4, Hillier to Clarendon, 4 October 1856, p. 289.

44 NA (UK): FO 69/4, Hillier to Bell, 27 September 1856, pp. 299-300, 302.

45 *Singapore Free Press*, 30 October 1856.

46 *Hillier Papers*: "Memorandum".

47 Ibid.

48 NA (UK): FO 69/4, Hillier to Clarendon, 4 October 1856, pp. 295-296.

49 Feltus, *Bradley's Journal,* 2 February 1852, p. 147.

50 Bowring in *Kingdom and People of Siam*, vol. 2, pp. 293-294, and Harris in Cosenza, *Journal of Townsend Harris*, p. 113, mention the prince's possession of an American medical diploma, while Wood, *Fankwei*, p. 150, refers to him as a fellow of the New York Academy of Medicine. See also Nopphanat and Komatra, "Wongsa and the House of Snidvongs".

51 Feltus, *Bradley's Journal,* 30 September 1856, p. 192.

52 Ibid.

53 NA (UK): FO 69/4, Hillier to Clarendon, 4 October 1856, p. 294.

54 Feltus, *Bradley's Journal,* 2 October 1856, p. 192.

55 NA (UK): FO 69/4, Consuls to Mongkut, 3 October 1856, p. 303.

56 NA (Fr): 120CP/1, Moor to de Montigny, 11 November 1856, p. 206.

57 NA (UK): FO 69/4, Hillier to Clarendon, 4 October 1856, p. 296.

58 NA (UK): FO 69/4, Consuls to Mongkut, 3 October 1856, pp. 303-306.

59 NA (UK): FO 69/4, Hillier to Clarendon, 4 October 1856, pp. 297-298.

60 Feltus, *Bradley's Journal,* 2 October 1856, p. 192.

61 *Hillier Papers*: "Memorandum".

62 NA (UK): ADM 53/6092: Ship's Log: H.M. Ship: *Saracen*, 5 October 1856.

63 *Hillier Papers*: "Memorandum".

64 Letter in the collection of Andrew Hillier, from Dr Hill to Revd Dr Medhurst, 22 October 1856.

65 NA (UK): FO 17/252, Richards to Bowring, 21 October 1856, p. 362.

66 NA (UK): FO 69/4, Bell to Clarendon, 22 October 1856, p. 308.

67 *Hillier Papers*: "Memorandum".

68 NA (UK): FO 17/252, Richards to Bowring, 21 October 1856, p. 361.

69 *The Observer*, 4 January 1857.

70 Khachon, "Moranakam nai insen", p. 62.

71 NA (UK): FO 17/252, Bowring to Clarendon, 2 December 1856, pp. 374-373; FO 69/9, Edward Hillier to Clarendon, 13 January 1857, pp. 11-13; Eliza Hillier to Clarendon, 10 February 1857, pp. 54-55; Davis to Clarendon, 1 March 1857, pp. 76-77; Eliza Hillier to Davis, 9 January 1857, pp. 78-81; *Singapore Free Press*, 13 November 1856.

72 NA (UK): FO 69/9, Wilson to Hammond, 15 June 1857, p. 119.

73 NA (UK): FO 69/14: Eliza Hillier to Clarendon, 12 January 1858, p. 52.

74 NA (UK): FO 69/15: Audit Office to Hammond, 11 March 1858 and 15 June 1858.

75 For more on the Hillier family, including Charles and Eliza's three sons who went on to hold important positions in China, see "Mediating Empire" by Andrew Hillier, Charles' great-great grandson.

76 Ibid.

Chapter 6: The king manages the consequences

1 NA (UK): FO 17/229, Mongkut to Bowring, 3 April 1855, enclosure 8 in Bowring to Clarendon, 28 April 1855, pp. 198-199.

2 Mongkut to Bowring, 31 July 1857 in Winai and Theera, *Writings of Mongkut to Bowring*, p. 63.

3 NA (UK): FO 17/229, Mongkut to Bowring, 27 March 1855, enclosure 3 in Bowring to Clarendon, 28 April 1855, p. 185.

4 Winai and Theera, *Writings of Mongkut to Bowring*, 26 May 1856, p. 40.

5 NA (UK): FO 17/267, Mongkut to Bowring, 19 March 1857, pp. 329-330, also in Cœdès, "Correspondence of King Mongkut", p. 130. Details of the king's losses were contained in a petition to Bowring from Kham dated 29 May 1857 in FO 17/269, pp. 242-245.

6 FO 17/262, Clarendon to Bowring, 17 June 1857, p. 39.

7 I am indebted to Ajarn Suchao Loychum for suggesting that แพมิศ แบล [*phaemisbel*] probably referred to Bell's floating house.

8 NL (Th): R4, 1218/100 & 100 Kor.

9 Feltus, *Bradley's Journal*, 18 May and 13 July 1844, p. 94.

10 Wyatt, "The Buddhist Monkhood", pp. 50-51.

11 Feltus, *Bradley's Journal*, 3 October 1856, p. 192.

12 NA (US): Mattoon to Marcy, 4 October 1856.

13 NA (UK): FO 17/252, Mongkut to Richards, 29 October 1856, p. 370.

14 Feltus, *Bradley's Journal*, 6 October 1856, p. 192.

15 NA (UK): FO 628/1/1, Bell to Bowring, 2 December 1856; FO 628/1/2, p. 90 and FO 69/4, Bell to Clarendon, 4 December 1856, p. 310.

16 NA (US): Mattoon to Marcy, 4 October 1856.

17 NA (UK): FO 69/4, Bell to Clarendon, 4 December 1856, pp. 310-311.

18 NA (US): Mattoon to Marcy, 4 October 1856.

19 NA (UK): FO 628/1/6, Mongkut to Puddicombe, 8 October 1856.

20 Feltus, *Bradley's Journal*, 24 October 1856, p. 192.

21 NA (UK): FO 628/2/20, Phraklang to Schomburgk, 21 May 1859; FO 628/2/20 and FO 628/3/27, Wongsa to Schomburgk, 20 December 1859.

22 NA (UK): FO 628/1/13, Gingell to Phraklang, 26 October 1857, p. 266; FO 628/1/12, Gingell to Phraklang, 5 November 1857; FO 628/1/11, Phraklang to Gingell, 2 and 9 November 1857, and Phraklang to Schomburgk, 18 December 1857.

23 NA (UK): FO 628/1/11, Phraklang to Gingell, 8 July 1857.

24 Sayomporn, "Phol krathop chak kantat thanon", pp. 18-27.

25 Feltus, *Bradley's Journal*, 6 October 1856, p. 192.

26 NA (US): Mattoon to Marcy, 10 November 1856.

27 Landy, "Maps of Bangkok", p. 73.

28 NA (UK): FO 17/252, Mongkut to Richards, 29 October 1856.

29 NA (UK): FO 17/252, Bowring to Mongkut, 3 December 1856.

30 NA (US), Phraklang to Bowring, 6 November 1856, enclosure in Mattoon to Marcy, 10 November 1856 for the translation seen by Mattoon; NA (UK): FO 17/264, Phraklang to Bowring, 6 November 1856, pp. 302-311 for the final version delivered to Bowring.

31 Cœdès, "Correspondence of King Mongkut", Mongkut to Clarendon, 24 July 1857, p. 136.

32 NA (UK): FO 69/6, Clarendon to Bell, 5 March 1857.

33 NA (UK): FO 628/1/13, Gingell to King Mongkut, 13 May 1857, p. 230.

34 NA (UK): FO 17/267, Bowring to Clarendon, 18 April 1857, p. 277.

35 NA (UK): FO 69/6, Clarendon to Schomburgk, 28 February 1857; FO 83/2339, Law Officers to Clarendon, 4 November 1857, p. 37.

36 NA (UK): FO 69/6, Clarendon to Gingell, 4 May 1857; FO 69/7, Gingell to Clarendon, 15 May 1857 and internal notes appended; and FO 17/262, Clarendon to Bowring, 31 August 1857, p. 128.

37 P. Bowring, *Free Trade's First Missionary*, pp. 146-147.

38 NA (UK): FO 69/7, Bell to Clarendon, 4 March 1857.

39 NA (UK): FO 69/6, Clarendon to Bell, 4 August 1857.

40 NA (UK): FO 69/6, Clarendon to Gingell, 23 December 1857.

41 NA (UK): FO 69/7, Gingell to Clarendon, 26 March 1857.

42 NA (UK): FO 69/7, Gingell to Clarendon, 1 July 1857.

43 NA (UK): FO 17/271, Phraklang to Bowring, 10 May 1857, pp. 30-33.

44 NL (Th), R4, 1219/63.

45 NA (UK): FO 69/7, Gingell to Clarendon, 14 and 25 April, 30 May, 3 June and 22 July 1857; FO 628/1/10, Gingell to Treasury, 1 July 1857, pp.151-153; FO 628/1/13, Gingell to Mongkut, 24 March, 9 and 30 April 1857, pp. 217, 220-222, Gingell to Phraklang, 20 May 1857, pp. 235-236.

46 NA (UK): FO 69/9, Foreign Office to Treasury, 23 September 1857, p. 251; Cœdès, "Correspondence of King Mongkut", Mongkut to Clarendon, 30 June 1858, p. 161.

47 NA (UK): FO 69/7, Gingell to Clarendon, 4 July 1857; FO 69/6, Clarendon to Gingell, 20 October 1857; FO 69/8, Gingell to Schomburgk, 10 December 1857, Schomburgk to Hammond, 20 October 1857, Gingell to Clarendon, 10 December 1857, Schomburgk to Clarendon, 26 December 1857.

48 NA (UK): FO 628/1/2, Schomburgk circular, 28 December 1857; FO 628/3/26, Schomburgk to Audit Office, 15 April 1859, p. 132.

Chapter 7: Legacies

1 References to the Seng affair can be found in Khachon's "Moranakam nai insen", pp. 59-65; Manich's *Anglo-Thai Relations*, pp. 90-91; and his *Mongkut and the British*, pp. 129-134; Moffatt's *Mongkut*, p. 101; Terwiel's *Thailand's Political History*, pp. 147-149; Viboon's "Khrokam khong nai insen", pp. 241-274; and Wilson's "State and Society"; pp. 371-375.

2 *The Observer*, 4 January 1857. The event was also covered in the *Singapore Free Press*, 30 October and 13 November 1856; the *Straits Times*, 11 November 1856; and the *Manchester Guardian*, 22 December 1856, which reprinted an article in the *Singapore Free Press.*

3 *Singapore Free Press*, 30 October 1856.

4 Ibid.

5 Feltus, *Bradley's Journal*, 3 October 1856.

6 NA (UK): FO 69/4, Hillier to Clarendon, 4 October 1856, p. 291.

7 Wilson, "State and Society", pp. 373-374.

8 Terwiel, *Thailand's Political History*, pp. 148-149.

9 Wilson, "State and Society", pp. 372, 375.

10 Khachon, "Moranakam nai insen", p. 59.

11 *Abolition of Slavery Act*, 1905.

12 Khachon, "Moranakam nai insen", pp. 63-65.

13 Manich, *Mongkut and the British*, pp. 130-131.

14 See Larsson, *Land and Loyalty*, for an analysis of the development of property rights in Thailand.

15 Ibid., pp. 54-56.

16 NA (UK): FO 17/229, "Bowring's Embassy: Journal", enclosure 15, Bowring to Clarendon, 28 April 1855, pp. 241-243.

17 NA (UK): FO 628/2/14, Schomburgk to Blundell, 11 January 1858.

18 Sayre, "The Passing of Extraterritoriality", p. 73.

19 NA (UK): FO 69/255, Beckett to Lansdowne, 17 November 1904, p. 367.

20 Batson, "American Diplomats", p. 61.

21 Van Roy, *Siamese Melting Pot*, p. 129.

22 Vikrom, "Siam in British Foreign Policy", pp. 137, 164, 201; NA (UK): FO 69/265, Paget to Lansdowne, 27 October 1905, pp. 309-312.

23 Larsson, *Land and Loyalty*, p. 158.

24 For more on the trade-off between extraterritorial rights and property rights, see Larsson, *Land and Loyalty*, pp. 39-44, 127-129; Vikrom "Siam in British Foreign Policy", pp. 137-139, 150-164, 220-221.

25 NA (UK): FO 628/2/20, Phraklang to Schomburgk, 21 May 1859.

26 Nithi, "Su prawatsat", p. 55.

27 Larsson, *Land and Loyalty*, p. 43.

28 Chatthip and Suthy, *Political Economy 1851-1910*, pp. 223, 225, which includes van der Heide's criticism of the scheme.

29 Chatthip, Suthy and Montri, *Political Economy 1910-1932* , pp. 1-5 and pp. 48-55, the latter a reprint from Carle C. Zimmerman, "An economic survey of the Central Plain, 1930-31", *Siam Rural Economy Survey, 1930-31,* Bangkok, Bangkok Time Press, 1931.

30 Landy, "99-year leases".

31 *Lease of Immovable Property Act, 1999.*

32 NA (UK): WORK 10/215, Simpson to Chief Architect, 15 March 1921.

33 Ibid.; and Lyle to Simpson, 6 April 1921.

34 NA (UK): WORK 10/215, Simpson memorandum, 2 February 1922.

35 *Remembering the British Embassy Bangkok*, p. 46.

36 NA (UK): WORK 10/215, Crosby memorandum, enclosure in Seymour to Curzon, 14 July 1921; Treasury to First Commissioner of Works, 18 August 1921; Crosby to Curzon, 22 October 1921; Simpson to Allison, 18 January 1922; Earl of Balfour to Secretary of the Office of Works, 24 June 1922; Bradley to Allison, 30 June 1922.

37 NA (UK): WORK 10/216.

38 Ibid., Waterlow to Sir Austen Chamberlain, 4 October 1926.

39 FCO Reports 2005-06, Ev 79-80; 2017-18, p. 114.

40 NA (UK): WORK 10/275: Archer to Marquess of Lansdowne, 28 August 1901; Lyle to Lord Curzon, 26 August 1919; *The Times*, 9 May 1905.

41 NA (UK): WORK 10/275: Bangkok report by Edward Muir, 31 July 1962.

Glossary

1 Thanyaporn and Jessica, *Economic History of Land Rights*, pp. 8-11.

Acknowledgements

The idea for this book came from the British foreign office's decision to sell its property in Bangkok and was spurred further by an unplanned encounter with its then chief, Boris Johnson. But neither impetus would have been sufficient to lead to a book-length output without the unflagging support, encouragement and, frankly, partner-management skills of Napaporn, my wife. She was also the first to read a draft and provided a continuous sounding board and sanity check. For reading early drafts, I am also hugely indebted to the generosity and perspicacity of Chris Baker, Alastair Laurence, Edward Van Roy and my other long-suffering family "volunteers", Patrick Barta and Salisa Landy. The book would be much reduced without their incisive and insightful contributions, but none can be held accountable for any faults or misinterpretations that remain, for which I claim full responsibility.

Those who have kindly given their time and input in other ways are likewise absolved. I have been fortunate to have been able to discuss aspects of the story with a variety of people who have kindly given their time, suggestions and support. Some of these meetings were brief, others engaged in longer discussions over email, especially during the Covid-19 pandemic, but all were very valuable to me. Among those who have helped me in this way I would like to thank Chao Khun Anil, Rozelle Bentheim, Brian Berenblut, Mark Bertram, Acharn Phutorn Bhumadorn, Pimpraphai Bisalputra, Simon Browne-Wilkinson, Philip Bowring, Tatiya Bunnag, Tej Bunnag, Nigel Gould-Davis, Andrew Hillier, Michel Houde, Sawanit Kongsiri, Padej Kumlertsakul, Tomas Larsson, Richard Le Page, Robin Phillips, Acharn Suchai Ploythong, Papisuti Saichampa,

Charin Satchayan, Jon Selby, Artyasit Srisuwan, Paul Michael Taylor, Chaiwat Thaipasert, Francisco Vazpatto, Jessica Vechbanyongratana, James Warren, Greg Watkins and James Wise. I am also indebted to the invaluable resources and staff of the Archives of the French Ministry of Foreign Affairs in La Courneuve, the National Archives in London, the National Library in Bangkok, the British Library, Leeds University Library, Mahidol University Library, the SOAS Library and Thammasat University Library.

Finally, a special thank you to my publisher, Narisa Chakrabongse, Ruetairat Nanta and Chris Shelley at River Books, and to Gwen Robinson, who not only provided excellent advice and encouragement, but also the serendipitous introduction to Narisa.

References

Adey Moore, R., "An Early British Merchant in Bangkok", *Journal of the Siam Soceity*, vol. 11.2 (1914-15), pp. 21-39

Akin Rabibhadana, *The Organization of Thai Society in The Early Bangkok Period 1782-1873*, Bangkok, Amarin, 1996

Baker, Chris and Pasuk Phongpaichit, *A History of Ayutthaya: Siam in the Early Modern World*, Cambridge, Cambridge University Press, 2017

Batson, Benjamin A., "American Diplomats in Southeast Asia in the Nineteenth Century: The Case of Siam", *Journal of the Siam Society*, vol. 64.2 (1976), pp. 39-111

Biblioasia, "A Missionary's Guide to Java and Bali", Ong Eng Chuan retrieved from, http://www.nlb.gov.sg/biblioasia/2016/01/18/a-missionarys-guide-to-java-and-bali/

Bowring, John, *The Kingdom and People of Siam with A Narrative of the Mission of That Country in 1855*, 2 vols, London, John W. Parker, 1857

Bowring, Philip, *Free Trade's First Missionary: Sir John Bowring in Europe and Asia*, Hong Kong, Hong Kong University Press, 2014

Bradley, Dan Beach, ed., *The Bangkok Calendar,* 15 editions, Bangkok, American Missionary Association, 1859-73

Dictionary of the Siamese Language, Bangkok, American Missionary Association, 1873

Bradley, William, *Siam Then: The Foreign Colony in Bangkok Before and After Anna*, Pasadena, California, William Carey, 1981

Brummelhuis, Han ten, *King of the Waters: Homan van der Heide and the origin of modern irrigation in Siam*, Chiang Mai, Silkworm Books, 2005

Burney, Henry et al, *The Burney Papers*, 5 vols, Farnborough, Hants, Gregg International, 1971

Chai-anan Samutwanit, *Sakdina kap phatthanakan khong sangkhom thai* (ชัยอนันต์ สมุทวณิช, *ศักดินากับพัฒนาการของสังคมไทย*) [Thai elites and social development], Bangkok, Nam Aksorn, 1976

Chaiyan Rajchagool, *The Rise and Fall of the Thai Absolute Monarchy: Foundations of the Modern Thai State from Feudalism to Peripheral Capitalism*, Bangkok, White Lotus, 1994

Charnvit Kasetsiri, ed., *Prachum prakat ratchakan thi 4* (ชาญวิทย์ เกษตรศิริ, *ประชุมประกาศรัชกาลที่ 4*) [*Collected Proclamations of King Mongkut*], Bangkok, Toyota Thailand Foundation, 2004

Chatthip Nartsupha, *The Thai Village Economy in the Past*, trans. Chris Baker and Pasuk Phongpaichit, Chiang Mai, Silkworm, 1999

Chatthip Nartsupha and Suthy Prasartset, eds, *The Political Economy of Siam, 1851-1910*, Bangkok, Social Science Association of Thailand, c197-

Socio-Economic Institutions and Cultural Change in Siam, 1851-1910: A Documentary Survey, Singapore, Institute of Southeast Asian Studies in co-operation with the Social Science Association of Thailand, October 1977

Chatthip Nartsupha, Suthy Prasartset and Montri Chenvidyakarn, eds, *The Political Economy of Siam, 1910-1932*, Bangkok, Social Science Association of Thailand, 1981

Coates, P. D., *The China Consuls: British Consular Officers, 1843-1943*, Oxford, Oxford University Press, 1988

Cœdès, George ed., "The English Correspondence of King Mongkut", *Journal of the Siam Society*, vol. 21.2 (1927-28), pp. 127-177

Cosenza, Mario Emilio, ed., *The Complete Journal of Townsend Harris: First American Consul General and Minister to Japan*, New York, Doubleday, Doran, 1930

Crawfurd, John, *Journal of an Embassy from the Governor-General of India to the Courts of Siam and Indo-China*, London, Henry Colburn and Richard Bentley, 1830

The Crawfurd Papers: A Collection of Official Records relating to the Mission of Dr. John Crawfurd sent to Siam by the Government of India in the year 1821, Bangkok, Vajiranana National Library, 1915

Cunha, Hélder de Mendonça e, "The 1820 Land Concession to the Portuguese", *Journal of the Siam Society*, vol. 59.2 (1971), pp. 145-149

Damrong Rajanuphab, "The Introduction of Western Culture in Siam", *Journal of the Siam Society*, vol. 20.2 (1926-27), pp. 89-100

"Laksana kanpokhrong prathet sayam tae boran", *Anusorn nai ngan phra ratchathan phloeng sop nai dao bupphawet* (สมเด็จพระเจ้าบรมวงศ์เธอ กรมพระยาดำรงราชานุภาพ, "ลักษณะการปกครองประเทศสยามแต่โบราณ", *พิมพ์เป็นอนุสรณ์ในงานพระราชทานเพลิงศพ นายดาว บุปผเวส จ.ม., บช.*) ["Ancient administration of Siam", *Funeral book of Mr Dao Bupphawat*], Bangkok, Liang Sieng Charoen, 1968 [1959]

Earl, George Windsor, *The Eastern Seas: or voyages and adventures in the Indian Archipelago in 1832-33-34, comparing a tour of the island of Java – visits to Borneo, the Malay Peninsula, Siam, &c.; also an account of the present state of Singapore, with observations on the commercial resources of the archipelago*, London, W. H. Allen, 1837

Endacott, G. B., *A Biographical Sketch-Book of Early Hong Kong*, Singapore, Donald Moore for Eastern Universities Press, 1962

Falkus, Malcolm, "Early British business in Thailand", *British Business in Asia Since 1860*, ed. R. P. T. Davenport-Hines and Geoffrey Jones, Cambridge, Cambridge University Press, 1989, pp. 117-156

Feeny, David, "The Decline of Property Rights in Man in Thailand, 1800-1913", *The Journal of Economic History*, vol. 49.2 (1989), pp. 285-296

Feltus, George Haws, *Samuel Reynolds House of Siam: Pioneer Medical Missionary 1847-1876*, New York and Chicago, Fleming H. Revell, 1924

ed., *Abstract of the Journal of Rev. Dan Beach Bradley M.D.: Medical Missionary in Siam 1835-1873*, Cleveland, Ohio, 1936

"Foreign & Commonwealth Office, Annual Report & Accounts: 2017-2018", retrieved from www.gov.uk/government/publications/foreign-and-commonwealth-office-annual-report-and-accounts-2017-to-2018

Hallett, Holt S., *A Thousand Miles on an Elephant in the Shan States*, Bangkok, White Lotus, 1988 [1890]

Hansard Parliamentary Debates, London, G. Woodfall & Son, 1846, col. 88, 4 August 1846

Hillier, Andrew, "Mediating Empire: An English Family in China, 1817-1927", Ph.D. thesis, Bristol, University of Bristol (now published under the same title by Folkestone, Renaissance Books, 2020)

Hillier, Eliza, "At Home in Siam", *Household Words: A weekly journal*, conducted by Charles Dickens, vol. 16.400, (21 November 1857), pp. 482-488

"A Pair of Siamese Kings", *Household Words: A weekly journal*, conducted by Charles Dickens vol. 17.422, (24 April 1858), pp. 447-451

"Siamese Women and Children", *Household Words: A weekly journal*, conducted by Charles Dickens, vol. 17.455, (11 December 1858), pp. 40-42

Hillier Family Papers, School of Oriental and African Studies Archive

Hills, Douglas Martin, "King Mongkut's Interactions with Christianity and the Failure of Early Protestant Missionary Efforts to Convert the Siamese", Master of Theology thesis, Vancouver, British Columbia, Regent College, 2009

Hong, Lysa, *Thailand in the Nineteenth Century: Evolution of the Economy and Society*, Singapore, Institute of Southeast Asian Studies, 1984

"'Stranger Within the Gates': Knowing Semi-Colonial Siam as Extraterritorials", *Modern Asian Studies*, vol. 38.2 (2004), pp. 327-354.

"House of Commons Foreign Affairs Committee: Foreign & Commonwealth Office Annual Report 2005-2006", retreived from https://publications.parliament.uk/pa/cm200506/cmselect/cmfaff/cmfaff.htm

Jit Poumisak (Somsamai Srisudravarna), "The Real Face of Thai Saktina Today", *Thai Radical Discourse: The Real Face of Thai Feudalism Today*, trans. Craig J. Reynolds, Ithaca, New York, Cornell University Press, 1987

Khachon Sukhaphanit, "Moranakam khong nai insen", *Sangkhomsat Prithat Khomun chak adit* (ขจรสุขพานิช, "มรณกรรมของนายอินแสน", *สังคมศาสตร์ปริทัศน์ข้อมูลจากอดีต*) ["The Death of Nai Insen", *The Social Science Review*], vol. 6.2 (1968), pp. 59-65.

Kullada Kesboonchoo Mead, *The Rise and Decline of Thai Absolutism*, Abingdon, Oxfordshire, RoutledgeCurzon, 2004

La Loubère, Simon de, *A New Historical Relation of the Kingdom of Siam*, London, 1693

Landy, Simon, "Are 99-year leases good for Thailand?", Colliers International Thailand, Bangkok, 2016

"Maps of Bangkok, 1856 to 1861: The Changing Face of the Capital in the post-Bowring Treaty Transition Period", *Journal of the Siam Society*, vol. 108.1 (2020), pp. 73-92

Lane-Poole, Stanley, *The Life of Sir Harry Parkes*, 2 vols, London, MacMillan, 1894

Larsson, Tomas, *Land and Loyalty: Security and the Development of Property Rights in Thailand*, Singapore, NUS Press, 2013

Lingat, R., *Prawattisat kotmai thai: kotmai thidin* (ร. แลงกาต์, *ประวัติศาสตร์กฎหมายไทย: กฎหมายที่ดิน*) [*History of Thai Law: Land Law*], Bangkok, Thammasat University, 1940

Longhurst, Henry, *The Borneo Story: The history of the first 100 years of trading in the Far East by The Borneo Company Limited*, London, Newman Neame, 1956

Lord, Donald C., "Missionaries, Thai, and Diplomats", *Pacific Historical Review*, vol. 35.4, (1966), pp. 413-431

Low, James, "On the Laws of Mu'ung Thai or Siam", *The Journal of the Indian Archipelago and Eastern Asia* (1847), pp. 328-426

Manich Jumsai, *History of Anglo-Thai Relations,* Bangkok, Chalermnit, 1970

King Mongkut of Thailand and the British: The Model of a Great Friendship, Bangkok, Chalermnit, 1991

Martin, Meredith,"Staging China, Japan, and Siam at the Paris Universal Exhibition of 1867", *Beyond Chinoiserie: Artistic Exchange between China and the West during the Late Qing Dynasty*, eds Petra ten-Doesschate Chu and Jennifer Milam, Leiden and Boston, Brill, 2019, pp. 122-148

Mattoon, Mary, "Sketch of the Life of Rev. Stephen Mattoon D. D.", 1928, retrieved from https://jcsu.contentdm.oclc.org/digital/collection/p15170coll6/id/13/.

McDonald, N. A., *A Missionary in Siam (1860-1870)*, Bangkok, White Lotus, 1999 [1871]

McFarland, George Bradley, *Historical Sketches of Protestant Missions in Siam 1828-1928*, Bangkok, White Lotus, 1999 [1928]

Moffatt, Abbott Low, *Mongkut, the King of* Siam, New York, Cornell University Press, 1961

National Archives of France (NA [Fr]): 120CP/1: Siam, Folios 206-208

National Archives of the UK (NA [UK]):
Admiralty: ADM 53/6092

Colonial Office: CO 129/45
Foreign Office (China): FO 17/210; 17/211; 17/214; 17/215; 17/216; 17/217; 17/223; 17/225; 17/226; 17/228; 17/229; 17/233, 17/234; 17/235; 17/236; 17/248; 17/249; 17/252; 17/262; 17/264; 17/265; 17/267; 17/269; 17/271; 97/368; 228/207; 228/221; 228/244; 230/56
Foreign Office (Siam): FO 69/1; 69/2; 69/3; 69/4; 69/5; 69/6; 69/7; 69/8; 69/9; 69/14; 69/15; 69/255; 69/265; 628/1/1; 628/1/2; 628/1/4; 628/1/6; 628/1/10; 628/1/11; 628/1/12; 628/1/13; 628/2/14; 628/2/20; 628/3/26; 628/3/27
Foreign Office (Great Britain and General): FO 83/2339
Office of Works: WORK 10/215; 10/216; 10/275

National Archives of the USA (NA [US]): Despatches from U.S. Consuls in Bangkok, Siam, 1856-1906, 1.1

National Library of Thailand, Ancient Manuscripts Department (NL [Th]), Chotmaihet Ratchakanthi 4, (จดหมายเหตุรัชกาลที่ 4) [Records of King Rama 4]: 1218 [1856], 86: Prakat rueang khon angkrit sue thidin chao thi din (ประกาศเรื่องคนอังกฤษซื้อที่ดินเช่าที่ดิน)
1218 [1856], 100 & 100 Kor: Chotmai rueang naikham mahatlek sonthana kap soe yon boring (จดหมายเรื่องนายขำมหาดเล็กสนทนากับเซอร์ยอนโบริง)
1218 [1856], 137: Khwam rueang khwam mueang khamen (ความเรื่อง ความเมืองเขมร)
1219 [1857], 63: Phraratchasan lae ratchabannakan krung angkrit (พระราชสาส์นและราชบรรณาการกรุงอังกฤษ)
1227 [1865], 117: Khwam mueang rueang khwam mueang trangkanu (ความเมือง เรื่องความเมืองตรังกานู)

Nattawut Suthisongkhram, *Somdetchaophraya borommaha srisuriyawong* (ณัฐวุฒิ สุทธิสงคราม, *สมเด็จเจ้าพระยา บรมมหาศรีสุริยวงศ์*), Bangkok, Sangsan Books, 2008 [1960]

Neale, Frederick Arthur, *Narrative of a Residence at the Capital of the Kingdom of Siam: with a description of the manners, customs, and laws of the modern Siamese*, London, Office of the National Illustrated Library, 1852

Neon Snidvongs, "The Development of Siamese Relations with Britain and France in the Reign of Maha Mongkut, 1851-1868", Ph.D. thesis, London, University of London, 1961

Newspaper articles: - "Siam", *The Straits Times and Singapore Journal of Commerce*, 12 September 1854 and 11 November 1856
"Siam", *The Singapore Free Press and Mercantile Advertiser*, 30 October and 13 November 1856
"Siam", *Manchester Guardian*, 22 December 1856
"A Difference at Siam Adjusted", *The Observer*, 4 January 1857
"The Queen Victoria Memorial at Bangkok", *The Times*, 9 May 1905

Nithi Aeusriwongse, "Su prawattiisat prachachon thai", *Sinlapawatthanatham*; (นิธิ เอียวศรีวงศ์ "สู่ประวัติศาสตร์ประชาชนไทย", *ศิลปวัฒนธรรม*) ["Towards a History of the Thai People", *Art & Culture*], vol. 9.3 (1988), pp.42-60

Nopphanat Anuphongphat and Komatra Chuengsatiansup, "Krom Luang Wongsa and the house of Snidvongs: Knowledge transition and transformation of medicine in early modern Siam", 2014, retrieved from https://www.academia.edu/2029073/Krom_Luang_Wongsa_and_the_House_of_Snidvongs_Knowledge_Transition_and_the_Transformation_of_Medicine_in_Early_Modern_Siam

Norton-Kyshe, James William, *The History of the Laws and Courts of Hong Kong: From the Earliest Period to 1898*, 2 vols, Hong Kong, Vetch and Lee, 1971 [1898]

Paisarn Piemmettawat, *Siam: Through the Lens of John Thomson 1865-66, including Angkor and Coastal China*, trans. Narisa Chakrabongse, Bangkok, River Books, 2015

Pallegoix, Jean-Baptiste, *Description of the Thai Kingdom or Siam: Thailand under King Mongkut*, trans. Walter E. J. Tips, Bangkok, White Lotus, 2000 [1954]

Peter Sek Wannamethee, "Anglo-Siamese Economic Relations: British Trade, Capital and Enterprise in Siam, 1856-1914", Ph.D. thesis, London, London School of Economics and Political Science, 2014

Praratchahatlekha phrabatsomdet phrachomklaochaoyuhua (*พระราชหัตเลขา พระบาทสมเด็จ พระจอมเกล้าเจ้าอยู่หัว*) [*Letters of King Mongkut Rama IV*], Bangkok, Mahamakut Buddhist University, 1978

Quaritch Wales, H. G., *Ancient Siamese Government and Administration*, London, Bernard Quaritch, 1934

Remembering the British Embassy Bangkok on Wireless Road, Bangkok, Thai Beverage, 2019

Ruschenberger, W. S. W., *A Voyage Round the World; including an embassy to Muscat and Siam in 1835, 1836, and 1837*, Philadelphia, Carey, Lea & Blanchard, 1838

Sayomporn Tongsari, "Phol krathop chak kantat thanon nai krungthep nai rachasamai phrabat somdet phrachulachomklao chao yu hua (pho so 2411-2453): sueksa chapoh korani kantat thanon nai kamphaeng phranakhon dan nuea lae dan tai phranakhon" ("ผลกระทบจากการตัดถนนในกรุงเทพฯ ในรัชสมัยพระบาทสมเด็จพระจุลจอมเกล้าเจ้าอยู่หัว (พ.ศ. 2411-2453): ศึกษาเฉพาะกรณีการตัดถนนในกำแพงพระนครด้านเหนือและด้านใต้พระนคร") ["The Impact of the Building of Roads in Bangkok during the Reign of King Rama V (1868-1910): A study in the area within the city walls, the northern and the southern parts of the city"], M.A. thesis, Silapakorn University, 1983

Sayre, Francis Bowes, "The Passing of Extraterritoriality in Siam", *The American Journal of International Law*, vol. 22.1 (January 1928), pp. 70-88

Seni Pramoj and Kukrit Pramoj, *King of Siam Speaks*, Bangkok, draft presented by Chulalongkorn University to the British Library, 1958 (later published as *A King of Siam Speaks*, Bangkok, The Siam Society, 1987)

Skinner, G. William, *Chinese Society in Thailand: An Analytical History*, Ithaca, New York, Cornell University Press, 1957

Smith, Samuel, ed., *The Siam Repository*, 6 vols, Bangkok, 1869-74

Sng, Jeffery and Pimpraphai Bisalputra, *A History of the Thai-Chinese*, Singapore, Editions Didier Millet, 2015

St John, Spenser, *The Life of Sir James Brooke Rajah of Sarawak*, Edinburgh and London, William Blackwood and Sons, 1879

Sunthari Asawai, *Panha kan thuekhrong kammasit thidin nai prathet thai khong khon tang chat: sueksa korani khong yipun pho so 2398-2480* (สุนทรี อาสะไวย์, *ปัญหาการถือครองกรรมสิทธิ์ที่ดินในประเทศไทยของคนต่างชาติ : ศึกษากรณีของญี่ปุ่น พ.ศ. 2398 – 2480*) *[Problems of foreign land ownership in Thailand: a case study of Japan, 1855-1937]*, Bangkok, Sathaban Thai Khadi Sueksa, 1990

Tanabe, Shigeharu, "Land Reclamation in the Chao Phraya Delta", *Thailand: A Rice-Growing Society*, ed. Yoneo Ishii, trans. Peter and Stephanie Hawkes, Honolulu, University Press of Hawaii, 1978, pp. 40-82

Tarling, Nicholas, "Siam and Sir James Brooke", *Journal of the Siam Society*, vol. 48.2 (1960), pp. 43-72
"Harry Parkes' Negotiations in Bangkok in 1856", *Journal of the Siam Society*, vol. 53.2 (1965), pp. 153-180
"The Bowring Mission: The Mellersh Narrative", *Journal of the Siam Society*, vol. 63.1 (1975), pp. 105-126

Terwiel, B. J., *Through Travellers' Eyes: An approach to Early Nineteenth century Thai History*, Bangkok, Duang Kamol Books, 1989
"The Bowring Treaty: Imperialism and the Indigenous Perspective", *Journal of the Siam Society*, vol. 79.2 (1991), pp. 40-47
Thailand's Political History: From the Fall of Ayutthaya in 1767 to Recent Times, Bangkok, River Books, 2005

Thanyaporn Chankrajang and Jessica Vechbanyongratana, *A Brief Economic History of Land Rights in Thailand: From the Sukhothai Period to the End of King Chulalongkorn's Reign*, Bangkok, Thailand Research Fund, 2017

Thongchai Winichakul, *Siam Mapped: A History of the Geo-Body of a Nation*, Chiang Mai, Silkworm Books, 1995
"The Quest for '*Siwilai*': A Geographical Discourse of Civilizational Thinking in the Late Nineteenth and Early Twentieth-Century Siam", *The Journal of Asian Studies*, vol. 59.3 (2000), pp. 528-549

Van Roy, Edward, *Siamese Melting Pot: Ethnic Minorities in the Making of Bangkok*, Chiang Mai, Silkworm Books, 2017

Vella, Walter F., *Siam Under Rama III: 1824-1851*, New York, J. J. Augustin, 1957

Viboon Wichitwathakan, "Khrokam khong nai insen", *Ruang sanook nai phaendin somdet phra chom klao* (วิบูล วิจิตรวาทการ, "เคราะห์กรรมของนายอินแซน", *เรื่องสนุกในแผ่นดินสมเด็จพระจอมเกล้า*) ["The unfortunate Nai Insen", *Interesting stories from the time of King Rama IV*], Bangkok, 1998, pp. 241-274

Vikrom Koompirochana, "Siam in British Foreign Policy 1855-1938: The Acquisition and the Relinquishment of British Extraterritorial Rights", Ph.D. thesis, Michigan, Michigan State University, 1972

Wilson, Constance M., "State and Society in the Reign of Mongkut, 1851-1868: Thailand on the Eve of Modernization", Ph.D. thesis, Ithaca, New York, Cornell University, 1970

Winai Pongsripian and Theera Nuchpiam eds, *The Writings of King Mongkut to Sir John Bowring (A.D. 1855-1868)*, Bangkok, Aksorn Thai, 1994

Wood, William Maxwell, *Fankwei; or, the San Jacinto in the Seas of India, China and Japan*, New York, Harper & Brothers, 1859

Wright, Arnold and Oliver T. Breakspear, eds, *Twentieth Century Impressions of Siam: Its History, People, Commerce, Industries, and Resources*, London, Lloyd's Greater Britain Publishing Company, 1908

Wyatt, David K., "The Buddhist Monkhood as an Avenue of Social Mobility in Traditional Thai Society", *Silpakon*, vol. 10.1 (1966), pp. 49-52

Index